MW00800747

Encyclopedia
of
Classic French
Pastries

ENCYCLOPEDIA

OF

Classic French Pastries

⁓⁓

HISTORY & LEGENDS OF THE GREAT PASTRIES OF FRANCE

⁓

Easy-to-Follow Recipes For Home Cooks

SUSAN WHATLEY

A Few Words Before You Begin:

Due to the extensive number of recipes, and the need to cross-refer, each Recipe is identified with 2 numbers. The first number (the Roman Numeral) indicates the Chapter in which the recipe is found. The second number identifies the recipe number in that chapter. So, the number (II-2) refers to the recipe found in Chapter II, Recipe 2.

Please note that all recipes are indexed according to their English titles and their French titles. In the back of the book, you will find a complete English Index and a French Index to help locate recipes by their French or English equivalents. In some instances, there is not an exact translation, so that the French name might appear in the English Index. Also, please note, that the recipes are indexed with their full title so that reference will be easier.

And before you begin, please know that you are entering the world of the great classic pastries of France. Recipes are very carefully written and detailed to assure you success every time. This book is especially useful for those times when you care enough to prepare only the very best, the most glorious dessert for your family and friends.

We hope the legends and anecdotes will enrich your pleasure and knowledge. And above all, we know that you will treasure this monumental work for years and years.

The Editors

The Contents

The Introduction

The richness of the French culture can never be considered complete without the inclusion of its stories about food. And, as any gourmand waxing eloquent over the subtlety of flavor, or the stunning tour de force of a gateau would tell you, knowing its antecedents only adds to the romance.

Numerous sources have been drawn upon to bring you the many anecdotes in this book. Indeed, legends, historical events, even tall but well-loved folk tales gathered on my travels around France have contributed to the wealth of these stories. It is my hope that you will enjoy reading them as much as I have savored the pleasure of compiling them for you.

Susan Whatley

The Basics

Ingredients

Would you expect a top-flight couturier to have his designer collection sewn from old burlap bags? Or a master cabinet-maker to build his creations with cardboard and plaster? Of course not. By the same token, it would be unrealistic to think that first-rate pastry can be made with second-rate ingredients. It just can't. That's one of the most important things to keep in mind, whether you want to prepare a simple crème caramel for tonight's dessert, or plan an elaborate creation to serve at a special occasion.

I've noticed that recipes in many modern cookbooks call for artificial substitutes and prepared foods. This, in an effort, I suppose, to save time and work. They're often more expensive, and can even be harmful to the health. Finally, they always do injustice to an otherwise well-prepared dessert, and what's infinitely worse, to the cook who made it. So banish them, mercilessly, from your kitchen. As we say in France, "C'est normal!" After all, your family, your friends--and you--deserve only the best, n'est-ce pas?

ACCOMPANYING WINES

The ideal wine to serve with French pastries? Champagne, of course! Whether you prefer it pink or white, dry or sweet, select it carefully. If you're unfamiliar with the numerous brands now available in wine shops, check the bottom of the label. Those marked with the initials "R.M." or "N.M." are excellent choices. If champagne isn't available to you, then white wine is a fine second choice. Many gastronomists recommend sweet white wines from Bordeaux, such as Mont Bazillac or Sauternes.

Both white wine and champagne should be chilled quickly on ice, shortly before serving. Slow chilling in the refrigerator would destroy their taste. There's one notable exception to the wine rule: chocolate desserts, whose distinctive taste would overpower even the finest wine. A cup of coffee or a goblet of ice water would be a better choice.

DAIRY PRODUCTS

Only a top-quality, unsalted butter (also known in some parts of the country as "sweet butter") should be used in French pastry making. Even butter labeled "lightly salted" is far too salty, and since the higher salt content prolongs shelf life, chances are that it won't be as fresh as the unsalted kind. As for artificial butter replacements such as margarine and hydrogenated shortening, don't ever use them. They contain chemical additives and have a poor taste.

The softened butter called for in many recipes should be the consistency of a thick pommade, but never runny. In fact, that's why French bakers refer to it as "beurre en pommade". The time it must spend out of the refrigerator depends mainly on the ambiant temperature of the kitchen, so judge it by its consistency, not by how long ago you removed it from the refrigerator.

Pans and molds are often buttered before use. This can be done with softened or melted butter, or with a more practical preparation, which remains soft, even when refrigerated. In a small saucepan, melt 1/2 cup (1 stick) butter over low heat. Clarify it by skimming off the foamy milk solids which have risen to the surface, then stir in 1/2 cup of cooking oil. Cool before using, and store in a tightly-covered container in the refrigerator.

Milk should always be fresh and whole, not canned, skimmed, or powdered. For whipping, use only heavy cream rather than products which contain only 1/2 cream and 1/2 milk. Needless to say, nondairy whipped toppings are unacceptable. Neufchatel cheese, a creamy, light cheese made in Switzerland, has a lower fat content than cream cheese, and can be substituted.

EGGS
Use large-sized eggs for all recipes. Much larger or smaller ones would throw off the proportions in a recipe, so if you're not sure about an egg's size, measure it. One egg should measure a scant 1/4 cup.

Egg whites can be kept, tightly covered and refrigerated, for 10 to 12 days. If you can't remember how many you've set aside, or want to use less than what you have, three whites measure about 1/2 cup, and five, about 3/4 cup. If you're lucky enough to have access to country-fresh eggs, be sure that they're at least three days old before using them, because brand new eggs don't whip or bake as well as older ones.

Many of the recipes in this book call for egg wash, which is made simply by beating a whole egg with a pinch of salt. The salt helps break down the egg white so that it will blend perfectly with the yolk and brush on smoothly.

FOOD COLORINGS
Natural food coloring made from plant extracts can be found in some specialty stores, but if you can't find it, the standard kind found in all supermarkets will do, because you'll be using it in minute quantities. It's used to give fondants and icings the traditional colors, which go with certain flavorings (such as pale green for kirsch, and pale pink or peach for Grand Marnier) or for adding a touch of color to some pastries (for instance, in making green buttercream stems and leaves on a bûche de Noël). Remember, a little bit of

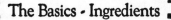

color will make a pastry attractive and appetizing. A lot will make it look like the garish work of an amateur.

DECORATIONS

Decorations are like food coloring: Judiciously applied, they add that finishing touch of elegance. Piled on with a heavy hand, they can make a pastry look like a Mardi-Gras queen's headdress. Silver pearls and Jordan almonds lend a particularly festive note to party cakes such as the croquembouche, red hots bring out the pinkness of a Grand Marnier-flavored salambo, and yellow mimosa balls on kirsch-flavored pastries bring to mind the French Riviera city of Nice.

Sugar-coated violets, a specialty from Toulouse, are especially striking on St. Honorés, meringues à la chantilly, and other whipped cream pastries. Angélique (formally called "herbe des anges" which means "angels' herb" because it was thought to neutralize poisonous snake bites) is a kind of stringy green plant which is dried, then candied. Use it along with candied cherry halves to decorate babas, savarins, and cakes aux fruits confits.

Chocolate desserts and layer cakes can be attractively garnished with chocolate sprinkles. As for multicolored sprinkles, they're an excellent example of what **not** to use for decorating! Almost all of these decorations can be found in supermarkets, but sugar-coated violets and angelique may have to be ordered from a gourmet shop.

FLAVORINGS

The kind of chocolate most often used for these recipes is semi-sweet, which is sold in one-ounce portions, larger flat bars, and as chocolate chips. All of these are fine, but if you don't have kitchen scales, the one-ounce portions are the most practical. In a few cases, powdered, unsweetened cocoa (never the kind mixed with sugar and used as an instant drink flavoring) and unsweetened chocolate are required.

Extracts, such as vanilla, coffee, and almonds must be natural, never synthetic, which automatically eliminates artificial butter flavoring. Dried vanilla pods can also be used for recipes in which they're infused in hot liquids.

Prâlin, unchanged since its creation over four hundred years ago, gives a luscious, nutty caramel flavor to icings, fillings, and notably the incomparable Paris-Brest. Cans of thick, dark brown prâlin paste can be found in or ordered from some specialty shops. If you have a blender or food processor, you can make powdered prâlin according to the recipe (II-9).

In French pastry making, alcohols are frequently used for heightening flavor. Here are the ones called for in this book, in order of their importance:

Rum: Dark rum from the French Antilles is considered to be among the world's finest tasting rums. In my kitchen, a big earthenware crock holds a permanent supply of raisins soaking in dark rum from Martinique.

Kirsch: This colorless brandy made from fresh cherries can enhance any dessert or pastry made with "red fruits" such as strawberries, raspberries, and of course, cherries.

Grand Marnier: This is the best-known and most flavorful of orange liqueurs. It's used in many orange-based pastries.

Calvados: This French apple brandy, made in Normandy, is used for heightening the flavor of apple desserts.

Sherry: The walnut casks in which this Spanish wine is aged give it a lovely walnut taste, which makes it perfect for enhancing the taste of walnut pie and, if you wish, chocolate desserts.

FLOUR

All recipes call for white, all-purpose flour. Don't use self-rising flour, which contains baking powder, or presifted flour because the volume is different from unsifted flour. Although whole wheat flour is too heavy for making French pastry, unbleached flour, which is available in all health food stores, gives good results. Whole wheat pastry flour can be substituted for part of the flour in the cake recipes, but results will be a little heavier. "Bleached" by a natural aging process rather than the standard chemical method, is more healthful than plain white flour, although the latter is fine, too.

FRUITS

Fruits should be ripe but, unless you intend to mash or blend them, firm enough not to fall apart when baked. Whatever kind of fruit you want to use, choose tart, flavorful varieties. You may have to pay more for them than for the milder, not to say insipid varieties, but the final results will be well worth it.

Raspberries and strawberries should be handled with the utmost care. Mismanagement will cause unsightly bruises, and soaking will rob them of their taste. In fact, if it's at all possible, they should be cleaned with a damp towel. You shouldn't have any trouble following this rule with raspberries, which almost never need to be cleaned at all, but sandy strawberries often pose a problem.

Clean them off one by one with a soft pastry brush, or use the following method which has always worked for me: Dunk a clean dishtowel in cold water and wring it out well. Place the strawberries in the middle and roll it up carefully to enclose the fruit, then twist the ends of the towel tightly to secure. Now, taking one end in each hand, shake the towel back and forth in front of you, in a sawing motion for about 20 to 30 seconds. The fruit will lose the dust and sand as it rolls gently on the damp towel, but will keep all its taste.

Untreated oranges and lemons from the health food store or other reliable sources should be used in recipes calling for grated rind.

Even though nothing can compare with the taste of fresh fruits, frozen and canned fruits in light syrup, or better yet, in natural juice, are acceptable for most (but not all) recipes during the off-season or for convenience' sake. For instance, frozen strawberries can be used for fruit sauce, but not for strawberry pie. In other words, let experience and, above all, common sense be your guide. Last of all, there are canned pie fillings, which are quite another thing. They contain large amounts of sugar, starch and artificial food coloring...and disappointingly little fruit. Stay away from them.

LEAVENERS

Yeast is widely available in granulated inactive form and in fresh compressed cakes. The former is easier to find, keeps for long periods of time without your having to take any special precautions, and is easy to use.

I recommend fresh yeast. It keeps well for several days in the refrigerator, and can easily be frozen. I like to buy large quantities and freeze it so that I'll have an ever-ready supply. Frozen yeast should be allowed to thaw completely before being used, so be sure to remove it from the freezer well ahead of time. That way, you won't be tempted to pour overly-hot liquids on it to help it thaw out.

By all means, use the kind that works better for you. One envelope of granulated inactive yeast is the equivalent of one cake (about 15 grams) of compressed fresh yeast. It should be completely dissolved in water or milk before being added to the other ingredients. Don't let either kind of yeast come into direct contact with sugar or salt, which would "burn" it chemically and reduce its rising power.

If there is any doubt about the freshness of the yeast, it should be proofed by dissolving it in 1/2 cup warm (105-degrees) water. Stir in 1/2 teaspoon sugar, and allow to stand for 10 minutes. At this point, yeast should start to foam. If it does not foam, it is inactive and should be discarded.

Baking powder, a chemical leavener which reacts when brought into contact with moist ingredients, but does most of its work in the oven, is often lumpy. If so, take the time to sift it before using.

NUTS

Nuts are widely used in French pastry for adding flavor and texture to pastry dough and fillings, serving as the basis for creams, and as a decoration. The most frequenly used nuts are:

Almonds: Whether chopped, slivered, sliced, or ground, they should generally be blanched beforehand. To blanch almonds: Drop shelled almonds into boiling water for 1 minute. Drain, allow to cool for a few minutes, then squeeze each nut out of its skin. Dry on a baking sheet in a 350-degrees oven until lightly browned, or about 10 to 12 minutes. Sliced and slivered almonds will take less time, about 5 or 6 minutes. Watch the nuts closely as they toast. Once browning begins, it progresses quickly and the almonds could burn very easily.

To grind almonds or any other kind of nuts: Use an electric blender or food processor. Grind in short bursts, stopping frequently to check the nuts' consistency. Remember, if you do it too long, you'll end up with nut butter. And don't try to grind them with a food mill or meat grinder. The results would be disastrous.

Hazelnuts: These small round nuts which can replace half the almonds in many recipes are generally used unblanched. However, if you want to toast them, do it like this: Heat nuts on a baking sheet at 350-degrees for 5 minutes. Place on a dishtowel, fold it over to enclose nuts, and rub vigorously to remove the dark skin.

Walnuts: In recipes which call for walnuts, use English walnuts, which have a delicate, mellow taste. Black walnuts have a much stronger taste which is undeniably good. And yet, it would be overpowering in most desserts.

Chestnuts: These nuts with a high starch and low fat content are frequently recommended for people with cholesterol problems. Their preparation is rather lengthy, since they must be heated in the oven, peeled, then cooked in water or milk and peeled a second time to rid them of their inner skin. Canned chestnuts eliminate the work of peeling and cooking, but don't taste nearly as good.

Whatever kind of nuts you want to use, be sure that they're perfectly fresh. A pound of unshelled nuts will yield about a half pound of nutmeats, so buy accordingly. If you buy shelled nuts, check to see that they're unsalted. Store nuts in a tightly covered container in the refrigerator, or, if possible, freeze them to conserve their qualities. If in doubt about a nut's freshness, throw it out. Rancid or stale nuts would ruin an otherwise good pastry.

SALT

Used primarily as a flavor enhancer, salt is also added in very small amounts to egg whites to aid in whipping, and to whole eggs for egg wash. It does the same thing in both cases: helps break down the white sufficiently to permit easy beating or brushing.

SUGAR

For centuries, honey was the world's most widely-used sweetener, while sugar was reserved for medicinal purposes. Now, paradoxically, honey is considered beneficial for the health, while sugar has taken honey's old place as a sweetener for desserts. The kinds called for in this book:

White Sugar: Whether made from beets or sugar cane, this refined sugar is used in the majority of recipes. Although cooking sugar goes through a number of different stages, the soft ball stage is the only one which is of major importance for these recipes. Testing with a thermometer, temperature should reach 238-degrees. An alternate method would be to pour a few drops of the cooked syrup in cold water. If it forms a soft ball (one that gently flattens when pressed together) it is ready.

Brown Sugar: It's made by mixing granulated white sugar with black molasses. It has a fuller, richer flavor than refined white sugar.

Powdered Sugar: Also called "confectioner's sugar", this is white sugar which has been ground to a very fine powder then mixed with a small amount of cornstarch to prevent lumping. It's used mainly for making icings and glazes, and for dusting over finished pastries.

Artificial sweeteners, of all kinds, have an unpleasant taste which becomes all the more so with baking. Don't ever use them.

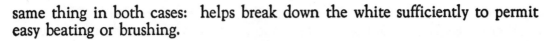

Equipment

Is equipment really all that important? Yes, it is. The kind you use can determine the way you feel about French pastry making. In fact, it can even mean the difference between a disgusted rejection of it...and a lifelong passion for it. If you don't believe me, try making croissant dough with a cheap rolling pin, slicing a rolled brioche with any old knife, or whipping cream with a fork! So don't hesitate to invest in good baking equipment. It's a joy to use, and even if it's sometimes (but certainly not always) expensive, it will bring you years of satisfaction.

BAKING SHEETS

The best kind to have is dark, heavy, and large: Dark because light metals reflect heat away from pastries, causing them to bake and brown more slowly, heavy because the lightweight kind tends to pop up on one side as it heats, and large because, if possible, you should use only one shelf in the oven at a time. If you can, have two or three heavy black steel ones cut to fit your oven, so that one sheet can be readied for the oven while others bake and cool. That way, you'll never be faced with the temptation to place unbaked dough or batter on a still-hot baking sheet in an effort to save time.

Allow one inch around all sides for proper heat circulation in the oven. A slight lip is recommended for filled pastries which bake directly on the sheet, like turnovers, and butter-rich ones, like croissants, to prevent leaks of fruit juice and butter from dripping to the oven floor and burning. A jelly roll pan with sides no more than one inch high is good for most baking needs, too. If you use flan rings a lot, a baking sheet with at least one straight, unlipped side is recommended, so that the pie can be slid off the sheet rather than lifted.

BOWLS

French "culs de poule" are perfectly designed to make pastry-making a pleasure. They're fairly deep, stainless steel, flat-bottomed bowls which are narrower at the bottom than the top. Excellent for just about every kind of mixing job, they can be heated over a gas flame, which is particularly handy when you're making génoise or heating crème au beurre.

Other mixing bowls can be of any kind of matter: pottery, clear glass, ceramic, etc. The smaller and lighter ones are good for holding chopped, sliced and beaten ingredients as they wait to go into the final mixture. Larger, heavier bowls are good for 1. hand-kneading, because they slide around less, 2. for storage in the refrigerator, and 3. for rising, since they retain heat and cold better.

CAKE BOARDS

The cake board acts as a base for delicate filled layer cakes and allows you to handle them with ease as you garnish and decorate. In most cases, it should be exactly the same diameter as the cake. A smaller board wouldn't support the cake correctly, and a larger one would hinder you when you try to coat the sides of the cake with nuts or chocolate sprinkles. And then, the overlapping board, unless hidden with cream or icing, would be unsightly. Cake boards can be found in any cake decorating shop, or you can make them yourself at a considerable savings, using heavy posterboard available almost anywhere. Just trace around the cake pan of your choice and cut out enough boards so that you'll always have plenty on hand.

CORNES

The name of this small, handleless scraper sounds rather bizarre to the American ear. Long ago, it was made out of horn, or "corne"...thus, its name. The standard-sized corne, which is also known in some supply houses as a dough scraper, measures about 3x5 inches. It has a curved, sharp-edged side for scooping dough and batter out of mixing bowls, and a flat side for smoothing creams and fillings.

DOUBLE BOILER

French bakers call it a "bain-marie" and use it for melting chocolate, preparing meringue, cooking delicate sauces, and so on. The classical double boiler consists of a medium-sized pot (containing the ingredients to be cooked or heated) which fits into a slightly larger pot (containing water, which heats, with the steam it produces, the contents of the smaller pot). The bottom of the small pot should never touch the hot water. If you don't have a double boiler, a large pot and a smaller one, or a mixing bowl (depending upon what you want to use it for) will do about as well.

Another kind of bain-marie, which is used for baking, is simply a large pan half-filled with very hot water, in which the mold is placed so that its contents will bake more gently and evenly. Crème renversée au caramel, ile flottante, and tarte tatin, for example, are baked this way.

FOOD MILL

This very practical utensil comes with a set of grills with holes in varying sizes for doing different grinding jobs, and a hand-turned crank. It's used primarily for grinding and puréeing cooked fruits, such as stewed apples or boiled chestnuts, and raw fruits, like strawberries and raspberries. Don't try to use it for grinding nuts, though. It would just mash them, squeeze out their oil, and turn them into an unrecognizable mess.

FLOUR SIFTER

The deluxe model with several layers of screen may look more efficient, but it's almost impossible to clean, once bits of hard flour and debris have become trapped between the layers of mesh, so the single-screen sifter is the wiser choice. Maintenance is easy: just shake off the flour, wipe the outside with a dry cloth, and store it in a dry place. If you have a small amount of ingredients to sift--for instance, baking powder, cocoa, or powdered sugar--the job can be done just as well with a small tea strainer.

KNIVES

For the recipes in this book, you'll be working with three different knives:

Serrated Knife: This long knife with a saw-like blade is used for slicing fragile génoise in layers, trimming jelly rolls, cutting baked pâte feuilletée, and so on. One with a 10 to 12-inch blade is best, so that you can slice génoises in one cut.

Chef's Knife: This heavy, wedge-shaped knife was designed for chopping nuts and chocolate, cutting croissant dough, and slicing soft brioche rolls, among other things. It's best to get one with a 10-inch blade, because it's small enough to be manageable, but large and heavy enough to meet you halfway.

Paring Knife: This modest looking but excellent knife is for peeling and slicing fruits, scoring pastries and making slits before baking. If you don't already have several, buy at least two or three, preferably with three-inch blades.

Whatever kind of knife you happen to be using, be sure that it's very sharp. Dull knives cause extra work and can even make you tear up delicate pastries as you saw away at them. Sharpening stones can be found in any department or hardware store. Invest in a good one, and use it religiously.

MACHINES

Have you ever tried grinding prâlin with a mortar and pestle? Or kneading a triple batch of baba dough by hand? Or maybe preparing a large quantity of hot meringue with a whisk? I have. And that's why I'm an unconditional advocate of machines which can take the toil out of pastry making. Here are the most common ones, one or more of which you probably already have:

Electric Beater: Even if you have a heavy-duty mixer, a small, hand-held electric beater can come in handy for mixing jobs done over a double boiler, and for preparing small quantities. Some brands even have kneading attachments, but they sometimes aren't powerful enough to work well with anything but very small quantities of dough.

Electric Blender: Thanks to it, fruits can be puréed, nappage liquified, and nuts or prâlin ground fine in a matter of seconds. The kind with a clear glass container is best, because you can keep an eye on the contents without lifting the lid, and stop blending the instant they've reached the right consistency. Look for one with low-lying blades, too, so that you can purée small amounts, if need be. High-lying blades would simply pack small quantities, intact, under them. Although the blender is a handy appliance to have, it isn't suited to every pastry-making operation. For instance, crème au beurre preparation in one is a total fiasco, and egg whites and cream, which require even whipping, shouldn't be beaten in it.

Food Processor: This sturdy, multiple-purpose machine was created in France about twenty years ago for professionals, but the home model is now firmly implanted in many American, as well as European kitchens. I've always thought of it as being a cross between an electric blender and a heavy duty mixer. It can chop, grind, purée, and mix pie dough, but unless it's a large model with a very powerful motor, it can't handle conveniently large quantities of dough and batter. For the pastry maker who prepares a lot of yeast-rising dough, especially, the more versatile heavy duty mixer with a dough hook would be a better choice.

Heavy Duty Mixers: All heavy duty mixers can be placed in one of two categories: those with fixed action, in which the beater or beaters turn on a stationary axis, and those with planetary action, in which a large beater turns on an axis which rotates simultaneously around the bowl. The second kind is highly superior for the obvious reason that the contents of the bowl get mixed more evenly and efficiently. The best mixers come equipped with a large-capacity (5 to 7 quarts) stainless steel bowl which locks into place, and three different kinds of beaters: a whisk for whipping egg whites, cream, and fluffy batters, a flat leaf beater or paddle for soft doughs like pâte à chou, and a hook for kneading yeast-leavened doughs. Some also have blender attachments. Although all the recipes in this book give instructions for hand kneading and mixing, a machine can be used without any modifications in the directions. You'll want to check the consistency of the dough from time to time during the kneading process, but don't forget to stop the machine first.

MANQUÉ PAN

Resourceful by nature, French bakers have always respected an age-old tradition of turning mistakes into saleable delicacies. A case in point: Centuries ago, cakes which had failed to rise properly in the oven or had broken when unmolded, were topped with prâlin, returned to the oven for browning, then sold as "manqués", which means, roughly, "failures". This kind of gâteau became so popular that bakers were soon forced to make them specially, to satisfy the demand. The manqué eventually fell out of popular favor, but did leave its name to the pan in which it was baked. I prefer the manqué pan to the traditional American cake pan because it's deeper. This makes it perfect not only for génoises and other layer cakes, but also for deep pies, such as tarte tatin, and for yeast-rising pastries which call for a round mold, like brioche roulée. Eight and ten-inch manqué pans are the most frequently used sizes.

MEASURING DEVICES

All of the recipes in this book have been adapted to the American measuring system, so you won't need anything you don't already have: a set of stainless steel cups, ranging from 1/4 cup to 1 cup, and a set of measuring spoons, ranging from 1/8 teaspoon to 1 tablespoon. Larger measuring cups with a several cup capacity should be transparent glass or plastic, for accuracy and ease in measuring.

European recipes always call for proportions by weight, so for the French cook, scales are an absolute necessity. Although this isn't so for the American homemaker, scales do come in very handy for weighing out correct quantities of dough taken from larger pieces, checking the weight of nuts after shelling, weighing chocolate, fruits, etc. Spring scales are the easiest kind to find, but if you get one, be very careful not to subject it to sudden jolts. The simple spring mechanism would be distorted without hope of readjustment. If you can find one, a beam balance scale which is sensitive enough to measure to the nearest 1/4 ounce, is a better choice.

MOLDS

The following descriptions of the molds called for in this book will help you in choosing.

Baba: The baba mold is a rather shallow, smooth-sided, ring-shaped pan. It can be made of oven-proof ceramic, but more commonly of lightweight aluminum.

Brioche: The brioche mold is deeply fluted and narrow at the base, then flares out to a wide top. Like the baba mold, it can be found in oven-proof ceramic or the more practical aluminum.

Charlotte: This deep, narrow round mold is perfect, not only for charlottes, but for pudding St. Martin, ile flottante, timbale Belle-Hélène, and other baked or molded desserts. The transparent glass kind is preferable to metal or ceramic because the contents can be watched more closely as they bake or chill.

Kugelhopf: This deep tube pan with diagonally fluted sides is traditionally made of glazed terra cotta. My aluminum molds, however, have always given me complete satisfaction.

Madeleine: Madeleine molds are somewhat reminiscent of muffin pans: they're flat metal sheets with six to eight shell-shaped wells per sheet.

Soufflé: The round, straight-sided soufflé dish comes in a variety of sizes. Besides the obvious soufflés, it can be used for making diplomate aux fruits, gâteau de semoule, biscuit Balzac, crème caramel, etc. For molded desserts, I prefer a transparent glass dish, so that I can keep an eye on the contents, but I like to use presentable white ceramic soufflé dishes for those served in the mold.

METAL SCRAPER

This is a blunt-edged metal rectangle mounted on a cylindrical wooden handle, which is especially useful for working fondant, cutting pieces of dough off of larger portions, cutting large quantities of cold butter, and scraping work surfaces clean. If you have the choice, buy a thin-bladed scraper rather than a thick-bladed stainless steel one. It's suppler and easier to use...and then, it's cheaper.

PASTRY BAGS

Many would-be French pastry makers find this utensil exotic and vaguely disconcerting. And yet, it's one of the most valuable and easiest to use tools of the art. It wasn't always that way. Its earliest ancestor, a kind of large syringe which dates back to about 1710, was infinitely better than nothing, but was somewhat tricky to use, and the results obtained weren't always satisfactory. Today, the descendants of this first model can be found in most cake decorating shops. You may be tempted by their deceptively simple

apppearance, but I suggest that you pass them up altogether. They haven't come very far in 275 years.

The invention of the pastry syringe was eventually followed by that of the paper pastry bag, whose obvious disadvantage was its tendency to get soggy and break open at the worst possible moment. These, too, still exist in an updated form. I know a lot of people who use them, but only for small quantities of dough, and quickly. Around 1820, someone came up with the canvas bag which French pastry chefs still use today. A few years ago, it was further improved by plastification, which prevented the contents from leaking through the canvas weave.

This kind is fine, but personally speaking, I prefer yet another sort: a supple all-plastic bag with nozzles which can be changed in seconds thanks to a system of screw-on rings which hold them in place. There's no need, as with the classical French bags, to empty the bag and fish out the nozzle in order to change it. It's best to have an assortment of sizes to be used according to the amount of dough or cream you're working with. I have purposely limited the number of different nozzles needed for the recipes in this book. The 1/8-inch star nozzle is a must for filling and decorating, the larger fluted nozzles are used principally for pâte à chou and, again, decorating. Round nozzles are for making round and oval meringues, succès, and, in the case of nids de pâques, for decorating. The bûche de Noël calls for a fluted ribbon nozzle.

PASTRY BRUSHES
Brushes which are perfectly suitable for pastry making can be found in any home improvement or hardware store for a fraction of what they cost in fancy bakery supply houses or gourmet boutiques. You'll need two basic kinds: a soft, flat brush about 4 inches wide, for brushing excess flour from the dough you're rolling out or from the work surface, and a 1 to 2-inch wide brush for applying melted butter, egg wash, and nappage. Buy several of the second kind, so that you'll always have one handy without having to wash it.

PASTRY CUTTERS
When cutting out pieces of pâte feuilletée, the layers of butter and pastry should never be pinched together by a dull cutter. This is why a water glass isn't a recommended cutting tool. Smooth-sided and fluted pastry and cookie cutters in varying sizes and shapes depending upon what you want to cut out, are essential.

There's also the sort which consists of a sharp wheel--again, fluted or not--mounted on a wooden handle, which is excellent for cutting thin strips of pastry for lattice-topped pies, and cutting croissant as well as other toured dough.

PIE PANS

There's an infinite variety of pie pans: Metal ones with removable bottoms so the baked pie can easily be pushed out, attractive ceramic or glass plates with straight or sloped sides, which do double duty for baking and serving, flan rings, which belong to the pie pan family and which are nothing more than metal rings with no bottom, so that the pie can be baked directly on the baking sheet. All the pie recipes here call for 10-inch pie pans, which doesn't mean that they won't work if made in smaller pie plates. You may just end up with a little leftover filling.

ROLLING PASTRY PIERCER

This wooden roller spiked with rows of sharp metal pins is simply for pricking holes in pastry to prevent it from rising excessively or unevenly in the oven. I must admit, a fork does just as good a job, unless you're dealing with an enormous quantitiy of dough.

ROLLING PINS

Although you can get by with using the cheaper, lightweight kind, it would be a good idea to invest in a good heavy rolling pin with ball bearing handles. The weight of the pin will help roll out the dough without your having to bear down on it excessivley, while the ball bearing handles allow it to turn smoothly and easily.

An old-fashioned, straight-sided glass bottle filled with ice cubes and water may seem like the ideal rolling out device. After all, the principal of the heavy cylinder pressing down on the dough while keeping it cold is, in appearance, a sound one. There's just one catch: the ice water makes the bottle sweat, which is catastrophic for any kind of pastry dough. Pour out the water, and it becomes like any other empty bottle: too light for doing an adequate job.

A slender wooden cylinder like the ones used by professional bakers in France is fine for rolling out small quantities of dough and especially useful for beating cold butter to make it more manageable.

RULERS

Many French pastries call for clean-cut edges and precise dimensions, so a washable 24-inch metal or wooden ruler is a necessity.

SPATULAS

Flexible-bladed metal spatulas are excellent for icing cakes and spreading on filling. Buy several in varying sizes for different needs.

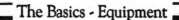

Stiff plastic spatulas are good for folding mixtures and scooping stiff doughs and batters out of mixing bowls. The softer rubber spatula is also fine for folding and for working with thinner, more supple doughs.

Wooden spatulas can be used for stirring and folding but, of course, aren't suitable for scraping bowls clean.

SUGAR DREDGER

This is a metal can with holes in the top, which is used for dusting powdered sugar or cocoa over pastries. If you don't have one, a small tea strainer will do just as well.

THERMOMETER

More often than not, ovens don't heat to the exact temperature marked on the dial, and that's why it's advisable to have a good oven thermometer. If your oven heats poorly, the maintenance center for the store where you bought it, or the city utility company, will usually adjust it at no cost. Afterwards, regular temperature checks will keep your oven in line.

TIMERS

They're not absolutely necessary, as most ovens are equipped with one, but they are convenient items for busy cooks who could get distracted long enough for a cake to burn or dough to overrise. An even handier kind is a small, round one on a soft cord to hang around your neck and accompany you wherever you go.

TURNING CAKESTAND

This makes decorating and icing faster and easier.

WHISKS

Whisks are wonderful! They can do just about any kind of mixing job with ease and rapidity, while the wires break up lumps before they have time to become a problem. In addition to the standard whisk, which comes in a wide range or sizes (I have a set of six stainless steel whisks, ranging from a 4-inch conversation piece with which I admittedly don't do much mixing, to a 19-incher, for whisking heroic quantities of batter and cream), there's also the balloon whisk, which has a rounder shape. It's perfect for whipping egg whites and cream because it aerates more efficiently. The job takes longer, but the results are lighter. For pastry makers with fragile enamel-lined saucepans and bowls, a plastic whisk is a must.

WAXED PAPER

Waxed paper eliminates the tedious chore of buttering and flouring baking sheets, allows easy removal of baked goods, and all but does away with washing up afterwards. Parchment paper, which can be found in bakery supply houses and comes in sheets and large rolls, serves the same purpose.

WORK SURFACE

When choosing a work surface, there are three things to take into consideration: size, type of surface, and height. Ideally, the work surface should be large enough so that all the ingredients can be set out and all operations called for in a recipe (such as mixing, kneading, rolling out, etc.) can be accomplished without your having to clear it off. This would undeniably save time and work. Still, it need be only big enough for maneuvering a large rolling pin: that is, about 24x24 inches. If you have too much dough for a small area, you can usually cut it into two or three pieces and roll them out separately.

Formica is certainly the most common type of work surface. In fact, most of my pastries are made on an old formica kitchen table which I'm not afraid of damaging. If you have a nice new formica table or countertop, you may not want to expose it to the perpetual danger of being scratched or nicked. In that case, an acrylic, anti-stick pastry board, available in most kitchenware shops, will protect it.

Wood makes a fine work surface, but must be scraped clean and scrubbed after every use. That's why it must be a very smooth, hard wood. Scrubbing can make a soft wood shred slightly, causing tiny splinters to get mixed in with the dough or fondant as it's worked on the table. I learned this the hard way. Since then, the table in question has found a new home in my study, and we're both the happier for it.

There's no doubt about it: Marble is the perfect matter for a work surface. On top of being a pleasure for the eyes, it's smooth, easy to clean, and retains cold for long periods of time. In most bakeries in France, enormous marble counters are placed on top of refrigerator units. Although few American kitchens can be set up that way, most home pastry cooks can find a place for a slab of marble, if not one big enough to cover the kitchen table or part of a countertop, at least a smaller rectangle which can be moved around at will and can be stored in the refrigerator.

While it's in place, you can set things on it to cool them more quickly. Remove it from the refrigerator and use it for rolling out pastry, working fondant, and so on. It's especially useful during the summer, when it keeps the butter from oozing out of pâte feuilletée as you tour (turn) it, and pie crust firm enough to handle. Another nice thing about marble is that it can be found in a variety of colors, ranging from classical white, black, and grey, to a more striking salmon pink and--my favorite--dusky green.

And then, you never know where you're going to find just the right piece of marble for your kitchen: at a junk dealer's, an antique shop, an estate sale...I found mine at the Salvation Army in France. If you're in a hurry, you could always buy it directly from a marble cutter, but it's less fun.

One more thing: The height of the work surface is just as important as the size and material. If it's too high, rolling out will be an arm-killing chore. Too low, it forces you to stoop, causing backache. The ideal height is when the edge of the work surface rests under the palms when the arms are slightly extended in front of the body. Check your work surface and, if need be (and if possible) shorten the table legs accordingly, or find a low footstool to raise you up.

Terms

The following section will help acquaint you with the most important terms used and techniques called for in this book. Read it over carefully before beginning work on any recipe.

Blanch: To remove the brown skin from almonds by dropping them into boiling water, draining, then squeezing each nut out of its skin.

Blind: When a pie shell is prebaked without filling, it's said to be baked "à blanc", or "blind". Shrinking and blistering are the most common problems encountered when baking blind. Allowing the rolled out crust to rest in the refrigerator for an hour before baking will greatly reduce the risk of shrinkage. You can cut down on blistering by pricking the crust before baking. A disk of foil or parchment paper covered with rice or dried beans can help, too, but don't forget to remove both paper and beans ten minutes before the end of baking so that the lighter bottom crust can catch up with the rest of the pastry shell.

Chop: To cut into very small pieces, using a chef's knife and working with a pivoting motion. In most cases, this can also be done with a food processor or electric blender.

Clarify: To remove the milk solids from butter by melting it, then skimming off the milk solids which rise to the top.

Cut: Generally speaking, it's better to cut dough with a chef's knife, using a quick downward motion rather than by dragging the knife through it. This is especially true for pâte feuilletée and croissant dough because the layers of butter and dough should never be pressed together, whether by a knife or by a dull-edged cutter such as a drinking glass. This is also the case for rolled brioche dough with soft fillings, since a sawing motion would tear up the dough and squeeze out the filling.

Détrempe: This is a kind of "starter dough" for pâte feuilletée or croissant dough, before it's toured with butter. The higher the butter content in the détrempe, the easier the dough will be to tour (turn).

Dust: To sprinkle dough or finished pastry (lightly, unless indicated otherwise) with flour or powdered sugar, using a dredger or small strainer.

Egg Wash: A mixture of beaten whole egg with a pinch of salt, for brushing over pastries before baking.

Fold: To blend ingredients or dough with beaten egg whites or whipped cream. It must be done very carefully to prevent the whipped mixture from falling. Usually, about 1/3 of the whipped mixture can be beaten into the stiffer mixture to make it lighter and easier to blend. Then the lightened mixture is blended into the rest of the whites or cream. It should be lifted carefully with a wide rubber or wooden spatula and turned over, rather than mixed or beaten.

Ganâche: A creamy mixture of semi-sweet chocolate and heavy cream which are heated together, then cooled. It's used for filling and icing pastries.

Gâteau: This is a tricky word to translate. As a general rule, it means "cake", but shouldn't always be taken too literally because it can be applied to cookies or even to puddings.

Grind: Nuts can be ground in an electric blender or food processor. So can chocolate, but it must be frozen first to prevent it from turning into chocolate paste. Whether you're grinding nuts or chocolate, neither machine should be operated for more than a few seconds at a time, until the desired consistency is obtained.

Knead: Kneading, which means, generally speaking, to work dough, is essential for a light, airy yeast-leavened dough. The correct amount of kneading varies with the kind of dough. Brioche and baba doughs, for instance, must be kneaded vigorously and lifted up (or "soufflé", to use a professional term) to permit maximum aeration. Croissant détrempe calls for a moderate amount of kneading, while pie crusts must be stirred and kneaded as little as possible, only until the ingredients are mixed. Otherwise, they'd become tough.

Liquids: The amount of liquids called for in pie crust or yeast-leavened dough recipes is always relative. Depending upon the kind of flour used, the humidity in the air the day it's used, and so on, you may need slightly more or less liquid than called for in the recipe. Add it little by little, until dough reaches the right consistency...which is easy to determine, with a little experience. You don't want to end up with a gummy, impossible-to-manage paste, nor do you want a crumbly ball of packed flour, either! All things considered, a too-soft dough which would become firmer with refrigeration is preferable to a too-dry one, which would become rock-hard when chilled.

Macerate: To soak fruit in liquid (usually some kind of alcohol) to soften it and give it flavor. The sort of fruit most often macerated is, by far, the raisin. However, bananas, pineapple, or any other fruit, for that matter, can be used.

Measuring: All measures in this book have been translated from the European metric system of weights and measures to standard American liquid measures, and when unavoidable (as with chocolate, nuts, fruits, and doughs), to American pounds and ounces. The liquid measures are level. That is, the measuring cup or spoon should be filled to overflowing, then leveled off with a flat knife blade drawn across the top. The excess shouldn't be smoothed down with a spoon (which would pack it down into the cup) or shaken off (which would remove too much).

Piping: To squeeze out dough, fillings, icings, etc., using a pastry bag. First, to fill the bag; place the nozzle, then fold over the open end of the bag to form a cuff, two to three inches wide. With one hand, hold the bag under the cuff, and with the other, fill the bag no more than 1/2 full. (The reason for filling the bag only 1/2 way is simple: no matter how careful you are, pressure caused by piping will force the excess up and out the wrong end. That's why I recommend large bags for large amounts of dough. The whole batch can go into the bag at once).

Now, unfold the cuff and twist the bag tightly closed. Holding the bag in one hand, and guiding it with the index finger of the free hand, begin piping the desired shapes by squeezing firmly and steadily as you move the bag. To help get the feeling of piping, I suggest that you practice on the work surface, using a small amount of dough or icing. When you've finished, scrape it up and put it back into the bag for re-use. Your first tries won't be perfect, but you'll be surprised how quickly you master pressure control, which is the key to making beautiful decorations and pastries.

Pommade: Softened butter is said to be "en pommade". It's best to remove the butter from the refrigerator long enough ahead of time for it to reach the right consistency, but if you forget, or if the butter simply hasn't gotten soft enough by the time you're ready to use it, you can work it with your hands as you would clay, to obtain the desired consistency.

Preheat: To heat the oven completely--that is, for 15 to 20 minutes--before baking anything in it. An oven which hasn't been preheated properly is too hot in some places and too cold in others, causing pastry to bake unevenly.

Prick: To punch holes in unbaked pastry dough, using a fork or rolling pastry piercer, to help it rise evenly during baking, or prevent blistering when baking pie crusts "blind". If, in spite of pricking, an unfilled pie crust blisters while in the oven, don't hesitate to pierce the air pocket, then press it flat with a fork.

Quantities: It's often just as easy to prepare large quantities of basic doughs and certain fillings as it is to make small quantities, especially if you have a heavy duty mixer. The extra cakes, doughs, and fillings can be frozen for later use.

Ribbon: When génoise batter poured from a spoon falls in a smooth stream, then rests on the surface of the batter in the mixing bowl for a few seconds before sinking in, it's said to "form a ribbon".

Rognures: These are bits and scraps of classical pâte feuilletée which are put aside for later use in making mille-feuilles and pie crust. Rognures obtained from pâte demi-feuilletée are suitable only if used immediately.

Refrigeration: Refrigeration is essential for firming up dough with a high butter content, notably pâte feuilletée, so be careful to respect refrigeration times scrupulously.

Scald: To heat liquid--usually milk--to the boiling point without letting it actually boil. This is done when preparing baked custard, for example.

Tour (Turns): A tour, or "turn", is the procedure of rolling out dough, folding it, and turning (thus, the name) it for rerolling. There are three ways of folding the dough, two of which are used in this book:

Demi-tour: (Which isn't called for in any of these recipes). Calls for folding the dough in half, like a book.

Tour complet: This is the most frequently used tour. It consists of folding the dough in three as for a letter, by folding one end over 2/3 of the way, then the other end over the first fold.

Double tour: This is also called a "tour portefeuille" because dough resembles a "portefeuille" or wallet. It's done by folding one end over to the middle, the other end the same way, then folding it in half again.

Unmolding: Cakes and other pastries baked in molds should come out with no trouble if the pans were buttered and floured before baking. As a general rule, they should be inverted on a cooling rack as soon as they come out of the oven, or after 5 to 10 minutes of cooling. Pie plates with removable bottoms and those which can be presented at the table solve the sometimes tricky problem of unmolding pies.

Molds for chilled desserts such as charlottes can be buttered or wet, but neither is really necessary. The secret to easy unmolding lies in the short freezing time right before unmolding, which causes a thin film of ice to form between the dessert and the inside of the mold. When the mold is dipped in hot water, the ice melts and the dessert lets go as if by magic. Still other desserts unmold easily thanks to the mold's caramel lining, which melts during refrigeration.

Chapter I

Basic Doughs and Cakes
(Pâtes et Gâteaux de Base)

I-1   GÉNOISE

Louis XIII hardly resembled the kings of his time: hungry for the simple pleasures of non-royal life, he waved a hand at rigorous court etiquette and learned to shoe horses, drive his own carriage, and cultivate a vegetable garden...the products of which, incidentally, he sold to his minister of finances for astronomically high prices! But his favorite pastime was undeniably cooking. With the help of his head cook Maître Georges, he quickly excelled in the preparation of a variety of pastries, including pies and "biscuits".

This classical "biscuit", a kind of plain cake like sponge cake, but not a true sponge, because of its butter content, is good enough to be eaten as is, but also serves as a basis for fancier cakes. As indicated by its name, it originated in Genoa, Italy.

(I-1)

Génoise
(Genoa Sponge Cake)

Ingredients: (for one 8-inch layer)

2	tablespoons butter
1/2	cup flour
1	tablespoon cornstarch
1/8	teaspoon salt
3	eggs
5	tablespoons sugar

butter and flour for pans

Ingredients: (for two 8-inch layers)

1/4	cup (1/2 stick) butter
1	cup flour
2	tablespoons cornstarch
1/4	teaspoon salt
5	eggs
3/4	cup sugar

butter and flour for pans

Preheat oven to 350-degrees. In a small saucepan, melt butter, then clarify (with a spoon, skim off milk solids which have risen to the surface). Set aside to cool.

In a medium mixing bowl, combine flour, cornstarch and salt. Sift twice, then set aside.

More→

(Génoise, Cont.)

Place whole eggs and sugar in a large mixing bowl over a pot of boiling water (the bowl shouldn't touch the water) and beat at high speed for about 1 minute, until the mixture is barely warm. Don't overheat...the finished cake would dry out rapidly. Remove from heat and beat another 10 minutes, or until the mixture "forms a ribbon". To test, dip a spoon in and hold it over the bowl. The batter should fall in a smooth ribbon and come to rest on the surface for a few seconds before sinking in.

Sift dry ingredients a third time, directly into the batter, and using a wide spatula, fold in very carefully to avoid making the whipped eggs fall. Last of all, fold in the melted butter. Pour the batter into buttered and floured 8-inch cake pans, and bake for about 30 minutes. The cake is done when it pulls away from the sides of the pan. Let cool for a few minutes, then turn out onto a cooling rack. Quickly invert the cake, so that it will cool right side up. If you don't want it to be marked by the wire rack, place a cloth over the rack before turning out the cake.

Génoise au Chocolat (Chocolate Genoa Sponge Cake) (I-1a): Add 1 tablespoon powdered cocoa (per layer of génoise), to the flour mixture and prepare as above. The génoise au chocolat isn't quite as light as the plain génoise.

Note: The cake should be a light golden brown all over. If the bottom is darker, then the cake is baking too quickly from below, which makes it heavier and more compact than it should be. This problem can be corrected by placing the cake pan in another, larger pan, or on a baking sheet to bake.

Storage: Wrap in plastic and keep in a cool, dry place for 3 to 4 days, or freeze for up to 2 months. Thaw several hours in the refrigerator before using.

I-2 BISCUIT ROULÉ

Centuries ago, the biscuit was a sort of bread, baked twice ("bis" - "cuit" in Latin means "baked twice") so that it would keep for long periods of time. It was used most often by religious communities, as well as soldiers and sailors, who took it with them on extended military campaigns and voyages.

France's modern-day biscuit is a kind of cookie or cake. In this particular case, it's the basis for jelly rolls, bûches de Noël, roulés aux fraises . . .

(I-2)

Biscuit Roulé
(Rolled Cake Base)

Ingredients: (for one 10 x 15-inch cake)

2   tablespoons butter

4   egg yolks
1/2   cup sugar
1/2   cup flour

3   egg whites
     pinch salt
1   teaspoon sugar

     butter for baking sheet

Preheat oven to 375-degrees. In a small saucepan, melt, then clarify butter. In a large mixing bowl, beat the egg yolks and sugar at medium speed for about 3 minutes, until thick and lemon colored. Blend in the flour without beating.

In another mixing bowl, beat the egg whites and salt at high speed until soft peaks form. Add the teaspoon sugar and continue beating until stiff but not dry. Carefully fold the whites, then the butter, into the egg yolk mixture.

Butter a 10x15-inch jelly roll pan and cover it with waxed paper. Butter the paper. With a metal spatula, spread the batter over the paper in an even 1/2-inch layer. Be very careful not to make any thin spots, which would become dry and brittle with baking. Bake for about 7 minutes, or until very lightly browned. A cake tester, inserted in the center, should come out clean. Remove from the oven, wait a few minutes and invert on a sheet of waxed paper. Carefully peel off waxed paper it was baked in. With a chef's knife, even out the edges. Place a sheet of waxed paper over the hot cake and roll it up tightly. Store it this way until ready to use.

Storage: Keep in a cool, dry place for several days, or freeze for up to 2 months. Allow to thaw for several hours before using.

I-3   BISCUIT JOCONDE

After almost five centuries, a group of art experts and historians claim to have resolved the enigma surrounding Mona Lisa del Giocondo's mysterious smile. According to them, the model for Leonardo Da Vinci's most famous portrait was not, as originally believed, a beautiful Florentine noblewoman, but . . . the artist himself! We can only wonder, in that case, why Mona Lisa's amused smile isn't even broader . . .

Mona Lisa, known in French as "La Joconde", gave her name to this almond sponge cake, which serves as a base for Opéra, rolled cakes, Yule Logs, Marjolaine...

(I-3)
Biscuit Joconde
(Almond Sponge Cake)

Ingredients: (for one 10 x 15-inch biscuit)

2/3	cup ground blanched almonds
1/3	cup sugar
2	eggs
3	tablespoons flour
3	egg whites
	pinch salt
1	tablespoon sugar
2	tablespoons butter, melted
	butter for baking sheet

Preheat oven to 350-degrees. Butter a 10x15-inch jellyroll pan and line with waxed paper. Butter the paper. In a large mixing bowl, stir together almonds and sugar, then whisk in whole eggs and beat until smooth. Add flour, and beat just until well blended.

In a deep mixing bowl, beat egg whites and salt at high speed until soft peaks form. Add sugar and continue beating until stiff but not dry. Beat 1/3 of whites into batter, then carefully fold in rest of whites. Last of all, fold in butter.

With a large metal or rubber spatula, spread batter evenly over baking sheet, being careful to avoid making thin or thick spots. Bake 8 to 10 minutes, until biscuit is light brown around the edges and cream colored elsewhere. Remove from oven, invert onto a sheet of waxed paper, and brush hot waxed paper on bottom with water. Wait a few minutes, then carefully peel off waxed paper.

Storage: Wrap in plastic and keep in a cool dry place for up to 48 hours. Or, freeze for one month. To use, thaw overnight in refrigerator.

I-4 BISCUIT À SUCCÈS

Tender disks of almond-rich pastry filled with flavored buttercream are sure to be a big success, whether served at tea time, or for dessert after Sunday dinner. This pastry base can be filled with a variety of frostings. The "chocolatine" calls for the same pastry base, filled with chocolate mousse, and the délicieux", yet another possibility, is filled with a praline-flavored buttercream.

(I-4)
Biscuit à Succès
(Almond Pastry Base)

Ingredients: (for two 8-inch layers)
Pastry base:

1	cup blanched ground almonds
1/3	cup granulated sugar
1/3	cup powdered sugar

4	egg whites
	pinch salt
1/3	tablespoon granulated sugar

1/4	cup sliced untoasted almonds

Preheat oven to 350-degrees. In a medium mixing bowl, stir together dry ingredients. In a large mixing bowl, beat egg whites and salt at high speed until soft peaks form. Add the 1/3 tablespoon of sugar and continue beating until very stiff. Dust whites generously with part of dry ingredients and fold in carefully with a rubber spatula. Repeat until all dry ingredients are mixed in.

Butter and flour 2 baking sheets, or line them with waxed paper, using a dot of batter in the corners and center to make it stick. With a pencil, and using an 8-inch cake board as a guide, trace a circle in the middle of each baking sheet. Spoon batter into pastry bag and pipe 2 8-inch disks, beginning in the center and piping in a closed spiral, ending just inside the traced circle. Sprinkle one of the disks with the sliced almonds.

Bake about 10 minutes, then switch the sheets around so the pastry will brown evenly (if necessary), and bake for another 10 minutes, until the disks are golden brown. With a metal spatula, remove immediately from baking sheets and cool on wire racks.

To make Individual Succès Shells (I-4a): With a 2 1/2-inch cutter, cut individual bases from the 8-inch disks. If you have a steady hand, pipe 2 1/2-inch disks and then trim them with the cutter.

To make Chocolate Succès Shells (I-4b): Add 2 tablespoons unsweetened cocoa to the batter. To make these into individual shells, see above (I-4a).

Storage: The pastry base can be made up to 2 weeks in advance, then wrapped in plastic and refrigerated. It can also be frozen for up to 2 months. Allow to thaw in refrigerator 12 hours before using.

I-5 BISCUITS À LA CUILLÈRE

These cookies, known also as "boudoirs" because they were a popular sitting room refreshment, are known to Americans under the more familiar name of "lady fingers". They were created centuries ago, long before the invention of the pastry bag. The name was purely functional, since they were originally shaped with a spoon, or "cuillère".

Serve them with tea or coffee, ice cream, fruit salad, or custard. They also go into many desserts such as charlottes, biscuit balzac, diplomate aux fruits…

(I-5)

Biscuits à la Cuillère
(Ladyfingers)

Ingredients: (for about 40 3-inch biscuits)

5	egg yolks
2/3	cup sugar
3/4	cup flour
5	egg whites
	pinch salt
1	tablespoon sugar
3/4	cup powdered sugar

Preheat oven to 350-degrees. In a large mixing bowl, beat egg yolks and sugar at high speed until thick and lemon-colored. Beat in flour. In another large mixing bowl, beat egg whites and salt at high speed until soft peaks form. Add sugar and continue beating until stiff but not dry.

Beat 1/3 of whites into yolk mixture, until well blended, then, with a rubber spatula, carefully fold in rest of whites. Cover baking sheets with waxed paper, making it stick with a dot of batter in the center and on the corners. Spoon batter into pastry bag and pipe out 40 3-inch biscuits, spacing them to allow for expansion during baking. Dust generously with powdered sugar and bake 12 to 15 minutes, until a deep cream color.

Watch them closely for the last 5 minutes, and remove if they brown too quickly. Immediately remove from baking sheets, using a metal spatula. If removed when cool, they will break.

Storage: Cover tightly and keep in a cool, dry place for up to 2 weeks. Freeze in same container for up to 1 month.

I-6 PÂTE BRISÉE

French pastry-making is said to have begun around 1270, with the "patissiers-oublayeurs", who supplied the Church, their principal client, with the consecrated wafers used during religious services, as well as a variety of pastries connected with religious holidays . . . "nieulles", for instance, which were attached to the feet of birds released in the sanctuary during the "Gloria in Excelsis", and "échaudés", the only pastry which could lawfully be sold on All Saints' Day.

And then there were "gaufres à pardon" (that is, "waffles of forgiveness"), baked in molds depicting sacred themes and sold to hungry churchgoers after mass. Traffic jams in front of churches (yes, even then!) became such a nuisance that a royal decree was finally issued, making it illegal to sell these popular pastries too close to places of worship. Later, a "pastry" was any kind of food—sweet or savory—encased in crust. An early version of pâte brisée was most frequently used.

This pastry is similar to pâte sablée but is less rich and easier to handle.

(I-6)
Pâte Brisée
(Short Pastry)

Ingredients: (for about 11 ounces dough)
1/2	cup butter, softened
1 1/2	teaspoons sugar
1	egg yolk
1 1/2	tablespoons milk
1	cup flour
1/2	teaspoon salt

In a mixing bowl, beat together butter and sugar until light and creamy. Stir in egg yolk, then milk. Add the flour and salt to creamed mixture and mix with the hands just until a smooth dough is formed. Cover and refrigerate at least 1 hour before using.

Note: If refrigerated overnight before use, the dough will be more tender.

Storage: Wrap in plastic and store in the refrigerator for up to 3 days, or freeze for up to 1 month. Allow to thaw overnight in the refrigerator or for several hours at room temperature. In the latter case, you may have to chill it slightly before using.

I-7 PÂTE SABLÈE

In the early Middle Ages, the term "dessert" was used only in reference to the various kinds of entertainment performed to amuse guests at royal banquets, while the tables were being cleared off and readied for the next course. Later, during the 14th and 15th centuries, it took on a more culinary meaning, referring to the third course of important dinners, when sweet dishes and jellies (twin sisters to our modern day "jello") were served alongside roasted swans, pheasants, and peacocks.

This rich, short pie crust can also be used for making sand tarts, as indicated by its name ("sable" meaning "sand"). The pastry chef who trained me, often reminded me that this delicate pastry must be "treated like a young bride."

(I-7)
Pâte Sablèe
(Sweet Short Pastry)

Ingredients: (for about 14 ounces dough)

1	cup flour
3	tablespoons sugar
1/4	teaspoon salt
3	tablespoons ground almonds
2/3	cup butter, softened
2	egg yolks
1	tablespoon milk

In a mixing bowl, combine dry ingredients, then mix in the butter with the hands, until mixture is like coarse crumbs. Add egg yolks and milk, and continue mixing with a wooden spoon just until a supple but firm dough is formed. Cover and refrigerate 1 hour before rolling out.

Note: If the dough is too dry, knead in a little milk. If you have trouble rolling it out because of its fragility, knead it lightly for a minute, to make it more elastic and consequently easier to handle. Overkneading would make it tough, though, so don't go overboard.

Storage: Wrap in plastic and refrigerate for 3 to 4 days, or freeze for up to 1 month. Let thaw in the refrigerator for several hours before using.

I-8 PÂTE FEUILLETÉE CLASSIQUE

An interesting medieval custom: During Lent, churches were equipped with "butter boxes" for those who wished to indulge their yearning for butter during that strict period of fasting. A small donation served as a religious dispensation, thereby satisfying Church and gourmets alike.

Although pâte feuilletée exists since at least the 14th century, as proven by a charter dated 1311, we have Antonïn Carême to thank for the recipe we use today. The classical technique of "touring" isn't as complicated as it will probably seem at first. With a little bit of practice, it will become easy.

(I-8)

Pâte Feuilletée Classique
(Classic Puff Pastry)

Ingredients: (for about 1 pound, 6 ounces dough)

1 3/4	cups flour
1	teaspoon salt
3	tablespoons butter, softened
3/4	cup water
1	cup (two sticks) butter

Ingredients: (for about 2 pounds, 12 ounces dough)

3 3/4	cups flour
2	teaspoons salt
1/3	cup butter, softened
1 1/2	cups water
2	cups (4 sticks) butter

In a large mixing bowl, stir together flour and salt. With hands, mix in butter, then stir in water to make a stiff dough. (This can be accomplished nicely in a mixer or food processor, providing you do not overbeat.) Dust lightly with flour, wrap in plastic, and refrigerate 2 hours.

Remove 1 cup butter from refrigerator 30 minutes before using. Place between 2 sheets of plastic wrap and beat with a rolling pin to form a solid sheet of butter about 1/2-inch thick. On a lightly floured surface, roll out the dough to a large square about 1/4-inch thick and place sheet of butter in the middle. Fold over edges to envelope completely and press well with fingers, to seal.

Sprinkle flour on dough, rolling pin, and working surface, then roll out dough into a 1/4-inch thick rectangle and fold it in thirds. Turn the dough 90-degrees, so that the single fold is perpendicular to you, and roll out again. Press with two

More→

(Pâte Feuilletée, Cont.)

fingers so you'll remember that you've done two tours (turns), then wrap and refrigerate 1 hour.

Remove from refrigerator and give dough two more tours (turns), as described above, then mark with four impressions, wrap and refrigerate. At this point, the dough can be refrigerated for 3 to 4 days, or frozen. Before using, give it two more tours and refrigerate 1 hour. If you plan to use it the same day, give the dough the last two tours after the second refrigeration time, then refrigerate 1 hour before using.

Storage: Wrap in plastic and refrigerate 3 to 4 days, or freeze for up to 1 month. If frozen, thaw in refrigerator 24 hours, then do the last two tours, and refrigerate 1 hour.

Note: Rognures (I-8a) are simply scraps of leftover pâte feuiletée. Whatever you do, don't throw them away! They're perfect for pastries like mille-feuilles and certain pie crusts, which should be light but shouldn't puff up too much. Pack them in a tight ball, wrap in plastic and refrigerate several hours or, better yet, overnight before using, so that the rognures will have time to relax.

To use, weigh, then cut off the quantity desired. After rolling out, refrigerate again at least an hour before baking, so that it will relax again and the risk of excessive shrinkage in the oven can be reduced. Rognures keep well, but don't forget them in the refrigerator: they'll turn black after several days, just like pâte feuilletée. Pâte demi-feuilletée isn't suitable for rognures because the resulting pastry wouldn't be light enough, and the rognures themselves wouldn't keep well while waiting to be used.

I-9 PÂTE DEMI-FEUILLETÉE

The reduced number of "tours" (turns) in this simplified recipe cuts down on the work. Also, the dough is easier to roll out and handle because the détrempe contains butter. However, it doesn't keep as well as classical pâte feuilletée, and doesn't puff up quite as much.

(I-9)
Pâte Demi-Feuilletée
(Quick Puff Pastry)

Ingredients: (for about 1 pound, 6 ounces dough)
1 3/4	cups flour
1 1/2	teaspoons salt
1/3	cup butter, softened
3/4	cup water (may need 1/4 cup more)
1/2	cup (1 stick) butter

Ingredients: (for about 2 pounds, 12 ounces dough)
3 3/4	cups flour
1	tablespoon salt
3/4	cup (1 1/2 sticks) butter, softened
1 1/2	cups water
1	cup (2 sticks) butter

In a large mixing bowl, stir together flour and salt. Add butter and water, and stir until a stiff dough forms. This is called a "détrempe". It should be stiff but not dry, so knead in a little more water, if necessary (or flour, if it's too soft). Turn out onto a lightly floured surface and knead for 1 minute. Cover and refrigerate 1 hour.

Remove butter from refrigerator 30 minutes before using. Place between 2 sheets of plastic wrap and beat with a rolling pin, or better yet, a smaller wooden cylinder, to form a solid sheet of butter about 1/4-inch thick.

On a lightly floured surface, roll out the dough into a long rectangle about 1/4-inch thick. Place the butter on top of the dough, toward the far end. If it doesn't cover 2/3 of the surface, break it into small pieces and spread them out some. Rather than folding in three, as for classical pâte feuilletée, fold one end over to the middle, fold the other end to the middle, then fold in half. This is called a "double tour" or "tour portefeuille" ("portefeuille" means "wallet" or "billfold"). Press with 2 fingers so you'll remember you've done one double tour, wrap in plastic, and refrigerate 1 hour.

Remove dough from refrigerator and place it with the single fold nearest to you. Turn it 90-degrees, so that the single fold is perpendicular to you, and roll it out to 1/4 inch thick. Fold as described above, then wrap and refrigerate 1 hour.

More→

(Pâte Demi-Feuilletée, Cont.)

Remove from refrigerator and repeat the above step, including refrigeration time. Use immediately after refrigeration. If it's allowed to sit, even in the refrigerator, the pastry will fail to rise properly when baked.

Note: If plaques of butter develop, give the dough one or even two extra tours. Also, if the butter comes through the dough (which shouldn't happen, if refrigeration times are respected) sprinkle on more flour.

Storage: Can be frozen after the second double tour. Thaw overnight in refrigerator, then do last double tour and refrigerate 1 hour before using.

I-10   PÂTE À BRIOCHE

According to France's great novelist Alexandre Dumas, brioche is so-called because the original recipe called for cheese from Brie. Over the years, the recipe evolved and the cheese was gradually eliminated, but the name has remained the same. This buttery, rich breakfast or tea bread is delicious all by itself, but also serves as the departure point for more elaborate creations.

(I-10)
Pâte à Brioche
(Rich Butter Bread)

Ingredients: (for about 11 ounces dough)

3	eggs
1 3/4	cups flour
3/4	teaspoon salt
1	tablespoon sugar
1	cake compressed yeast
3	tablespoons milk

1/2   cup (1 stick) butter, softened

Break the eggs into a large mixing bowl, then, without stirring, add the unsifted flour. In three different places, place the salt, sugar, and crumbled yeast. (If the salt or sugar come into contact with the yeast, they'll burn it.) Gradually add the milk, then, holding the bowl with one hand and mixing with the other, knead for 10 minutes, bringing the cupped hand up and away from the side of the bowl in a lifting motion, so that the dough will be well aerated.

(If the bowl slips around too much, a folded dishtowel underneath will help keep it in place.) Add the butter, and knead for another 5 minutes. The dough should be soft and elastic, but not runny. When it's ready, it will pull away from your hands. With a rubber spatula, clean the sides of the bowl, then cover and refrigerate overnight before using.

More➤

(Pâte à Brioche, Cont.)

Storage: Cover tightly and refrigerate for up to 48 hours. It can also be frozen for up to 1 month. Allow to thaw overnight in the refrigerator before using.

I-11   PÂTE À CHOUX

These small round puff pastries, well known and loved by most Americans, bring to mind the vegetable which gave them their name. After all, "chou", in French, also means "cabbage". While we're on the subject, I'd like to clear up one longstanding misconception about a popular French endearment. "Mon chou" is in direct reference to . . . the pastry, of course, and not the vegetable!

Profiteroles, cream puffs, éclairs, Paris-Brest...there's almost no end to the array of pastries made with this base.

(I-11)
Pâte à Choux
(Cream Puff Pastry)

Ingredients: (for about 1 1/4 cups dough)
- 1/2 cup, plus two tablespoons, water
- 2 tablespoons butter
- 1/2 teaspoon salt
- 1/2 teaspoon sugar

- 1/2 cup flour

- 2 eggs

In a medium saucepan, heat water, butter, salt and sugar to a boil. Remove from heat and add flour all at once, then stir until a stiff, slightly lumpy dough is formed. Return to heat and cook for a minute or so, stirring constantly with a wooden spoon, until dough pulls away from sides of pan and forms a ball. Don't let it get too dry or mixing in the eggs would be difficult.

Turn the hot dough into a large mixing bowl, and beat in the eggs, one at a time. If the eggs are very large, separate the last one and stir in the yolk, then if the dough is still too stiff, stir in the white. This is more trouble than adding it all at once, but it helps to avoid a runny dough. Stop beating as soon as the eggs are blended in, since overbeating causes lopsided choux. The dough must be baked immediately; otherwise, it would dry a little and tend to crack while baking.

If you can, use a pastry bag with a fluted nozzle to shape the dough. The rippled texture made by the fluted nozzle helps the dough rise straight and puff up well. Baking sheets should be very lightly greased to prevent sticking. If they're too

More➔

(Pâte à Choux, Cont.)

oily, wipe them off with a paper towel. Pipe out the desired shapes, brush with beaten egg so they will brown well, and, if you didn't use a fluted nozzle, drag the tines of a fork lightly across the dough.

Bake in a preheated 425-degrees oven for the first 15 minutes, then lower heat to 400-degrees, prop oven door open with a spoon (this is done to allow the steam, created by the baking choux, to escape — if trapped, it would cause them to crack or even fall) and finish baking. As a general rule, pâte à choux should be rather well-baked. It tends to soften when cooled, and if underbaked, would get soggy shortly after being filled.

Storage: Although the dough itself can't be frozen, the baked choux can. Store them in plastic bags in the freezer for up to 1 month. To use, heat for a few minutes in a preheated 300-degree oven. They can also be stored, wrapped in plastic, in a cool, dry place for up to 2 days.

I-12.   MERINGUE FRANÇAISE

Meringue was invented in 1720 by a Swiss pastry chef: a certain Mr. Gasparini, but it was named after the Polish town of Mehrinyghen, where it was created. King Sanislas Leszczynski, in giving his daugher Marie in marriage to King Louis XV, was indirectly responsible for introducing this specialty to the French people. Marie-Antoinette, the ill-fated wife of Louis XVI, adored meringues and enjoyed preparing them herself, using a recipe given to her by Marie Leszczynski.

There are three different kinds of meringue, two of which are cooked twice. Meringue Francaise is the easiest and quickest to prepare, and adapted to most dessert recipes.

(I-12)
Meringue Française
(French Meringue)

Ingredients: (for 24 individual shells)
- 1/2   cup granulated sugar
- 1/2   cup powdered sugar, sifted if lumpy

- 3   egg whites (about 1/2 cup)
-      pinch salt

Preheat oven to lowest setting. In a small bowl, mix together the sugars. In a large mixing bowl, beat egg whites and salt at high speed until soft peaks form, then add 1 tablespoon sugar and continue beating until very stiff. Lower speed and beat in rest of sugar. Stop beating as soon as it's blended in.

More →

(Meringue Française, Cont.)

Butter and flour baking sheets. Spoon meringue into pastry bag and pipe out one of the following:

> **Têtes de Nègre:** 24 (2 x 2-inch) round meringues
> **Meringues à la Chantilly:** 24 (1 1/2 x 2 1/2-inch) ovals

Note: In most cases, meringue should be dried rather than baked. Place in preheated oven, crack the door with a spoon, and dry for 1 to 1 1/2 hours, or until completely dried. It should be, at the very darkest, a deep cream color. Be sure to keep the oven door ajar, so that the steam formed during baking can escape rather than soften the meringue and make it fall. Watch it closely, if it browns too quickly, turn off the oven.

Storage: Wrap in plastic and store in a cool, dry place for up to 3 weeks.

I-13 MERINGUE SUISSE

In L'Histoire à Table, Andre Castelot tells the following story: During the early 1800's, when an English blockade created a severe sugar shortage on the Continent, the bourgeois of Paris created a new custom: "sugar on a string". A piece of rock candy was suspended from the ceiling by a string, and each family member was allowed to dip it into his coffee. There was no risk of anyone leaving it in too long, since the permitted number of seconds was strictly monitored.

Swiss meringue differs from French meringue in that it is whipped over a double boiler. The resulting meringue is smoother and has less of a tendency to fall when baked.

(I-13)
Meringue Suisse
(Swiss Meringue)

**Ingredients: (for about 5 cups meringue or 36 individual meringues,
1 3/4-inch in diameter)**

4	egg whites
1 1/4	cups granulated sugar

In a 2-quart double boiler (over, hot but not boiling water) beat egg whites and sugar at high speed for 10 minutes. The meringue should be thick, smooth and glossy. Remove from heat, reduce speed to medium, and continue beating for 5 minutes, or until cool and very thick.

Use for meringue shells (see I-12).

More➤

(Meringue Suisse. Cont.)

Variations: Beat in 1 teaspoon vanilla extract and:

Almond (I-13a): 2 cups chopped, untoasted or toasted almonds. (Pecans can also be used for this.)

Coconut (I-13b): 2 cups unsweetened, coconut flakes.

Chocolate (I-13c): 2 to 3 tablespoons unsweetened cocoa powder.

Coffee (I-13d): 1 to 2 teaspoons coffee extract. (Extreme care should be taken to avoid adding too much coffee extract, which would make the meringue too moist and keep it from drying properly in the oven.)

Preheat oven to lowest setting. Drop meringue by teaspoons onto buttered and floured baking sheets. Space 1/2-inch apart. Crack oven door open with a spoon to allow steam to escape, and bake 1 1/2 hours. The meringues should darken only very slightly. If they darken too quickly, turn off oven and leave them in until dry.

Storage: Wrap in plastic and store in a cool, dry place for up to 3 weeks.

I-14 MERINGUE ITALIENNE

Up until the 16th century, sugar was so expensive that it was sold only by apothecaries. It was during this era that an expression was coined: "apothecary without sugar", which meant "a boutique where nothing of consequence can be found."

Sugar, cooked to the soft ball stage, then blended with whipped egg whites, makes a more voluminous, less fragile meringue.

(I-14)
Meringue Italienne
(Italian Meringue)

Ingredients: (for about 7 to 8 cups meringue or about
48 individual 1 3/4-inch meringues)

1 1/4	cups granulated sugar
1/3	cup water
4	egg whites
2	tablespoons granulated sugar

In a small saucepan, cook sugar and water over low heat until it reaches the soft ball stage (238-degrees).

More➔

(Meringue Italienne, Cont.)

While the sugar is cooking, in a large mixing bowl, beat egg whites at high speed until soft peaks form. Beat in 2 tablespoons sugar, and continue beating until stiff peaks form.

When the sugar has reached the soft ball stage, drizzle it in slowly, between beaters and bowl, beating all the while. Stop when sugar is completely blended in.

Use as for meringue shells **(see I-12).**

Variations: Beat in 1 1/4 teaspoons vanilla extract and add:

Almond (I-14a): 2 1/2 cups chopped almonds (can also use pecans.)

Coconut (I-14b): 2 1/2 cups unsweetened flaked coconut

Chocolate (I-14c): 3 to 4 tablespoons unsweetened cocoa powder

Coffee (I-14d): 1 to 2 teaspoons coffee extract. (Add it a few drops at a time, and stop when meringue reaches desired color. As for Swiss Meringue, too much moisture will not let it dry properly.)

Preheat oven to lowest setting. Drop teaspoons of meringue onto buttered and floured baking sheets, spacing 1/2-inch apart. Crack oven door open with a spoon to allow steam to escape, and bake 1 1/2 hours. The meringues should darken only very slightly. If they darken too quickly, turn off oven and leave them in until dry.

Note: Although the same number of egg whites are called for in this recipe, as for Meringue Suisse, Meringue Italienne is more voluminous because the whites haven't been heated. When flavorings are stirred in, the volume will be reduced slightly.

Storage: Wrap in plastic and store in a cool, dry place for up to 3 weeks.

Chapter II

Basic Creams, Syrups and Fillings
(Crèmes et Sirops de Base)

II-1   CRÈME CHANTILLY

"Ah! It will be the death of me...I will never survive the dishonor!" the little man in white murmured faintly, wringing his hands as he paced back and forth in the royal kitchens. Ever since King Louis XIV had announced his intention to visit the Prince de Condé, the Château de Chantilly had been one immense flurry of activity, and François Vatel, the prince's head cook, hadn't slept in over a week.

In his overwrought mind, the minor problems encountered during that day's luncheon had been blown to colossal proportions, and now, the catastrophe he'd been dreading all along had actually happened: the fish for that evening's formal dinner had failed to arrive! He hurried to the top of a tower and looked out over the peaceful countryside...no sign of the long-awaited convoy from the coast.

Running a hand through his disheveled hair, he murmured again, "The dishonor ...the dishonor!" Back at the kitchens, he grabbed a small boy who had just come in the back door, carrying a crateful of fish.

"Is that all?" The cook's voice involuntarily rose an octave as he thought of the prince's numerous guests. Round-eyed, the boy took a step backward. "Yes, yes... it is sir, but the convoy will soon..."

Without a word, Vatel wheeled around and fled toward his living quarters. If only he had waited for the boy to finish. Minutes later, a group of men broke down his door, only to find the "dishonored" cook, run through on his own sword. They had come to tell him that the fish had finally arrived...

The unfortunate Vatel is better known for his dramatic suicide than for his delicious invention: crème chantilly.

(II-1)
Crème Chantilly
(Whipped Cream)

Ingredients: (for about 1 cup whipped cream)
- 1/2   cup heavy cream, well chilled
- 2   tablespoons sugar

Ingredients: (for about 2 cups whipped cream)
- 1   cup heavy cream well chilled
- 1/4   cup sugar

In a deep, preferably metal mixing bowl, beat the cream at high speed for 7 or 8 minutes, until the cream is firm and fluffy. Don't overbeat - - unless you want a bowlful of butter! Delicately fold in the sugar.

Crème Chantilly au Chocolat (Chocolate Whipped Cream) (II-1a): Flavor with 1 1/2 ounces semi-sweet chocolate per cup of whipped cream. Over a double boiler, melt the chocolate, stir in 1 teaspoon water until the mixture is smooth, then let cool until barely warm. Whip the unsweetened cream as above. Beat 1/3 of the cream into the melted chocolate, then carefully fold the chocolate mixture into the rest of the cream. Chill thoroughly before using.

Note: To help keep the cream from turning into butter, chill the bowl and utensils before use. That's why a metal bowl is preferable—it chills faster and stays cold longer.

Storage: Refrigerate, tightly covered, for no more than 48 hours.

II-2 CRÈME PATISSIÈRE

Vanilla and the new world were discovered at the same time: The Aztecs served the Spanish conquistadors a chocolate drink flavored with pods from a species of orchid. Both chocolate and vanilla were taken back to Spain, along with the Aztecs' fabulous treasures.

French pastry cream is used as a filling for pâte à chou (cream puffs), millefeuilles (Napoleons), layer cakes, pies and the like.

(II-2)

Crème Patissière
(French Vanilla Pastry Cream)

Ingredients: (for about 1 1/8 cups crème patissière)

1/3	cup sugar
3	tablespoons flour
	pinch salt

3/4	cup milk
2	egg yolks

1/4	teaspoon vanilla extract

Ingredients: (for about 2 1/4 cups crème patissière)

2/3	cup sugar
6	tablespoons flour
1/8	teaspoon salt

1 2/3	cups milk
4	egg yolks

1/2	teaspoon vanilla extract

In a medium saucepan, mix together the dry ingredients, then, with a wooden spoon, stir in enough milk to make a thick paste. Stir until smooth, then whisk in the egg yolks, followed by the rest of the milk. Cook over medium heat, stirring constantly, for another minute or two. Remove from heat and stir in vanilla extract.

Au chocolat (Chocolate) (II-2a): Add 2-ounces semi-sweet chocolate per cup of pastry cream or 1/3 cup chocolate chips. Stir into the hot pudding and allow to cool, stirring from time to time.

Au café (Coffee) (II-2b) : Add 1 1/2 teaspoons instant coffee, or 1 teaspoon coffee extract per cup of pastry cream. Stir until blended.

Crème Légère (Light Buttercream) (II-2c): Beat one part crème au beurre (II-4) with two parts chilled crème patissière until smooth. This is an especially good filling, since it's lighter and creamier than crème patissière alone. It also dries less quickly.

Storage: Cover tightly and refrigerate up to 48 hours.

II-3   CRÈME ANGLAISE

As in some French provinces, peasants in Lancashire, England never throw their eggshells in the fire because their hens, according to an old superstition, would become permanently sterile.

As indicated by the name, this rich custard sauce originated in England, but is used in many French desserts. For an even richer sauce, just add one or two more egg yolks -- but you must be even more vigilant, since it curdles more quickly.

(II-3)
Crème Anglaise
(English Custard Sauce-Vanilla)

Ingredients: (for about 1 1/2 cups crème anglaise)

1/3	cup sugar
	pinch salt

1 1/2	cups milk
3	egg yolks

1/4	teaspoon vanilla extract

In a medium saucepan, mix together sugar and salt. With a wooden spoon, stir in enough cold milk to make a thick paste, then whisk in the egg yolks until blended. Pour in the rest of milk and cook, stirring constantly, over medium heat until the mixture thickens slightly and reaches the boiling point, but doesn't actually boil. Remove from heat and stir in vanilla extract.

Place saucepan in cold water to stop cooking and stir until partially cooled. Serve warm or chilled. This recipe should generally be doubled when served with desserts.

Au Café (Coffee) (II-3a): Per cup crème, whisk in 1 1/2 teaspoons coffee extract. (Preferably not strong coffee).

Au Chocolat (Chocolate) (II-3b): Whisk in 2 teaspoons unsweetened cocoa powder per cup hot crème. (Preferably not semi-sweet chocolate or chocolate chips).

Note: - To serve cold, stir 1/2 cup cold milk into 1 1/2 cups hot crème, allow to cool to room temperature, then refrigerate until use. Be very careful not to let the sauce boil. If it does, even for a few seconds, it will curdle. Placing the saucepan in cold water and beating vigorously can sometimes, but not always, repair the damage.

Storage: Cover tightly and refrigerate up to 48 hours.

II-4   CRÈME AU BEURRE

Laws designed to protect the consumer by insuring the quality of foodstuffs aren't a modern invention. In the Middle Ages, for example, the fabrication of butter was strictly regulated, and unscrupulous "crèmiers" who added pork fat or dye made from yellow flowers were subject to heavy fines. This rich buttercream frosting is also mixed with fillings to make them lighter and creamier.

(II-4)
Crème au Beurre
(Rich Buttercream Frosting)

Ingredients: (for about 2 1/2 cups crème au beurre)
- 1   cup (two sticks) butter
- 2/3   cup sugar
- 2   tablespoons water

- 2   eggs

Cut the butter into small chunks and set aside.   In a small saucepan, cook the sugar and water over low heat to the soft ball stage, 242-degrees on the candy thermometer.

While the sugar cooks, beat the whole eggs at high speed in a deep mixing bowl until light and fluffy. When the sugar is ready, pour it over the eggs, between the side of the bowl and the beaters, beating all the while to avoid cooking the eggs.

Beat for another 10 minutes, until almost cool, then beat in the butter, 2 or 3 chunks at a time. The frosting, liquid at first, will suddenly thicken as you add the last third of the butter. Continue beating until perfectly smooth and creamy.

Au chocolat (Chocolate) (II-4a): Use 2 ounces melted semi-sweet chocolate per cup of crème au beurre. Beat until smooth.

Au café (Coffee) (II-4b): Beat in about 1 teaspoon coffee extract per cup of crème au beurre. Don't flavor with strong coffee.

Au prâlin (Praline) (II-4c): Beat in about 1/4 cup prâlin (II-9) per cup crème au beurre.

Au kirsch (Kirsch) (II-4d): Beat in 1 tablespoon kirsch and 1 or 2 drops green food coloring per cup crème au beurre.

Au Grand Marnier (Grand Marnier) (II-4e): Beat in 1 tablespoon Grand Marnier and 1 or 2 drops red food coloring per cup of crème au beurre.

A la vanille (Vanilla) (II-4f): Beat in 1 teaspoon vanilla extract per cup of crème au beurre

Crème au Beurre au Lait (Light Buttercream) (II-4g): Beat together 3/4 cup crème au beurre with 1/3 cup crème patissière (II-2). This kind is softer and less rich.

More➔

(Crème au Beurre, Cont.)

Crème au Beurre Meringuée (Meringue & Buttercream) (II-4h): Beat together 2/3 cup crème au beurre with 1/3 cup meringue française (I-12).

Note: To use refrigerated or frozen crème au beurre: let stand at room temperature for 30 minutes, then place quantity desired in a saucepan and heat **very** gently and briefly over low heat, beating all the while, preferably with a wire whisk, until the crème is smooth and spreadable. Avoid overheating.

Storage: Cover tightly and refrigerate for up to 1 week, or freeze for up to 1 month.

Afterword: *Butter seems to have had somewhat the same beginnings as sugar: apparently of Middle Eastern origin, its rarity and elevated price caused it to be used for centuries as a remedy rather than an aliment. Although Pline had a dim view of that vaguely barbaric product, the ancient Romans were especially confident of the healing powers of butter churned in May.*

II-5   CRÈME CHIBOUST
Italian meringue makes this basic pastrycream—named after the 19th century pastry chef who created it—particularly delicate. Use it as an alternate filling for St. Honorés, and cream-filled "baskets", or as a topping for Tarte Princesse.

(II-5)
Crème Chiboust
(Italian Meringue Pastrycream)

Ingredients: (for about 4 1/2 cups crème)

3	tablespoons sugar
2	tablespoons cornstarch
1/8	teaspoon salt
3/4	cup milk
3	egg yolks
1	teaspoon unflavored gelatin
1/4	teaspoon vanilla extract
3/4	cup sugar
3	tablespoons water
3	egg whites
	pinch salt

More➔

(Crème Chiboust, Cont.)

In a small saucepan, stir together sugar, cornstarch and salt, then stir in enough milk to make a thick, smooth paste. Whisk in the egg yolks, followed by rest of milk. Cook, stirring constantly with a wooden spoon over medium heat until crème thickens and boils. Lower heat and continue cooking for another minute or so. Stir in gelatin and vanilla. Remove from heat, cover, and set aside.

In another small saucepan, cook sugar and water over medium heat, to soft ball stage, 242-degrees on a candy thermometer. Meanwhile, in a deep mixing bowl, beat egg whites and salt at high speed until very stiff. When sugar has reached soft ball stage, drizzle it slowly over whites, between the beaters and the side of bowl, beating all the while to avoid cooking the whites. Stop beating as soon as sugar is completely mixed in.

Whisk a big spoonful of meringue into the warm pastrycream, then pour this mixture over the rest of meringue and with a rubber spatula, fold together carefully. Cover tightly and refrigerate until using: within 2 hours.

II-6   CRÈME AU CITRON

The Ancients clearly prized the lemon tree as much as the laurel: they often wove crowns of lemon leaves to adorn statues of their gods. The French borrowed this tangy lemon cream from the British Isles, where it originated, and found typically continental ways of enjoying it: in rolled cakes, doughnuts, chaussons, mousses...But don't eat it plain...it's far too tangy.

(II-6)
Crème au Citron
(Lemon Curd)

Ingredients: (for about 1 1/2 cups crème)
- 1/2   cup (1 stick) butter
- 3/4   cup sugar
- finely-grated rind of one lemon (about 1 tablespoon)
- juice of 1 1/2 lemons (about 5 to 6 tablespoons)
- 1   egg
- 1   egg yolk
- 2   tablespoons flour

In a double boiler, melt butter, then whisk in rest of ingredients and cook, stirring constantly, until thick. Cook a few minutes longer, still stirring, then remove from heat.

Crème au Citron (Lemon Cream) (II-6a): To use it as a filling for beignets and chaussons, mix one part crème au citron with two parts crème patissière (II-2)

Storage: Cover tightly and refrigerate for 3 to 4 days.

II-7 FRANGIPANE

During the Italian Renaissance, refinement in dress and cuisine reached its zenith, as illustrated by the Marquess of Frangipani, who launched a new fashion when he began scenting his gloves with almond extract. In honor of the refined marquess, a rich almond cream, created about the same time, bears his name: frangipane.

Many desserts owe their flavor and high nutritional value to this almond-rich pastry cream, which is also called "crème d'amandes".

(II-7)

Frangipane
(Almond Pastrycream)

Ingredients: (for about 1 3/4 cups frangipane)

1/2	cup (one stick) butter, softened
2/3	cup sugar
1	cup blanched, ground almonds
1	egg (whole)
1	egg yolk
1 1/2	tablespoons cornstarch
1	tablespoon rum
	pinch salt

In a large mixing bowl, beat together the butter and sugar until creamy, then beat in almonds alternately with eggs. Continue beating until light, then beat in cornstarch, rum, and salt.

To use refrigerated frangipane, let stand at room temperature for 30 minutes, then beat by hand or with an electric mixer until smooth.

Variation: Beat together until smooth: 1 part crème patissière (II-2) with 2 parts frangipane. Use the same way as frangipane.

Note: If you can't find ground almonds, you can grind them yourself in a blender or food processor. 1/2 pound of shelled, blanched almonds makes about 2 cups ground. Be careful not to grind them at too high a speed or for too long, or you'll end up with "nut butter".

Storage: Cover tightly and refrigerate for up to a week. Can also be frozen for up to 1 month.

Afterword: *Some gastronomists assert that frangipane was really created by a certain Brother Frangipani, companion of St. Francis of Assisi, and not by the Marquess of Frangipani.*

II-8 CARAMEL

In the 7th century A.D., the Arab nations discovered sugar cane, from which they extracted a kind of thick syrup called "Kurat al Milh". The name has changed, over the centuries, to "caramel".

In hard or liquid form, caramel is used for topping a wide variety of desserts.

(II-8)
Caramel

Ingredients: (for about 2/3 cup caramel)

1	cup sugar
4	tablespoons water
1	teaspoon lemon juice

Dur (Hard Caramel) (II-8a): In a medium saucepan, cook the sugar, water, and lemon juice over medium heat until the mixture begins to bubble. Lower heat and continue cooking. When the sugar begins to darken, tilt the pan slightly in a rotating motion so that it will color evenly. Don't stir. When the caramel has taken on a deep amber color, it's ready to use. Pour it quickly into the prepared mold or over the dessert. It will harden immediately.

Liquide (Liquid Caramel) (II-8b): Add 1/2 cup water to the finished caramel. It will splatter when the cold water hits it, so stand back a little until the splattering has died down. Stir the mixture to be sure that it has melted completely. It should be very liquid, since it thickens upon cooling. If it gets too thick, add a little water.

Note: If you're like me, you'll be tempted to stir the sugar as it cooks. Resist the urge! Stirring aerates the sugar, and you'd end up with a lumpy granulated mess.

Storage: Cover tightly and refrigerate for up to 2 weeks.

II-9 PRÂLIN

The Maréchal du Plessis-Praslin gave his name to a kind of candy invented by his cook: a simple bonbon made from almonds and caramelized sugar. Later, a creative pastry chef ground up this rich almond brittle and used it to flavor and garnish desserts, such as Paris-Brest, choux pralinés, crème au beurre…

(II-9)

Prâlin
(Ground Caramelized Almonds)

Ingredients: (for about 2 1/2 cups prâlin)
- 2   cups finely-chopped, blanched almonds

- 1   cup sugar
- 4   tablespoons water
- 1   teaspoon lemon juice

   butter for cooling surface

On a baking sheet, in a low oven, toast almonds lightly. In a medium saucepan, cook sugar, water, and lemon juice until amber colored, (238-degrees on a candy thermometer.) Stir in almonds, bring to a boil, then pour out onto a generously buttered cooling surface (formica or marble table or counter top, baking sheet, etc.). Cool completely, then break into small pieces and blend to a coarse powder in food processor or blender.

Note: You may have seen prâlin recipes which call for grinding it by hand with a mortar and pestle. It's possible, but only if you have a very big mortar and pestle, a lot of time, and plenty of muscle power!

Storage: Cover tightly and refrigerate or freeze several months.

II-10 FONDANT

During the Middle Ages, many products owed their wide availability to the Crusades, and sugar was no exception. Medieval Europeans, who curiously referred to it as "Indian salt", could find it in numerous shapes and forms, flavored with rose petals, violets, orange blossoms, and even musk. Its exorbitant price made it prohibitive for pastry making, so it was carefully locked away and doled out in miserly portions to treat illnesses.

This may seem like a lot of trouble to go to, when a powdered sugar glaze would surely do as well. Unfortunatly, it won't. That kind of glaze tends to become hard and dull-looking once it dries, whereas cooked fondant remains shiny and firm, but never hardens.

(II-10)

Fondant
(Fondant Icing)

Ingredients: (for about 1 1/2 cups fondant)

2 1/2	cups sugar
3/4	cup water
1 1/2	teaspoons lemon juice

In a medium saucepan, heat ingredients over medium heat, without stirring, to soft ball stage (242-degrees), about 10 to 12 minutes. Pour out onto a cool, clean surface (marble is the best because it cools the sugar quickly, but a formica table or counter top will do) and let cool 1 minute. With a wooden spatula, begin stirring it in a circular, back and forth, or figure eight motion. The main thing is to work and aerate it.

With a large metal spatula or scraper, scrape the sugar on the edges into the center from time to time, so that all the sugar will be aerated. After a few minutes, the sugar will begin to thicken and turn translucent. Stir it for another 10 minutes, or until it becomes dull, dry, and compact. Scrape up with a metal spatula and store in a tightly covered plastic or glass container. Allow to rest at least 24 hours before using.

To use, place quantity desired in a saucepan and heat very gently and briefly, usually no more than 1 minute, beating vigorously with a wooden spoon all the while. To test, dip a knuckle into the warm fondant. It's ready if you can feel a uniform warmth.   Be careful not to overheat it, as it would turn hard and dull with cooling.

Some pastry chefs recommend heating it over a double boiler, but I prefer not to use this method. It's too much trouble, and the fondant gets too hot too quickly. When at the right consistency, it should be soft, and should pour easily, without being runny. If it gets too thin, stir in a little powdered sugar. If it's too thick after being flavored, colored and heated, then stir in a little corn syrup, not water. If it gets too hot, place pan in cold water and beat until fondant reaches the right temperature and consistency.

More➜

(Fondant, Cont.)

Au chocolat (Chocolate) (II-10a): Use 2-ounces unsweetened chocolate per cup of fondant. Melt the chocolate over a double boiler, then beat into the fondant.

Au café (Coffee) (II-10b): Beat 4 teaspoons coffee extract into 1 cup plain fondant.

Au kirsch (Kirsch) (II-10c): Beat 1 tablespoon kirsch and 1 drop green food coloring into 1 cup plain fondant. It should be pale green.

Au Grand Marnier (Grand Marnier) (II-10d): Beat 1 tablespoon Grand Marnier and 1 drop red food coloring into 1 cup plain fondant to make it a pale pink. It can also be pale peach colored: add 1/2 drop yellow food coloring and 1 drop red food coloring per cup of fondant.

Au rhum (Rum) (II-10e): Beat 1 tablespoon rum into 1 cup plain fondant. It usually isn't colored.

Storage: Keeps indefinitely in a cool, dry place. Cover tightly to prevent drying.

Most historians consider the ancient Greeks to be the world's first pastry cooks. Even centuries after the decline of that great empire, the most renowned pastry chefs in Rome were Greek. Their creations, composed mainly of flour or semolina, ground almonds and dates, then heavily spiced—strangely enough—with black pepper, were fried, then drenched with honey. Since then pastry toppings have greatly evolved. Lighter and less sweet, they add that last refined touch, as well as a subtle flavor to the finished dessert. This tangy glaze is what gives that appetizing shine to fruit pies, babas and savarins, brioches roulées, and other pastries.

(II-11)

Nappage
(Fruit Glaze)

Abricotage (Apricot Glaze) (II-11a): The most widely-used nappage is simply apricot preserves, homemade or a good brand from the store, blended, with an electric blender to a perfectly smooth, brushable consistency, then strained to remove any stray lumps or fibers.

Fruites Rouges (Currant/Raspberry Glaze) (II-11b): For strawberry or raspberry-topped pastries, use equal portions of red currant or plum jam, and seedless raspberry jam. Don't use strawberry jam or preserves. Too heavy and sweet, they would overpower rather than enhance the flavor of fresh fruit Prepare as above. To use either kind, heat gently and add a little kirsch or a few drops of lemon juice to thin and add flavor.

Storage: Cover tightly and refrigerate for up to 1 month.

II-12 SIROP À ENTREMETS

The Gauls, ancestors of the modern-day Frenchman, used only honey to sweeten their food. Sugar was known to them (they called it "reed honey" because of sugar cane's resemblance to reeds) but they employed it only in case of illness or injury, since they believed it to have medicinal properties. Throughout the Middle Ages, people continued to regard it as a drug, just as they did any rare spice.

Flavored with vanilla or coffee extract, or the alcohol of your choice, this syrup is used most often for garnishing cakes before frosting.

(II-12)
Sirop à Entremets
(Dessert Syrup)

Ingredients: (for about 1 1/4 cups syrup)
- 3/4 cup sugar
- 3/4 cup water

Flavorings:
A l'alcool (Alcohol) (II-12a): 1/4 cup alcohol (rum, kirsch, or Grand Marnier)

À la vanille (Vanilla Syrup) (II-12b): 1/4 cup water and 1 teaspoon vanilla

Au Café (Coffee Syrup) (II-12c): 1/4 cup water and 1 teaspoon coffee extract

In the saucepan, heat sugar and water to a boil. Cool, then stir in flavoring.

Storage: Cover tightly and refrigerate for up to 2 weeks.

II-13 COULIS DE FRUITS

Centuries ago, all sauces, including meat gravies, were called "coulis" (from the word "couler"—"to flow"). Since then, the term gradually became limited to fresh fruit sauces.

This refreshing sauce, which can be made with any kind of fresh or frozen fruit, accompanies numerous desserts.

(II-13)

Coulis de Fruits
(Fresh Fruit Sauce)

Ingredients: (for about 3 cups sauce)

1	pound fresh or frozen, unsweetened fruit
2/3	cup sugar
1	teaspoon kirsch (optional)

Wash the fruit, peel, and remove stones or seeds. If you're using strawberries, remove stems and if very sandy, rinse quickly and pat dry with paper towels. Place in blender with sugar and kirsch, and blend at medium speed for about 2 minutes, or until smooth.

Note: Whenever possible, avoid excessive washing of strawberries and raspberries. Never allow them to soak, they'd quickly become waterlogged and lose their taste.

Storage: Refrigerate, tightly covered, for 3 to 4 days, or freeze for up to 1 month. Thaw several hours at room temperature, then beat until smooth.

II-14 CÔMPOTE DE POMMES

"I want to see her right now! No, don't bother to announce me, I know she's home." A small, plump woman in flowing robes of seaweed pushed past the butler and burst into the living room.

"Thetis, darling, what a lovely surprise! Do come in..." the elegant blond called languidly from the divan by the window. *"I do wish, though, that you'd change clothes before coming,"* she added, frowning slightly at the pool of sea water gathering on the carpet, *"or at least dry off."*

Thetis ignored the second remark. *"Lovely surprise, my eye!"* She strode over to where her rival was lounging. *"What's this about golden apples? I hear that Paris was handing them out like peanuts, yesterday afternoon."*

"Golden apples?" Venus' blue eyes opened wide in innocent astonishment. *"Just one, actually. After all, it's hardly the kind that grows on trees!"* White teeth flashed as she smiled over her own joke. *"And he wasn't just 'handing it out' as you put it. There was a contest, and if you must know, I happened to be the winner."*

Thetis clearly wasn't about to be put off. *"And you conveniently forgot to tell me, so I could compete. Afraid I'd win?"*

"Darling, you must be joking!" Venus' eyes danced with amusement as they wandered over the stout figure, the scraggly hair.

The little woman drew herself up proudly. *"I may not be pretty, but I have even better things to offer."* With a wave of the hand, she indicated the ocean beyond the vast picture window. *"My kingdom is much more extensive than yours."*

"Oh, no. That's where you're wrong!" The goddess of love suddenly sprang to her feet and faced Thetis. *"I rule over hearts, which makes me more powerful than all the kings on Earth put together! So say what you like. One fact remains: I deserved that apple because I gave Paris something no one else could—love."*

"You may have the prize now, but we'll see just how long you manage to hang onto it!" Thetis declared as she turned and stomped out, her seaweed dress trailing on the white carpet.

And the goddess of the sea was true to her threat. Shortly thereafter, she stole Venus' golden apple, and to perpetuate the memory of her revenge, she triumphantly scattered its seeds along the northern shores of Gaul. That, according to Bernardin de St. Pierre, an 18th century writer and historian, is the origin of Normandy's famous apple orchards.

More➤

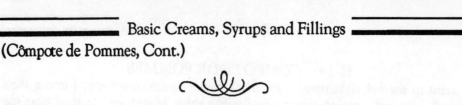

With plain cake or cookies, in a pie or turnovers, or all alone, these tart stewed apples always make a welcome dessert. It's equally good made with fresh peaches.

(II-14)

Cômpote de Pommes
(Applesauce)

Ingredients: (for about 2 cups compote)

    4   medium-sized apples (about 12 ounces)
  1/2 cup sugar
  1/3 cup water
    2   tablespoons lemon juice
    1   vanilla bean, split lengthwise

With a paring knife, peel, core, and quarter apples. Place in saucepan with other ingredients. Cover and cook in a medium saucepan over low heat for about 15 minutes, or until tender. Whirl in blender or put through a food mill with fine grill.

Storage: Refrigerate, tightly covered, for about 4 to 5 days, or freeze for up to 1 month. Thaw overnight in the refrigerator, then stir until smooth.

II-15   SAUCE AU CHOCOLAT

The pre-Columbian Aztecs and Mayas believed the cocoa tree to have mysterious powers, and thus respected it to the point of veneration. Although only kings, nobles, and warriors were allowed to drink the coveted beverage, a monetary system based on the cocoa bean was established for the commoners. A rabbit cost ten cocoa beans, for example, and a wife—indispensable commodity of the day—went for the bargain price of one hundred.

Serve this hot fudge sauce over ice cream, profiteroles, plain génoise...I even know someone who eats it with fresh strawberries. Why not!

(II-15)

Sauce au Chocolat
(Hot Fudge Sauce)

Ingredients: (for 2/3 cup sauce)

4	ounces semi-sweet chocolate, broken into small pieces or 2/3 cup chocolate chips
1	tablespoon water
2	tablespoons sugar
1/3	cup milk
1/4	teaspoon vanilla extract

In a small saucepan, melt chocolate in water over very low heat. With a wooden spoon, stir in sugar and milk, and heat to a boil. Lower heat and cook, stirring constantly with a wooden spoon, until candy thermometer registers 238-degrees, or the soft ball stage. (A drop of sauce in a glass of cold water will form a soft ball which holds its shape). This will take about 5 minutes. Stir in vanilla extract and serve immediately.

Cold Chocolate Sauce (II-15a): To serve cold, stir 1/2 cup cold milk into 2/3 cup hot sauce, allow to cool to room temperature, then refrigerate until use.

Storage: This sauce tastes best when served fresh, but will keep, tightly covered in the refrigerator, for a few days. To serve, reheat gently in a double boiler.

II-16 GLAÇAGE AU CHOCOLATE

In the 16th century, the cocoa trade between Central America and Spain was carried on in such great secrecy, that when Dutch pirates captured a Spanish merchant ship, they threw the entire cargo overboard. They'd taken the cocoa beans for sheep droppings!

An amazing array of pastries can be dressed up with this bittersweet chocolate glaze.

(II-16)
Glaçage au Chocolate
(Chocolate Glaze)

Ingredients: (for about 5/8 cup)
- **4** ounces semi-sweet chocolate
- **1/2** tablespoon butter
- **1/4** cup heavy cream

Ingredients: (for about 1 1/4 cups)
- **8** ounces semi-sweet chocolate
- **1** tablespoon butter
- **1/2** cup heavy cream

In a double boiler (or a small saucepan placed over another pan half full of water) heat all ingredients over low heat, stirring from time to time, until melted, and glaze is perfectly smooth. Cool partially or completely before using.

Storage: Keep, tightly covered in a plastic container and refrigerated for 1 week. To use, heat very gently over double boiler.

II-17 GANÂCHE

According to an ancient Central American legend, the high priest and king Quetzalcoatl journeyed to the Fields of the Sun and brought back an inestimable gift for mankind: the cocoa tree.

This rich concoction made of semi-sweet chocolate and cream is used as a filling for layered cakes such as Forêt Noire, Opéra, and Marjolaine.

(II-17)
Ganâche
(Chocolate Cream Frosting)

Ingredients: (for about 1/3 cup ganâche)
- 2 1/2   ounces semi-sweet chocolate
- 3   tablespoons heavy cream

Variations:

Au rhum (Rum) (II-17a): 2 teaspoons rum

Au kirsch (Kirsch) (II-17b): 2 teaspoons kirsch

Au café (Coffee) (II-l7c): 1 teaspoon coffee extract

À la vanille (Vanilla) (II-17d): 1/2 teaspoon vanilla extract

In a small saucepan over very low heat, or in a double boiler, heat chocolate and cream until chocolate is compeltely melted. With a wooden spoon, stir until smooth, then stir in flavoring. Cool thoroughly before using. Ganâche should be very thick, but if you find, after its cooled, that it's too dry to spread, beat in the appropriate liquid (heavy cream, strong coffee, alcohol) a few drops at a time, until the ganâche becomes spreadable.

Storage: Keep in an airtight container in the refrigerator for 3 to 4 days.

II-18 PÂTE D' AMANDES

Long before metal coins or paper money existed, each country carried out trade with an established monetary unit. For instance, Tibetans used blocks of compressed tea, Aztecs traded with cocoa beans, and Indian merchants bought their products with almonds.

(II-18)

Pâte d' Amandes
(Almond Paste)

Ingredients: (for about 10 ounces almond paste)
- 2/3   cup ground blanched almonds
- 1 3/4   cups powdered sugar
- 1   egg white

In a medium mixing bowl, blend together all ingredients until a smooth paste is formed. (You may need to use your hands since the paste becomes very stiff after a few minutes). It's best to tint almond paste just before you use it. Add the food coloring of your choice, one drop at a time, and work the paste on a countertop with the hands until the color is uniform.

To roll out, use a rolling pin and sprinkle work surface lightly with powdered sugar as you would with flour.

Almond paste can also be fashioned into tiny snowmen, birds, mushrooms, gingerbread houses, and so on for your Christmas bûches. Work with it as you would modeling clay.

Note: Leftover almond paste can be used to stuff dates or prunes. Split open fruit, stuff with a ball of almond paste (about 1 teaspoon) and roll stuffed fruit in granulated sugar.

Storage: Wrap in plastic and refrigerate up to 1 week.

Chapter III

Breakfast and Tea Pastries
(Patisseries Pour le Petit Déjeuner et le Thé)

III-1 CROISSANTS

On a moonless night in 1529, the Turkish army stealthily entered Vienna, intent upon taking the city by surprise. Since the town guards were fast asleep at their posts, Vienna would surely have fallen without a fight, if it hadn't been for the audacity of a young baker's apprentice, who, busy at his ovens, heard the troops' footsteps and clinking arms. He managed to alert the authorities in time to save the city, and in honor of his courage, it was decreed that the breakfast rolls so popular among the Viennese would thereafter take on the form of the Turkish crescent.

Simple but elegant, the crescent roll is the uncontested king of breakfast pastries. Its preparation, easy with a little practice, is nonetheless lengthy, so I've given you a recipe for a large quantity.

(III-1)
Croissants

Ingredients: (for about 1 pound 8 ounces dough, or 24 croissants)
I.   1   cake compressed yeast
     3   tablespoons warm water (not hot) (105-degrees)

II. 1/3   cup sugar
  2 1/2   teaspoons salt
     3   tablespoons milk

III.1/2   cup butter, (one stick)
   1/2   cup milk
   1/2   cup water

   3 3/4   cups flour

     1   cup butter, (two sticks)

     1   egg, beaten with a pinch of salt

I. In a small bowl , crumble the yeast into the water.

II. In another small bowl, mix together sugar, salt, and milk.

III. In a small saucepan, heat butter, milk, and water until butter is melted.

In a large mixing bowl, place flour, then add mixture II and mix by hand for a few seconds. Mix in III, then I. Mix for several minutes, until the dough becomes slightly elastic and detaches from the sides of the bowl. Turn into a

More➤

(Croissants, Cont.)

large baking dish, cover, and let stand at room temperature for 30 minutes. Punch down, cover tightly with plastic, and refrigerate overnight. This is known as "détrempe".

Remove the butter from the refrigerator 30 minutes before using, so that it will soften some and be easier to handle. Place it between two sheets of heavy-duty plastic wrap, and with a rolling pin, beat it to form a solid sheet of butter about 1/2-inch thick.

On a lightly-floured surface, roll out the dough to about 1 1/2-inch thick. Place the butter on top of the dough, fold edges over to envelope completely, and press well with the fingers to seal. Sprinkle flour on dough, rolling pin, and work surface, then roll out dough to a long rectangle about 1/4-inch thick, and fold it into thirds, as for pâte feuilletée classique (I-8).

Turn the folded dough 90-degrees, so that the single fold is perpendicular to you, roll it out and fold again. Press with two fingers, so you'll remember that you've done two "tours", wrap in plastic, and refrigerate 1 hour.

Remove dough from refrigerator, turn it 90-degrees, roll it out, and fold. Repeat, wrap, and refrigerate 1 hour.

After the last refrigeration time, roll out the dough into a 36x12x1/8-inch rectangle. (If your work surface is small, roll it out one half at a time). Cut in half, lengthwise, then cut each strip into 12 triangles, 3 inches wide at the base. Roll up each triangle, beginning at the base, and curl the ends to give the pastries a crescent shape.

Place on ungreased baking sheets, about 8 per sheet. Brush with beaten egg to prevent drying and thus aid in the rising process, and let rise in a warm place (not too warm—the butter would melt and run out over the baking sheets) for 1 to 1 1/2 hours, or until doubled in size. Brush again with egg and bake in a preheated 375-degrees oven for 20 minutes, until puffed up and golden brown. Serve warm with coffee or tea

Note: Professional bakers in France give the dough exactly 2 1/2 tours, but the homemaker handles the dough much more, which necessitates 4 tours. The dough should have a uniform appearance, with no lumps of butter showing through. If this happens, give it 1 or 2 more tours, until the color is even.

Storage: Wrap baked croissants in plastic and store in a cool, dry place for several days. To freeze for up to 2 weeks, place warm croissants on a baking sheet or tray and freeze, uncovered. When frozen, place in a plastic bag. To serve, heat unthawed croissants in a preheated 325-degrees oven for 5 minutes. The "détrempe" (that is, the dough before adding the butter and touring) can be frozen for up to 1 month. Allow to thaw in the refrigerator for 12 hours before using.

Afterword: *According to another old legend explaining the crescent roll's origin, the Polish King John III Sobieska saved Vienna from a later Turkish siege which occurred in 1683. To celebrate the liberation, the Viennese bakers used the last of their flour to make pastries resembling the enemy's symbol: the crescent.*

III-2 ORANAIS

At the beginning of the Christian era, the Arab nations considered the apricot to be a "cursed" fruit, and consequently excluded it from their diet. Its undeservedly bad reputation caused it to be ignored for hundreds of years, until its rehabilitation in the 15th century.

Oran is an important Algerian port and former headquarters of the French Foreign Legion. It's also known for its eternal sunshine, imitated, in this pastry given its name, by apricot halves.

III-2

Oranais
(Apricot Croissants)

Ingredients: (for 12 pastries)

1/2	recipe croissant dough, 12 ounces, (III-1) or
1/2	recipe pate feuilletée, 11 ounces, (I-8)
2 1/4	cups crème patissière (II-2), cooled
12	fresh apricots or 2 (28 ounce) cans apricot halves in light syrup, drained
1	egg, beaten with a pinch of salt, (egg wash)
	abricotage (apricot glaze) (II-11a) or powdered sugar

If you're using fresh apricots, wash them, split in half, and poach in a small amount of sugar water until tender. In any case, the apricot halves must be drained and patted dry with paper towels.

On a lightly floured surface, roll out dough to an 18x6x1/8-inch rectangle. If your work surface is very small, you can make 2 half-sized rectangles. With a sharp knife, cut in half, lengthwise, then cut each half into 6 3x3-squares.

In the center of each square, drop 1 tablespoon crème patissière (beaten with a very small amount of milk, if necessary, to make it creamy and spreadable, but not runny) and spread in a diagonal 2-inch wide band. Place an apricot half over the two corners covered with crème patissière. Fold one ungarnished corner over, well past the middle. Brush with beaten egg, then fold over the other ungarnished corner, covering the first by at least an inch, since rising and baking always make them separate some. Press to make them stick.

Brush with egg, if you are using pate feuilletée, or brush with egg wash, if you're using croissant dough, let rise in a warm place for 1 to 1 1/2 hours, or until doubled in size. Brush again with egg, and bake at 350-degrees for 20 to 30 minutes, or until puffed up and golden brown. Brush with warm abricotage or dust with powdered sugar, and serve warm.

Storage: Same as for croissants.

Afterword: *Apricots, which were first grown in Armenia, were quickly adopted by the ancient Romans and renamed "Armenian plums" in honor of their origin. The Persians, who next became acquainted with the apricot, immediately named it "sun egg".*

III-3 PETITS PAINS AU CHOCOLAT

Discovered in the early 16th century by the conquistadors during the conquest of Mexico and brought back to Spain by Fernando Cortez, cocoa beans were roasted, ground, and mixed with sugar by Spanish monks to make what we now call "chocolate".

An all-time favorite among French school children, these will quickly become a "regular" at your breakfast or tea table.

(III-3)

Petits Pains au Chocolat
(Chocolate Croissants-Chocolate Rolls)

Ingredients: (for 24 pains au chocolat)

1   pound, 8 ounces croissant dough (III-1)

8   ounces semi-sweet chocolate or 1 cup chocolate chips

1   egg, beaten with a pinch of salt (egg wash)

If you're not using chocolate chips, break or cut the chocolate into small pieces and set aside. On a lightly floured surface, roll out the croissant dough into a 36x12x1/8-inch rectangle. Cut in half, lengthwise, then cut each strip into 12 3-inch wide rectangles.

Divide the chocolate bits evenly between the pieces of dough, and arrange them in a straight line across each rectangle, toward one end. Fold the dough over the chocolate, then roll up—not too tightly, to allow for rising.

Place seam-side down on ungreased baking sheets and brush with beaten egg. Let rise in a warm place for 1 to 1 1/2 hours, or until doubled in size. Brush again with egg and bake in a preheated 350-degrees oven for about 20 minutes, or until puffed up and golden brown. Serve warm.

Note: Look closely at a cross-section of the croissant dough. You should be able to see the layers of butter which, during rising and baking, will make the pastry light and flaky.

Storage: Same as for croissants.

III-4   BRIOCHES INDIVIDUELLES

When told that the Parisians had no bread, Marie-Antoinette allegedly shrugged and declared, "Let them eat cake!" And yet, French gazettes of the time had really quoted her as saying, "Let them eat brioche!" Actually, it's doubtful that she said either...but we can see that in pre-revolutionary France, brioche was reserved for the privileged classes.

The crystalized sugar which tops these diminutive tea brioches gives them a glittery, jeweled appearance. If your local supermarket doesn't carry crystalized sugar, you can use rock candy. Grind it very coarsely with a mortar and pestle, or a hammer, then sift it to remove the fine powder. If possible, the remaining pieces of sugar should measure about 1/8-inch in diameter.

(III-4)
Brioches Individuelles
(Individual Petit Brioche Rolls)

Ingredients: (for 16 individual brioches)

11	ounces pâte à brioche (I-10)
1	egg beaten with a pinch of salt (egg wash)
1/2	cup crystalized sugar

On a lightly-floured surface, roll the brioche dough under your palms to form a long cylinder. With a chef's knife, cut it into 16 equal portions, then roll each piece as for the brioche parisienne (III-13). Place on lightly greased baking sheets and let rise in a warm place for about 1 to 1 1/2 hours, or until doubled in size. With wet scissor blades, make a cross-shaped slit in the top of each brioche. Brush with egg wash, sprinkle with sugar, and bake at 375-degrees for 10 to 12 minutes. Serve warm.

Storage: Same as for other brioches. To serve frozen brioches, heat, unthawed, in a 350-degree oven for about 5 minutes.

III-5   BRIOCHES AUX AMANDES

The almond tree may have originated in the Far East, but the ancient Greeks discovered it and began cultivating it in their own country, where it thrived in the hot, dry climate. It was highly regarded for its oil, but the nut itself was the more appreciated of the two. Plutarch himself recommended almonds as a preventive treatment for hangovers.

This is a wonderful way to "accommodate" leftover brioche, or croissants and pains au chocolat.

(III-5)

Brioches aux Amandes
(Almond Brioche Slices)

Ingredients: (for 10 slices)

  1/2   loaf, baked brioche nanterre (III-14)

   1   cup frangipane (II-7)

  1/2   cup sirop à entremets au rhum or à la vanille (II-12)
  1/2   cup sliced almonds
         powdered sugar

Preheat oven to 350-degrees. With a large serrated knife, cut brioche into 10 1/2-inch slices. Brush both sides with sirop à entremets, then spread one side with a thick layer of frangipane. Sprinkle generously with sliced almonds and place on a lightly greased baking sheet. Bake about 10 minutes, until golden brown. Dust with powdered sugar and serve warm.

If the brioche is very dry, use more sirop à entremets. Pour it in a shallow dish and dip the pieces of brioche, turning them quickly to avoid soaking, which would make them too fragile.

Note: You can also do the same thing with leftover croissants and pains au chocolat. Soak them in the warm sirop for 1 minute (they are less fragile than brioche, so you can do this without the risk of their falling apart) then let drain on a wire rack for a few minutes. With a serrated knife, split open, lengthwise, and fill with frangipane. Spread more frangipane on top and sprinkle with sliced almonds. Bake as directed above.

Storage: Freeze, unbaked, on a tray or baking sheet, then remove with a pancake turner and store in a plastic bag. Bake, unthawed, as directed above, for about 5 minutes longer.

III-6   PETITS PAINS AUX RAISINS

A proclamation issued in 1775 reads: "Whosoever takes a bunch of grapes from another's vineyard shall pay a fine of five sous or lose an ear."

Fortunately for us, grapes are no longer so rare or coveted, be they fresh or dried, as in this recipe for breakfast rolls garnished with raisins and pastry cream.

(III-6)

Petits Pains aux Raisins
(Raisin Buns)

Ingredients: (for about 12 petits pains)

11	ounces pâte à brioche (I-10)
2 1/4	cups crème patissière (II-2)
2/3	cup raisins
1/4	cup rum
1	egg, beaten with a pinch of salt (egg wash)
	nappage (II-11a) (optional)

In a small bowl, macerate the raisins and rum for 1 hour. On a floured surface, roll out brioche dough to an 8x12x3/16-inch rectangle. Drain the rum off of the raisins into the crème patissière and beat until smooth. Then, with a metal spatula, spread the crème patissière evenly over the dough. Sprinkle with raisins.

Roll up into a 12-inch long roll and cut in 12 1-inch wide slices. If possible, do this with a sharp chef's knife, and rather than using a sawing motion, do it with a single, sharp downward movement, which cuts without pressing out the crème or tearing the fragile dough.

Place on ungreased baking sheets, spacing well to allow for rising—generally no more than 4 per sheet—and press down gently in a dabbing motion with the fingertips, to make them spread some while rising. Let rise in a warm place for 1 to 1 1/2 hours, or until doubled in size. Brush with beaten egg and bake in a preheated 375-degree oven for 15 to 20 minutes, or until golden brown. Brush with nappage, if you like, and serve warm.

Storage: Keep, wrapped in plastic, in a cool, dry place for several days. They can also be frozen while still warm. Leave off the nappage and place on a tray or baking sheet in the freezer. When frozen, place in plastic bags. To serve, heat unthawed rolls for 5 minutes at 350-degrees.

Afterword: *The first grapes were said to have been discovered by Noah when he left the Ark after the great deluge, and thus became a symbol of abundance.*

III-7 CHAUSSONS

Because of its shape, this flaky fruit-filled pastry is called a "chausson", which is the French word for "slipper". In addition to the fillings below, you can make chaussons with almost any kind of stewed fruit, such as peaches or prunes. Be careful to drain the cooked fruit well, so the juice won't make the pastry soggy or leak out during baking, then whirl it briefly in the blender to eliminate big chunks.

(III-7)

Chaussons
(Turnovers)

Ingredients: (for about 12 chaussons)

    1   pound, 6 ounces pâte feuilletée classique (I-8) or
            pâte demi-feuilletée (I-9)
 1 1/2   cups filling: myrtilles (blueberries), crème au citron* (II-6),
            compote de pommes (II-14), or frangipane (II-7)
    1   egg, beaten with a pinch of salt (egg wash)
         powdered sugar (optional)

Preheat oven to 375-degrees. On a lightly floured surface, roll out dough to 3/16-inch thick, and cut out 12 6-inch disks. With a rolling pin, or a smaller wooden cylinder, flatten them slightly in the middle, but not the two edges destined to form the "lip". (The thicker edge will puff up nicely in the oven, giving the pastry its characteristic shape). Brush entire rim with egg wash and drop 1 heaping tablespoon of filling in the center of each disk. (Lemon filling is richer, so use less).

Fold over and press firmly to seal, but don't flute: the chaussons wouldn't rise properly. Brush with egg wash, and, if you're using more than one kind of filling, score the surface with a sharp paring knife, using a different design for each filling. Don't be afraid to press down firmly enough to make deep cuts— lighter cuts wouldn't show up. Bake 20 to 30 minutes, until puffed up and golden brown. Serve warm, plain or dusted with powdered sugar.

Storage: Freeze unbaked chaussons on a tray, then store in a plastic bag. Bake, unthawed, as directed above, allowing about 10 minutes more. Freeze and store baked chaussons as above. To serve, heat, unthawed, at 300-degrees for about 10 minutes.

Note: * Crème au citron (lemon curd), can be made less tart and lightened by mixing 1 cup plain crème patissière and 1/2 cup crème au citron.

III-8   BEIGNETS DE CARNAVAL

Although doughnuts, or "beignets", date back to the mists of Antiquity, they became very popular around the Middle Ages, when they were eaten during Carnival, a period of feasting and merriment which immediately preceded the austere forty days of Lent. Financial problems were no excuse for not observing this almost sacred custom, as proven by the old Alsacian saying, "During Carnival, make doughnuts, even if the bill collector is sitting on the frying pan handle."

These light, yeasty doughnuts are delicious plain or filled. I always double or triple the recipe, then freeze the extra dough for future use.

(III-8)
Beignets de Carnaval
(Yeast Doughnuts)

Ingredients: (for about 12 doughnuts)

3/4	cup milk
1	cake compressed yeast
2	cups flour
1	teaspoon salt
1/4	cup (1/2 stick) butter, softened
2	tablespoons sugar
4	egg yolks
1	teaspoon vanilla extract or rum
1	quart frying oil
	powdered sugar

In a small bowl, crumble yeast into milk. In a medium mixing bowl, stir together flour and salt. In a large mixing bowl, beat butter and sugar until creamy. Beat in egg yolks, flavoring, then milk-yeast. Add flour and, with the hand or a wooden spoon, stir until a firm dough is formed.

Knead with the hand for about 10 minutes, as for brioche dough. That is, bring the cupped hand up and away from the side of the bowl in a lifting motion to aerate the dough while kneading. It's ready when it becomes elastic and pulls away from the kneading hand. With a rubber spatula, clean sides of bowl, then cover with a cloth or plate and let rise in a warm place for 30 minutes.

On a lightly floured surface, knead dough lightly for a few minutes. Roll out to 1/2-inch thick, cut out 12 3-inch disks, and place on a floured cloth covering a large tray or baking sheet. Let rise in a warm place for another 30 minutes, or until doubled in size.

More➤

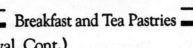

(Beignets de Carnaval, Cont.)

Lift off carefully by lifting the towel from underneath and taking dough in other hand. If the dough sticks to your hands, flour them lightly. Fry in hot oil about 2 minutes, turning once. Be careful not to overheat the oil, as the doughnuts wouldn't puff up properly and would tend to be raw in the middle. With slotted spoon, remove from oil and drain on paper towels. Dust with powdered sugar and serve immediately.

If you wish to fill them with jelly, applesauce ((II-14), or lemon curd (II-6), you'll need about 1 to 1 1/2 cups filling for 12 doughnuts. Spoon into a pastry bag with 1/8-inch star nozzle, make a small hole in the side with the tip, and pipe in a small amount of filling. Excess filling would leak out after you remove the nozzle, and eating would be messy. Dust with powdered sugar and serve immediately.

Storage: The doughnuts must be served fresh and hot, but the dough can be wrapped in plastic and frozen. Thaw in refrigerator several hours before using.

III-9 BEIGNETS PARMENTIER

Charged with robbing soil of its nutritive elements, considered unfit for human consumption, the potato was even accused, up until the late 1700s, of giving leprosy tothose who dared to eat it. Thanks to Antoine Parmentier, this long misunderstood vegetable has since become one of the occident's most widely consumed foodstuffs.

Mashed potatoes add body, and cream cheese gives a rich flavor to these hearty doughnuts.

(III-9)

Beignets Parmentier
(Potato Cream Cheese Doughnuts)

Ingredients: (for about 12 doughnuts)

2	eggs
2/3	cup cooked mashed potatoes
1 2/3	cups flour
1	teaspoon salt
2	tablespoons sugar
1	cake fresh yeast
3	tablespoons milk
2	tablespoons butter, softened
2	tablespoons cream cheese, softened
1	teaspoon vanilla extract
1	quart frying oil

In a large mixing bowl, place whole eggs, then, without stirring, add mashed potatoes, flour, and, in three different places, the salt, sugar, and crumbled yeast. Mix as for a brioche dough. That is, stir with one hand, lifting up and away from the side of the bowl, to aerate the dough. (This can be done more quickly and easily in a heavy duty mixer with a dough hook). Add milk little by little as you knead, so that the dough will be supple but not liquid. You may need a little more or less milk than called for.On a plate, mash together butter and cream cheese with a fork until smooth and creamy, then stir in vanilla. Add to dough and continue kneading until dough is elastic and pulls away from the kneading hand or dough hook. With a rubber spatula, scrape sides of bowl, cover with a dishcloth or plate, and let rest 30 minutes at room temperature.

On a generously floured surface, turn out dough and knead lightly for a minute or two, adding a little flour if necessary, then roll out to 1/2-inch thick and cut out 12 disks 2 1/2-inches, each. Place on a generously floured dishcloth, and cover with another cloth. Let rise 30 minutes. Fry about 2 minutes in hot oil, turning once. Drain on paper towels, dust with powdered or granulated sugar, and serve immediately.

Storage: Although these doughnuts must be eaten immediately, the dough can be frozen for one month. Thaw in the refrigerator for several hours. Be careful not to leave it in the refrigerator too long- - even chilled dough will rise and pop out of the aluminum foil.

III-10   PETS DE NONNE

A popular medieval legend would have us believe that these light, airy pâte à chou doughnuts were named during a church dignitary's visit to a convent. With the first bite, he allegedly beamed with satisfaction and exclaimed, "Paix aux nonnes!" ("Peace to nuns!") Did time and widespread use simply deform the name? I like to think so, since the literal translation of the name that came down to us is, I'm afraid, unprintable!

Wherever they got their name, they make a quickly-prepared and delicious surprise for breakfast guests, especially when accompanied by strawberry preserves and a pot of steaming café au lait.

(III-10)

Pets de Nonne
(Cream Puff Doughnuts)

Ingredients: (for about 30 bite-sized doughnuts)
1 1/4   cups pâte à choux (I-11)

1   quart vegetable oil for frying
powdered sugar

Prepare pâte à choux. In fryer, heat oil for deep fat frying. It should be hot but not smoking (overhot oil would make greasy doughnuts).   Drop in dough by teaspoonfuls. If it sticks to the spoon, push it off with a wet finger. Fry 2 to 3 minutes, until golden brown and puffed. If they brown too quickly, lower the heat. There's no need to turn them, as they turn by themselves as soon as they're done on one side. Remove with a slotted spoon, drain well on paper towels, and dust with powdered sugar. Serve immediately.

III-11 GAUFRES

Does the word "walfre" look vaguely familiar to you? It's the 12th century frankish word meaning "Honeycomb", and, by extension, the name of a honeycomb-shaped pastry—the simple but exquisite waffle, which has delighted royalty as well as commoners down through the ages. King François I was so fond of them, in fact, that he built up an impressive collection of silver waffle irons.

What a shame that Americans limit waffle eating to breakfast time! French homemakers serve "gaufres" at teatime, as after-school snacks, and dressed up with whipped cream and fruit, for dessert.

(III-11)
Gaufres
(Waffles)

Ingredients: (for about 12 6 x 6-inch waffles)

1 3/4	cups flour
1/2	teaspoon salt
1	tablespoon sugar

2	cups beer
2	egg yolks
2	tablespoons butter

2	egg whites
	pinch salt
1	tablespoon sugar

In a small saucepan, melt butter, then clarify. In a large mixing bowl, stir together dry ingredients, then whisk in enough beer to make a smooth, thick batter. Whisk in the egg yolks, butter, and finally, the rest of the beer. Cover with a cloth and let stand at room temperature for 1 hour.

In a medium mixing bowl, beat egg whites and salt at high speed until soft peaks form. Add sugar and continue beating until whites are stiff but not dry. Fold 1/2 cup batter into whites, stirring gently until perfectly smooth, then fold in rest of batter. Bake immediately in waffle iron.

To serve, top with powdered sugar, jam, whipped cream, butter, Fresh Fruit Sauce (II-13), maple syrup...

III-12   CRÊPES DE LA CHANDELEUR

The Chandeleur, celebrated on February 2, got its name from the candles carried in processions honoring the Blessed Virgin. In medieval Rome, the crowds of pilgrims were so dense that the pope began distributing free crêpes...a custom which eventually replaced the religious meaning altogether. In France's provinces, this minor feast day is still observed, and it is believed that to have good luck for the rest of the year, you must hold a gold louis in one hand, and with the other, flip the crêpes three times without dropping it on the floor. Successful flipping takes a little practice. As for finding a gold louis to hold...that's what I call real luck!

Serve them with grated chocolate, sugar and lemon juice, strawberry preserves and cream cheese, whipped cream and chocolate sauce, jam...or, unsweetened, with grated cheese.

(III-12)
Crêpes de la Chandeleur
(Crêpes)

Ingredients: (for about 18 8-inch crêpes)

1 1/2	cups flour
1/2	teaspooon salt
1	tablespoon sugar (optional)

1/2	cup heavy cream
2	eggs
1 3/4	cups milk
2	tablespoons butter, melted
1	tablespoon liqueur of your choice (optional)

   butter for pan

In a large mixing bowl, combine dry ingredients. Whisk in cream to make a thick paste, then whisk in rest of ingredients until smooth. Cover and let stand at room temperature at least 30 minutes. When ready to cook, the batter should be the consistency of heavy cream. If it has thickened too much while standing, stir in a little milk. To cook, follow directions in Crepes Suzettes (VIII-1).

Afterword: *In Brittany, where crêpes have always been the nourishment par excellence, riches and poverty are gauged by the number of times per day they're served. But rich or poor, every rural household reserves the last crêpe of the day for the house elf. Vindictive to the end, the elf is said to punish forgetfulness or neglect by a streak of bad luck for the offender.*

III-13   BRIOCHE PARISIENNE

At Marie-Antoinette's "Petit Trianon", the sheep and cows were bathed every morning, then perfumed and decorated with multicolored ribbons, before being presented to the queen for milking. Butter made from the royal milk was prepared daily, and stored in ceramic jars decorated with Marie-Antoinette's personal seal.

(III-13)
Brioche Parisienne
(Parisian Brioche)

Ingredients: (for one large brioche)
   11   ounces pâte à brioche (I-10)

   1   egg, beaten with a pinch of salt (egg wash)
   butter for mold

Cut off 1/3 of dough and set aside. Sprinkle the larger piece of dough with flour, and, cupping the hands lightly around it, roll gently on an unfloured surface in a circular motion, until a perfect ball is formed. With the middle finger, make a hole in the center and place in the buttered mold.

Shape the smaller piece of dough the same way, then roll it under the palm of one hand in a back and forth motion as you press down gently but firmly on one end, until a point is formed. Place the point in the hole and press down gently on the sides of the "head" as you turn the mold, so that it will be firmly attached to the "body".

Let rise in a warm, preferably moist place (for instance, an unlit oven with a large pan of hot water in the bottom) for 1 to 1 1/2 hours, or until doubled in size. With scissors, make 3 to 4 vertical slits in the top of the body as you carefully hold the head to one side to avoid cutting it. If the blades stick, dip them in water first. Brush with beaten egg and bake in a preheated 400-degree oven for 30 to 40 minutes. Turn out immediately onto a cooling rack. Serve warm.

Storage: Wrap in plastic and keep in a cool, dry place for up to 3 days. Can also be frozen. Allow to thaw at room temperature for 1 hour, then heat at 350-degrees for 10 minutes.

III-14 BRIOCHE NANTERRE

Nanterre, a large community to the north of Paris, is best known for being the birthplace of intrepid Geneviève, Paris' patron saint. It also gave its name to this loaf-shaped brioche.

Its loaf shape makes it practical to serve, and whatever is left over can be transformed into brioches aux amandes.

(III-14)

Brioche Nanterre
(Loaf-Shaped Butter Bread)

Ingredients: (for one 9-inch brioche)
- **11** ounces pâte à brioche (I-10)
- **1** egg, beaten with a pinch salt (egg wash)
- butter for mold

Divide the dough into 6 equal portions. Roll them as for the brioche parisienne (III-13), then press down gently with the palm of the hand, to form ovals. Place them side by side in a 9-inch loaf pan and let rise in a warm place for about 1 1/2 hours, or until doubled in volume. (Take care not to let the brioche overrise. It would fall some during baking, and the finished brioche would have a coarse texture).

With scissors, cut two cross-shaped slits in each section, wetting the blades if they stick to the dough. Brush with beaten egg and bake in a preheated 400-degrees oven for 30 to 40 minutes, or until golden brown. Immediately turn out onto wire cooling rack. Serve warm, plain or with blackberry preserves.

Brioche aux Raisins (Raisin Brioche) (III-14a): On a lightly floured surface, roll out dough to a 9 x 12-inch rectangle and sprinkle evenly with 2/3 cup raisins (macerated in dessert syrup). Roll up, place in buttered mold, let rise, and bake as above.

Storage: Same as for brioche parisienne (III-13).

III-15 KUGELHOPF

Marie-Antoinette, whose favorite breakfast consisted of a slice of kugelhopf and a steaming demitasse of chocolate, was responsible for making this specialty, from the French province of Alsace, fashionable at the French court.

This characteristically fluted raisin and almond brioche has graced Alsacian breakfast and tea tables for centuries.

(III-15)
Kugelhopf
(Alsacian Raisin & Almond Brioche)

Ingredients: (for one 9-inch kugelhopf)

1/2	cup sirop à entremets à la vanille (II-12b) or plain sirop with 1 tablespoon rum (II-12a)
1/2	cup raisins
	butter for mold
1 1/2	cups finely-chopped almonds, lightly toasted
11	ounces pâte à brioche (I-10)
1	egg beaten with a pinch of salt (egg wash)
	powdered sugar

In a small saucepan, heat sirop à entremets to a boil. Remove from heat, stir in raisins, cover and allow to soak for at least 1 hour. (Exceptionally, raisins macerated in rum shouldn't be used—they would have a bitter, overpowering taste).

Butter 9-inch kugelhopf mold generously, and sprinkle all over with 1 cup chopped almonds.

On a lightly floured surface, roll out brioche dough to a long rectangle about 1/4-inch thick. Drain raisins, sprinkle them evenly over the dough, then sprinkle on remaining 1/2 cup of almonds. Roll up tightly to form a long cylinder, and place in prepared mold, with the seam neither up nor down, but against the tube in the center.

Let rise in a warm place for about 2 hours, or until doubled in size. Brush with egg wash and bake in a preheated 400-degree oven for about 30 minutes. A long knifeblade inserted in the center should come out clean. Turn kugelhopf out onto a wire rack. Dust with powdered sugar immediately before serving.

Storage: Wrap in plastic and store in a cool, dry place for several days, or freeze for up to 1 month. Thaw frozen kugelhopf for 2 to 3 hours, then heat in a 350-degree oven for 15 minutes. Dust with powdered sugar before serving.

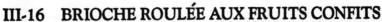

III-16   BRIOCHE ROULÉE AUX FRUITS CONFITS

In the southern French region of Provence, parishioners enjoy an old custom which allies piety with the sweet tooth: On Palm Sunday, the traditional palms sold in front of the church after services are decorated with gaily-colored candied fruit.

This brioche laced with crème patissière and candied fruit will dress up any Sunday-morning brunch table.

(III-16)
Brioche Roulée aux Fruits Confits
(Brioche Coffeecake with Candied Fruit & Pastrycream)

Ingredients: (for one 10-inch brioche)

11	ounces pâte à brioche (I-10)
2 1/4	cups crème patissière (II-2)
1/2	cup raisins
3	tablespoons rum
1/2	cup finely-chopped candied fruit
	butter for pan
1	egg, beaten with a pinch of salt (egg wash)
3/4	cup powdered sugar
1	tablespoon rum
1	tablespoon lemon juice
1/4	cup chopped candied fruit for decoration

In a small bowl, macerate raisins in rum for 1 hour. Cut off 1/4 of brioche dough, and, on a lightly-floured surface, roll it out to 1/8-inch thick. Line buttered 10-inch manqué mold, and trim edges.

Drain the rum off of raisins, into the crème patissière, then beat until smooth. Spread a thin layer in the bottom of the pastry shell.

Roll out the rest of the dough to a 10 x 16 x 3/16-inch rectangle. Using a metal spatula, spread on the rest of crème patissière and sprinkle evenly with raisins and candied fruit. Roll up to form a 16-inch cylinder and cut into 8 slices. Rather than cutting with a sawing motion, do so with a quick, firm downward motion to avoid pressing out the crème or tearing the delicate dough.

More→

(Brioche Roulée, Cont.)

Place the slices side by side in the pan, leaving 1/8-inch between them to allow for rising, and let rise in a warm place for 1 1/2 hours, or until doubled in size. Brush with beaten egg and bake in a preheated 375-degrees oven for 40 minutes, or until puffed up and golden brown.

If the brioche browns too quickly, tent it loosely with aluminum foil. Cool 10 minutes before turning out onto a cooling rack. Mix together the powdered sugar, rum, and lemon juice, and drizzle over the hot brioche, then sprinkle on the candied fruit. Serve warm.

Storage: Wrap in plastic and refrigerate for up to 3 days, or freeze, unglazed, for up to 1 month. Thaw for 1 hour at room temperature, then heat in a preheated 350-degrees oven for 15 minutes. Glaze and decorate, then serve warm.

III-17 ESCARGOT AU MIEL

Beginning with the ancient Gauls, each farm in France has always had its own beehive, the occupants of which are treated like respected members of the family. Deaths in the family are always solemnly announced to them, and the hive is discreetly draped in black as a sign of mourning, while for weddings they are decorated with white ribbon streamers. To this day, farmers firmly believe that if excluded from family events, or if exposed to quarrels and cursing, bees will waste away and die of grief. Compliments and encouragement are the rule: they're generally called "my little beauties", and if anyone is so rude as to refer to them as "animals", he's quickly rewarded with a sting. Who can resist this hot brioche filled with honey and cinnamon, then crowned with a lemon glaze? No one!

(III-17)

Escargot au Miel
(Honey Brioche Snails)

Ingredients: (for one 8-inch brioche)

11	ounces pâte à brioche (I-10)
2	tablespoons butter
1/2	cup honey
1/3	cup ground almonds
2	teaspoons cinnamon
	butter for mold
1	egg, beaten with pinch of salt (egg wash)
3/4	cup powdered sugar
2	tablespoons lemon juice
2	tablespoons lightly toasted, slivered almonds

In a small saucepan, melt butter, then whisk in honey, almonds, and cinnamon. Cut off 1/4 brioche dough, and on a lightly-floured surface, roll it out to 1/8-inch thick. Line an 8-inch buttered manqué mold. Roll out rest of dough into a 10 x 16 x 3/16-inch rectangle. With a metal spatula, spread on filling in an even layer, then roll up and place, seam-side down in lined pan, curling loosely to resemble a snail.

Let rise in a warm place for 1 1/2 hours, or until doubled in size. Brush with beaten egg and bake at 375-degrees for about 40 minutes, or until golden brown. Turn out immediately onto a cooling rack.
In a small bowl, mix together powdered sugar and lemon juice, drizzle over hot brioche, and sprinkle with slivered almonds. Serve warm.

Storage: Same as Brioche Roulée aux Fruits Confits (preceding recipe III-16).

Afterword: An old belief dating back from the 15th century: if someone appropriates a swarm of bees without giving it some money, the offended bees will never love their new master, and will consequently sting him and refuse to produce honey.

III-18   BISCUIT DE SAVOIE

Henri, Duc de Garonne, could hardly believe it. The official dinner for the Emperor of Germany had begun hours before, and Amédée IV de Savoie, host to the emperor, had yet to make an appearance. Henri had always considered Amédée, with his eternal green trappings, to be a bit eccentric. But the Green Count's ignoring such an important guest wasn't merely eccentric. It was suicidal.

Henri drummed his fingers on the richly polished table top and leaned toward his neighbor. "Where do you suppose he is?" he asked in a low voice.

"Who, Amédée?" Robert, Comte de l'Indre, shrugged and held out his goblet to a passing servant. "How should I know?"

"No one else seems to know, either," Henri muttered. "He was seen talking to his head cook before the banquet. Then poof! Vanished!"

"Calm down, Henri. He can't be far away." Robert guzzled the contents of his refilled goblet and held it out again.

Henri threw down his napkin. "In any case," he remarked sarcastically, "I find your concern very touching."

"I'm just saying there's no reason to panic."

"And I'm saying there is. Do you realize what could happen if the emperor has decided he's been insulted?"

Robert let out a heavy sigh. Henri was beginning to get on his nerves. "Look, if it makes you feel any better, I saw him just before the banquet. He told me he's planned a surprise."

"A surprise?"

"You know Amédée. Always up to something!"

"What kind of surprise?" Henri insisted, feeling himself break out into a cold sweat. He didn't always find Amédée's surprises in the best of taste.

Before Robert could answer, an elaborate fanfare sounded forth. A horse mounted by a green-clad rider charged in and galloped around the banquet hall, bringing shouts and applause from the guests who had recognized the Green Count.

Robert smiled triumphantly. "What did I tell you!" he shouted over the clamor. Henri only pursed his lips and frowned. He didn't like the look of the covered object Amédée was balancing precariously in one hand as he capered around the room. The horse finally clattered to a stop in front of the emperor's table. Renewed applause drowned

More➤

out Henri's sigh of relief when Amédée dismounted and, with a flourish, unveiled his surprise: a magnificent cake depicting the province of Savoie complete with lakes and mountains...topped, of course, by the imperial crown. The emperor, delighted, named Amédée "Vicaire Général de l'Empire".

Henri felt a nudge. "Well?" Robert's grin was unbearably irritating.

The Duc de Garonne waved a hand. "Cher ami, I knew it all along!" he said with a sniff, and turning his back to Robert, went to pay his respects to the new Vicaire Général.

This amazingly moist sponge cake is so good that there's no need to imitate the Green Count's extravagant presentation! Plain, it's the perfect accompaniment for oeufs à la neige, ile flottante, custard, ice cream... For added refinement, serve it alone with a chocolate glaze or with fresh fruit and whipped cream.

(III-18)
Biscuit de Savoie
(Savoy Sponge Cake)

Ingredients: (for one large biscuit)

5	egg yolks
3/4	cup sugar
1/2	teaspoon vanilla extract
2/3	cup cornstarch
5	egg whites
1/4	teaspoon salt
2	tablespoons sugar
	softened butter for pan
2	tablespoons sugar
2	tablespoons flour

Preheat oven to 325-degrees. In a medium mixing bowl, whisk egg yolks and sugar until thick and lemon-colored, then whisk in vanilla extract and cornstarch. Don't overbeat.

In a large mixing bowl, beat egg whites and salt at high speed until soft peaks form. Add sugar and continue beating until stiff but not dry. Beat 1/3 of whites into yolk mixture, then fold the softened mixture into rest of egg whites.

More➤

(Biscuit de Savoie, Cont.)

Generously butter a bundt pan (or other 10-inch decorative tube pan). In a small bowl, mix together sugar and flour. Dust inside of pan with this mixture, which will make a nice brown crust.

Spread batter in pan and bake 40 to 50 minutes, or until the cake is puffed up and a long knife blade inserted in the center comes out clean. Do **not** open oven door while it is baking. Allow to cool for 2 to 3 minutes, then invert onto a wire rack. Present whole or sliced, with oeufs à la neige, ice cream, etc.

Biscuit de Savoie Glacé au Chocolat (Savoy Sponge with Chocolate Glaze) (III-18a): Prepare 1 1/4 cups chocolate glaze (II-16). Cool slightly (about 10 minutes). Place cooled cake on a wire rack and slowly pour warm glaze over cake. For perfect coverage, use a small metal spatula to spread some, if necessary. Sprinkle with toasted, sliced, or slivered almonds. Allow to set 15 minutes before cutting.

Biscuit de Savoie aux Fruits (Savoy Sponge with Fresh Fruit)(III-18b): Fresh peaches, raspberries, and strawberries—combined or alone—are the best fruits to serve with the biscuit de savoie. You'll need 1 1/2 to 2 pounds fruit, for 8 servings. Wash and peel peaches. Cut in half, then in medium-sized slices. Clean strawberries with a soft pastry brush or a damp cloth. Unless very small, cut in half. Raspberries should be used "as is"—unwashed and whole. In a large bowl, mix fruit with just enough sugar to sweeten, a few drops lemon juice, and a spoonful of kirsch. Immediately before serving, fill center of cake with fruit.

Prepare 2 cups crème chantilly (II-1). Spoon about half the chantilly into a pastry bag with a 1/2-inch fluted nozzle, and pipe rosettes of crème around the base and top of cake. Decorate chantilly with whole raspberries, half or whole strawberries, or peach slices. Serve rest of fruit and chantilly on side.

III-19 QUATRE-QUARTS

"Quatre-quarts", in French, simply means "four-fourths", which is only logical, since this cake is made with equal weights of four ingredients. In many regions of France, it's also known as a "tôt-fait" because it's so quick and easy to make.

(III-19)

Quatre-Quarts
(Butter Pound Cake)

Ingredients: (for one 10-inch loaf cake)

2/3	cup butter, softened
3/4	cup sugar
3	eggs
1/4	teaspoon vanilla extract
1	cup flour
1	teaspoon baking powder, sifted if lumpy
1/4	teaspoon salt
	butter and flour for pan

Preheat oven to 350-degrees. In a large mixing bowl, cream butter and sugar until light, then beat in eggs, one by one. If the mixture separates, place the bowl over a large pot of hot water and continue beating until creamy.

In a small mixing bowl, stir together dry ingredients, then beat into creamed mixture until well blended. Spread in a buttered and floured loaf pan and bake 45 minutes, or until a cake tester, inserted in the center, comes out clean. Turn out immediately onto a wire rack. Serve warm.

Quatre-Quarts Marbré au Chocolat (Chocolate Marble) (III-19a): Beat together 1/2 cup batter with 1 teaspoon sifted cocoa. Spread 1/2 of plain batter in pan, then drop in chocolate batter by tablespoons. Spread on rest of plain batter. There's no need to stir for a marbled effect. It will happen by itself during baking.

Quatre-Quarts au Chocolat (Chocolate) (III-19b): Sift 2 teaspoons unsweetened cocoa powder into dry ingredients. Finish preparation and baking as above.

Quatre-Quarts Marbré au Café (Coffee Marble) (III-19c): Beat together 1/2 cup plain batter with 1 teaspoon coffee extract. Prepare as for quatre-quarts marbré au chocolat.

More➤

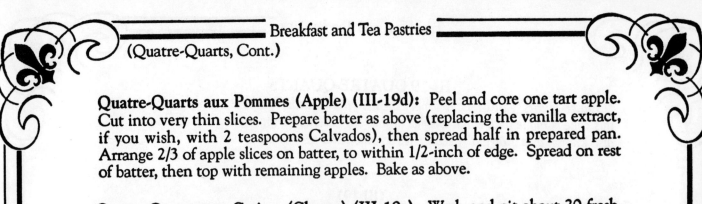
Quatre-Quarts aux Pommes (Apple) (III-19d): Peel and core one tart apple. Cut into very thin slices. Prepare batter as above (replacing the vanilla extract, if you wish, with 2 teaspoons Calvados), then spread half in prepared pan. Arrange 2/3 of apple slices on batter, to within 1/2-inch of edge. Spread on rest of batter, then top with remaining apples. Bake as above.

Quatre-Quarts aux Cerises (Cherry) (III-19e): Wash and pit about 20 fresh cherries. Dry carefully with paper towels. With a paring knife, cut in half or in quarters. (If left whole, the smooth, whole cherries would fall to the bottom of the pan. The irregular half or quarter shape helps keep them suspended in the batter during baking). Prepare batter as above (substituting the vanilla extract, if you wish, with 2 teaspoons kirsch), then gently stir in cherries. Bake as above.

Storage: Same as for cake aux fruits confits (see following recipe, III-20).

III-20   CAKE AUX FRUITS CONFITS

As early as the Middle Ages, candying was a widespread method of treating fruits for longer conservation. During the Italian Renaissance, it became popular to throw candied fruit wrapped in paper—called "frutti confetti"—when religious processions and parades passed. Today, only the bits of paper—and the last half of the name—remain to remind us of the old custom.

This buttery cake accented by nuts and candied fruit is generally eaten in the afternoon, with tea or coffee. French fruitcake is not the same as the American fruitcake.

(III-20)
Cake aux Fruits Confits
(French Fruitcake)

Ingredients: (for one 10-inch loaf cake)

1/2	cup (1 stick) butter, softened
2/3	cup sugar
3	eggs
1	cup flour
1	teaspoon baking powder, sifted if lumpy
1/2	teaspoon salt
3/4	cup finely-chopped candied fruit, nuts, and raisins
	butter and flour for pan
2	tablespoons blanched, slivered almonds
3	tablespoons rum
3	candied cherries
	angélique (optional)
	nappage (II-11a)

Preheat oven to 350-degrees. In a large mixing bowl, beat together butter and sugar until light and fluffy. Beat in the eggs, one at a time. If the mixture separates, place the mixing bowl over a large pot of hot water (but not touching the water) and continue beating until creamy.

In a small mixing bowl, mix together flour, salt and baking powder. Stir in the candied fruit. (This will help prevent it from sinking to the bottom during baking.) Stir flour mixture into sugar mixture, then spread in a generously buttered and floured 10-inch loaf pan. Sprinkle with almonds. Bake for 45 minutes, or until a cake tester inserted in the center comes out clean. Immediately turn out onto a cooling rack, and pour the rum over the hot cake. Before serving, brush with warm nappage and decorate with candied cherry halves or with angélique, if available.

Storage: Wrap in plastic and store in a cool, dry place for several days. Or, freeze while still warm. Thaw 4 hours in the refrigerator, brush with nappage and decorate before serving.

III-21 PAIN D' EPICES

Pain d'epices is among mankind's oldest forms of pastry. We see it in ancient Egypt, where bakers kneaded honey and spices into bread dough for their wealthy clients, and again in medieval Europe, where street vendors tempted and amused potential customers with pain d'épices in bawdy, not to say obscene shapes. Up until WWII, the provincial Frenchman declared his love by presenting the object of his desire with an elaborately decorated heart-shaped pain d'épices.

Gingerbread's form may have changed over the centuries, but its warm, spicy taste hasn't. The recipe for this moist loaf-shaped version came from Brittany.

(III-21)

Pain d'Epices
(Gingerbread)

Ingredients: (for one 10-inch gâteau)

1 3/4	cups flour
1	teaspoon cinnamon
1/4	teaspoon ginger
1/4	teaspoon cloves
	pinch nutmeg
1/4	teaspoon salt
1 1/2	teaspoons baking powder, sifted if lumpy
1/3	cup butter, softened
1/2	cup sugar
2	eggs, slightly beaten
1/2	cup plain, unsweetened yogurt
1/2	cup honey
1/4	cup unsweetened strong black coffee
1/3	cup raisins or chopped dates
	butter and flour for pan

Preheat oven to 350-degrees. In a medium mixing bowl, stir together dry ingredients.

In a large mixing bowl, cream butter and sugar until light, then lower speed and beat in eggs, yogurt, honey, and coffee. With a wooden spoon, stir in dry ingredients until well blended. Don't overbeat, as the cake would be tough. Stir in raisins or dates and spread in a buttered and floured 10-inch loaf pan. Bake 30 to 40 minutes, or until a cake tester inserted in the center comes out clean. Immediately turn out onto a wire rack. Serve warm, plain, or a la Normande: with a compôte de pommes (II-14) or crème chantilly (II-1).

Storage: Wrap in plastic and store in a cool, dry place for several days. Can be frozen for up to 2 months. Thaw for 4 hours in the refrigerator, then heat, wrapped in foil, at 350-degrees for 10 minutes.

III-22   ORANGERIE DE LA LANGUYOTTE

Although France's first orange grove was planted in the Tuilleries during the reign of Henri IV, the Orangerie de Versailles, an architectural marvel created by Mansart especially for Louis XIV, marked the beginning of the orange's career in French gastronomy. The orangerie became so famous, in fact, that royal houses all over Europe had similar ones designed and built.

Mounette, a dear friend from my au pair girl days, gave me her old family recipe for another kind of "orangerie": a fragrant orange cake perfect for mid-afternoon gatherings, whether served with a cup of tea…or a flute of champagne.

(III-22)
Orangerie de la Languyotte
(Glazed Orange Tea Cake)

Ingredients: (for one 10-inch cake)

1 1/2	cups flour
1 1/2	teaspoons baking powder
1/8	teaspoon salt
1/2	cup butter
2/3	cup sugar
3	eggs
	juice of 2 oranges and 1 lime (about 3/4 cup in all)
	finely-grated rind of 1 1/2 oranges and 1 lime
1	tablespoon Grand Marnier

Glaze:

3/4	cup powdered sugar
	juice of 1/2 orange and 1/2 lime
1	tablespoon Grand Marnier

Preheat oven to 350-degrees. In a small mixing bowl, stir together dry ingredients. In a small saucepan, melt butter, then remove from heat. Clarify and set aside. In a large mixing bowl, whisk together sugar and eggs, then whisk in juices, rinds, and Grand Marnier, followed by the partially cooled butter. Add the dry ingredients and whisk just until well blended. The batter should be fairly liquid. Pour it into a buttered and floured 10-inch manqué pan and bake 30 to 40 minutes, or until a cake tester, inserted in the center, comes out clean. Turn out onto a rack or a serving plate.

In a small bowl, stir together powdered sugar and just enough juice to make a smooth paste, then stir in the rest of juice and the Grand Marnier. Pour over the hot cake. The juice and Grand Marnier will soak into the cake, while the powdered sugar stays on the surface to form a glaze. Serve warm.

Storage: Although it's best when served almost immediately after coming out of the oven, this cake will keep well for a few days, if covered and stored in a cool, dry place.

III-23 GÂTEAU DE STE. GENEVIEVE

In 451, when Attila the Hun began his destructive sweep through Gaul, she prevented a massive exodus from Lutèce by predicting that the "Scourge of God" would exclude the city of the Parüsi from his list of victims. Words inspired by divine vision, or simply by a developed sense of tactics and psychology? In any case, they luckily proved to be true, and later, young Geneviève was named patron saint of the city which would one day change its name to "Paris".

This simple but tasty tea cake was created in the Parisian suburb of Nanterre, St. Geneviève's birthplace.

(III-23)
Gâteau de Ste. Geneviève
(St. Genevieve's Cake)

Ingredients: (for one 9x9-inch cake)

1 1/2	cups flour
1 1/2	teaspoons baking powder
1/2	teaspoon baking soda
1/8	teaspoon salt
3/4	cup sour cream
1/2	cup sugar
1	tablespoon rum or kirsch
1/3	cup lemon juice
2	egg yolks
2	egg whites
	pinch salt
2	tablespoons sugar
	butter and flour for cake pan
	powdered sugar

Preheat oven to 350-degrees. In a small mixing bowl, stir together dry ingredients. In a large mixing bowl, whisk together sour cream, sugar, rum or kirsch, lemon juice, and egg yolks. Stir in dry ingredients and beat just until a smooth batter is formed.

In a deep mixing bowl, beat together egg whites and salt at high speed until soft peaks form. Add sugar and continue beating until stiff but not dry. Beat 1/3 of whites into cake batter, then with a rubber spatula, carefully fold in rest of whites. Bake in buttered and floured 9x9-inch cake pan for 30 minutes, or until cake pulls away from sides of pan, and a cake tester, inserted in the center, comes out clean. Cool a few minutes, then turn out onto a wire cooling rack Place a 9x9-inch paper doily on top of the cake, for an attractive presentation, and dust generously with powdered sugar, . Remove doily and serve.

Storage: Wrap in plastic and store in a cool, dry place for several days, or freeze for up to 1 month. Thaw several hours in the refrigerator before serving, then decorate.

III-24   GÂTEAU PROVENÇAL

Orange flower water, a flavoring often used in Mediterranean cuisine and in pastries from the south of France, is derived from neroli oil, an essence brought to France around 1680 by Anna Maria Trémoille, Princesse de Néroli.

Raisins and orange flower water add dimension to this moist, orange-flavored cake, a typical gâteau from the southern region of Provence.

(III-24)
Gâteau Provençal
(Provence Cake)

Ingredients: (for one 9x12-inch cake)

1 1/2	cups flour
2	teaspoons baking powder
1/4	teaspoon salt
3/4	cup raisins
1	cup sugar
1/2	cup butter, softened
1/2	cup heavy cream
3	eggs
2	teaspoons orange flower water

butter and flour for pan

juice of 1 orange and 1/2 lemon
| 1 | cup powdered sugar |

chopped candied orange peel, or coarsely grated orange peel

Preheat oven to 350-degrees. Butter and flour a 9x12-inch cake pan. In a medium mixing bowl, stir together dry ingredients. In a large mixing bowl, beat together the sugar and butter until light and creamy, then whisk in cream, whole eggs, and orange flower water. Whisk in dry ingredients and beat just until well mixed. Spread in prepared pan, and bake 30 to 40 minutes or until a cake tester, inserted in the center, comes out clean. Cool 5 minutes, then turn out onto a wire rack. In a small mixing bowl, whisk together juices and powdered sugar. Pour over warm cake. Sprinkle with chopped candied orange peel, or coarsely grated fresh orange peel. Serve warm.

III-25 GÂTEAU DE POMMES À LA NORMANDE

Jean Boivin Champeaux, senator from Calvados, often declared with pride, "Calvados is to the apple what cognac is to the grape." Normandy's renowned apple brandy lends its incomparable flavor to this spicy apple cake and to its whipped cream garnish.

(III-25)

Gâteau de Pommes à la Normande
(Norman-Style Apple Cake)

Ingredients: (for one 10-inch gâteau)

1 3/4	cups flour
1/4	teaspoon salt
2	teaspoons baking soda
1	teaspoon cinnamon
	pinch ground cloves

3/4	cup sugar
1	tablespoon Calvados
3/4	cup melted butter
2	eggs
1/3	cup heavy cream
3	tablespoons orange juice
1 1/2	cups compote de pommes (II-14)
	butter and flour for pan

Chantilly au Calvados:

3	tablespoons sugar
1	teaspoon unflavored gelatin
2	tablespoons Calvados
1	cup heavy cream

Preheat oven to 350-degrees. In a medium mixing bowl, stir together dry ingredients. In a large mixing bowl, whisk together all other ingredients. With a wooden spoon, beat dry ingredients into sugar-egg mixture. Stop beating as soon as batter is mixed. (Don't use an electric beater for this, as the cake would have a tough texture). Spread batter in buttered and floured 10-inch decorative tube or bundt pan, and bake 40 to 50 minutes, or until a cake tester, inserted in the center, comes out clean and cake pulls away from sides of pan. Allow to cool 5 minutes, then carefully invert onto a cooling rack.

In a small bowl, stir together sugar, gelatin, and Calvados. Let stand about 15 minutes, until gelatin is dissolved. In a deep mixing bowl, beat cream at high speed until very firm. (Stop beating immediately, to avoid making butter). With a rubber spatula, fold Calvados mixture into whipped cream.

To garnish cake, spoon 2/3 of chantilly into center, then spoon rest of chantilly into a pastry bag with a 1/2-inch fluted nozzle, and cover surface of chantilly with rosettes or "shells". If you don't have a pastry bag, this last step can be omitted. Simply spoon all of chantilly into center and make small peaks with the back of a spoon. Serve within 2 hours, if possible.

Storage: Refrigerate until serving.

Chapter IV

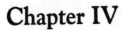

Cold Desserts
(Desserts Froids)

IV-1   CRÈME RENVERSÉE AU CARAMEL

Just as some idealistic botanists spend their lives in search of the elusive and probably non-existant black orchid or black rose, La Varenne spent his in quest of a black custard. He thought he'd found it when, to his colleagues' horror, he mixed a large quantity of soot into the ingredients for a plain custard. He was mistaken. After being severely ridiculed for his inedible creation, he was forced to admit defeat, and went on to create more palatable desserts.

This classical egg custard topped with liquid caramel is a favorite with children.

(IV-1)

Crème Renversée au Caramel
(Baked Caramel Custard)

Ingredients: (for 6 servings)
    2/3   cup caramel (II-8a)

    2   eggs
    3   egg yolks
    1/2   cup sugar
    1/2   teaspoon vanilla extract
    1/8   teaspoon salt

  2 1/2   cups milk

Preheat oven to 400-degrees. Prepare caramel and pour into 6 individual custard cups. In a large mixing bowl, whisk eggs, egg yolks, sugar, vanilla extract and salt until frothy. In a medium saucepan, heat milk to boiling point, then pour slowly over the egg mixture, whisking vigorously all the while to avoid cooking the eggs. Skim off foam and pour into custard cups. Place cups in a small saucepan half full of hot water, and bake about 20 minutes, or until the tip of a knife, when inserted in the center, comes out clean. Cool. To serve, run a knife blade around the rim and invert on individual saucers.

Crème Renversée aux fruits (Custard with Fruit Sauce) (IV-1a): Prepare as above, omitting caramel, and serve with a coulis de fruits (II-13).

Storage: Refrigerate, unmolded, until serving. Serve within 48 hours.

IV-2   OEUFS À LA NEIGE

"Here!" A young woman decked out in fig leaves placed a bowl in front of a moody young man.

"What!" he muttered, drawing back so suddenly that his own suit of leaves crackled loudly. "Another one of your big ideas?"

The woman only smiled and nudged his shoulder. "Taste it. It's a new dessert I just invented."

"What do you take me for, some kind of moron? No thanks!" He turned away, but couldn't help casting a sidelong glance at the bowl's contents. He had only one weakness: an incurable sweet tooth.

"Just one little bite…" the young woman coaxed gently. "I know you'll like it."

He wasn't about to give in so easily, though. "Ah, no! Do you think I've already forgotten what happened the last time you had me take 'just one little bite'?" He picked a leaf off of his suit and waved it at her. "Remember?"

His companion scuffed her feet around in the dust. "But you liked it, didn't you?" she pointed out, smiling up through her lashes, "And you'll like this, too. Look, there's even hard caramel on top…"

"Really?" The man's nostrils trembled in spite of his resolution.

"Uh-hmmm." She held out a spoon.

Later, a little smile stole across his face as he savored the last mouthful and declared, "Even better than apples!"

Eve laughed and threw a handful of leaves at him, "Oh, Adam!"

This is what an old Alsacian legend would have us believe to be the origin of "oeufs à la neige". Although this popular dessert of poached meringues, crème anglaise and caramel may not date back quite that far, it is firmly anchored in French tradition.

More➤

(Oeufs à la Neige, Cont.)

(IV-2)

Oeufs à la Neige
(Snow Eggs)

Ingredients: (for about 8 servings)
- 6 egg whites
- pinch salt
- 3/4 cup sugar
- 2 1/2 cups milk

- 6 egg yolks
- 3/4 cup sugar
- 1/8 teaspoon salt
- 1/2 teaspoon vanilla extract

In a large mixing bowl, beat egg whites and salt at high speed until soft peaks form. Add sugar gradually as you continue to whip, then beat until stiff peaks form. In a large saucepan, heat milk to the boiling point, then lower heat so that milk will gently simmer but not boil.

With 2 large spoons, shape meringue into egg-shaped ovals and drop into the simmering milk, leaving some space between them, since they swell some while poaching. Poach about 2 to 3 minutes on each side, turning once. Remove with a slotted spoon and place on a large plate. They're somewhat fragile, so don't pile them up. Set aside to cool. When completely cool, refrigerate. Reserve milk for the custard.

In a medium saucepan, whisk together the sugar, egg yolks, salt and vanilla extract until thick and lemon-colored. Pour a small amount of reserved hot milk over the yolk mixture, whisking vigorously all the while, to avoid cooking the yolks. Continue pouring the milk slowly until all has been added. Over medium heat, cook the mixture, stirring constantly with a wooden spoon, until custard thickens slightly and coats the spoon. (Don't let it boil, or it will curdle.) Remove from heat and pour into a large serving bowl. Cool to room temperature, stirring occasionally to speed up cooling, then refrigerate.

Remove custard and meringues from the refrigerator. Some milk will have collected under the meringues. Pour it off into the custard and stir until smooth. Place custard in a serving platter with a 1-inch rim. With a large spoon, place the meringues on top of the custard and return to the refrigerator. Immediately before serving, drizzle with hard caramel (II-8a) and sprinkle with toasted sliced or slivered almonds.

au Café (Coffee) (IV-2a): Whisk 1 tablespoon coffee extract into hot custard. (Very strong coffee isn't recommended for flavoring, because it has less flavor, and would "water down" the crème). Top finished dessert with hard caramel (II-8a) and toasted, sliced or slivered almonds.

au Chocolat (Chocolate) (IV-2b): Whisk 4 teaspoons unsweetened cocoa powder into hot custard. (Cocoa powder is preferable to semi-sweet chocolate or chocolate chips, which would thicken the crème too much). Top finished dessert with hard caramel (II-8a) and chocolate sprinkles.

IV-3   MARQUISE AU CHOCOLAT

In a letter to her daughter, the Marquise de Sévigné, one of the 17th century's most impenitent gourmands, speaks out against the immoderate consumption of chocolate: "...the Marquise de Coëtlogon drank so much chocolate during her pregnancy last year, that she gave birth to a baby boy who was 'dark as the devil'..."

Whoever created this rich molded chocolate dessert doubtless had the two Marquises in mind. Whisky exalts the full chocolate flavor, but if you prefer a milder taste, it can be replaced by vanilla extract.

(IV-3)
Marquise au Chocolat
(Molded Chocolate Marquise)

Ingredients: (for one 6-inch marquise, serving 8)

9	ounces semi-sweet chocolate
3/4	cup butter, softened
4	egg yolks
2	tablespoons whisky
4	egg whites
1/4	teaspoon salt
1/3	cup sugar

Base:

5 to 6	biscuits à la cuillère (ladyfingers) (I-5)
1/4	cup sirop à entremets (dessert syrup) (II-12)
1	tablespoon whiskey

Crème Chantilly au Whiskey:

3	tablespoons sugar
1	teaspoon gelatin, softened in 2 tablespoons whiskey, and dissolved over hot water
1	cup heavy cream
6 or 7	candied cherries
	angelique (optional)

In a double boiler, melt chocolate over medium heat. Remove from heat, add butter, egg yolks, and whisky, and beat until smooth. Set aside.

More➤

(Marquise au Chocolat, Cont.)

In a large mixing bowl, beat egg whites and salt at high speed until soft peaks form. Add sugar and continue beating until stiff but not dry. Add about 1/3 of whites to cooled chocolate mixture, beating until smooth, then pour all of chocolate mixture into rest of whites. Fold in with large spoon or rubber spatula. Mixture should be perfectly smooth. Pour into unbuttered 6-inch charlotte mold.

Pour the sirop à entremets (dessert syrup) and whiskey into a shallow dish and dip biscuits, turning quickly to avoid soaking. Place on top of chocolate mixture, cutting and fitting in pieces, when necessary, to make a solid layer. Cover with plastic or aluminum foil and refrigerate at least 6 hours, but preferably overnight.

Place marquise in freezer 30 minutes to 1 hour before unmolding. To unmold, place in hot water for about 1 minute. Dry off mold, then invert onto serving plate. With a small metal spatula, smooth surface of marquise, and return to refrigerator.

In a small bowl, mix sugar and gelatin mixture. In a deep mixing bowl, beat cream at high speed until very firm. Stir sugar and gelatin mixture into whipped cream. Refrigerate until using.

To present: Spoon whipped cream into pastry bag with 1/2-inch fluted nozzle and pipe large "shells", or rosettes, of chantilly around the base. Cover the top in the same way. Decorate with cherry halves and, if you wish, angélique. Refrigerate until serving. To serve, dip a sharp knife blade into hot water. Dry off quickly, then cut.

Variation: Replace whiskey in chocolate mixture with 1/2 teaspoon vanilla extract, whiskey in base, with 1 teaspoon vanilla, and use plain crème chantilly (II-1). In this instance, soften gelatin in 2 tablespoons of water and dissolve it over hot water as described above.

Storage: The decorated marquise should be eaten the same day as made. Molded, it can be kept for 24 hours before unmolding and decorating.

IV-4 GÂTEAU DE RIZ

France's southern province of Camargue is known for its herds of pale, semi-wild horses, its pink flamingos in salt marshes, and...its extensive fields of round rice, a regional specialty.

This creamy, caramel-topped rice pudding is naturally best when made with round rice from Camargue, but if it's unavailable in your specialty store, just use one of the cheaper brands of rice which are sticky when cooked. Whatever you do, don't make it with the special long grain, "guaranteed not to stick" kind. The pudding wouldn't hold together correctly.

(IV-4)
Gâteau de Riz
(Caramel Rice Pudding)

Ingredients: (for one 6 or 8-inch gâteau)

1 1/4	cups round rice
2 1/2	cups milk
1/8	teaspoon salt
1/2	vanilla bean, split lengthwise

1 1/3	cups crème anglaise (II-3)
1/4	cup raisins, macerated in rum or kirsch

2/3	cups caramel (II-8)

In a large saucepan, cook the rice in about 1 quart of boiling water for 5 minutes, then drain thoroughly. Return rice to the saucepan, stir in milk, salt, and vanilla bean, and heat to a boil. Lower heat, cover pan and simmer, stirring occasionally, until rice is tender, about 15 minutes. Remove vanilla bean. The mixture should be very thick and somewhat mushy.

While the rice is cooking, prepare the crème anglaise. Stir it into the hot rice, along with the raisins. Prepare the caramel, pour into unbuttered mold, rotating quickly to coat inside evenly. Spread rice mixture in the mold, let cool to room temperature, then cover with aluminum foil and refrigerate overnight. To serve, simply invert on a plate. There's no need to place the mold in hot water, since the caramel dissolves during refrigeration and allows for easy unmolding.

IV-5   GÂTEAU DE SEMOULE

Semolina is simply the gritty, coarse part of the wheat left over after grinding. This highly nourishing product, which is widely used in North African cuisine and pastry making, was discovered by the French colonists who settled in newly-conquered Algeria over 150 years ago.

A very popular dessert among French children, this creamy semolina pudding is quick and easy to prepare.

(IV-5)
Gâteau de Semoule
(Caramel Semolina Pudding)

Ingredients: (for about one 6-inch gâteau, serving 6)

2/3	cup hard caramel (II-8a)

2 3/4	cups milk
1/8	teaspoon salt
2/3	cup semolina

2	egg yolks
1/2	cup sugar
1/2	teaspoon vanilla extract

1/3	cup raisins macerated in rum

Prepare caramel and pour into a 6-inch soufflé dish, rotating quickly to coat bottom and sides evenly. In a large saucepan, heat milk and salt to the boiling point, then whisk in semolina. Cook, stirring constantly with a wooden spoon, until mixture boils, then cover and cook over very low heat for another 10 minutes. The semolina should be completely cooked and the mixture creamy. Remove from heat.

In a large mixing bowl, whisk together egg yolks, sugar, and vanilla extract. Add a small amount of the hot semolina mixture and whisk vigorously to prevent the egg yolks from cooking. Beat in the rest of the semolina little by little, then stir in the raisins. Pour the hot preparation into the caramelized mold. Cool to room temperature, then cover with foil and refrigerate for several hours before serving. To unmold, place a serving plate (with a slight lip, if possible, to catch the liquid caramel) on top and invert quickly. During refrigeration, the caramel dissolves, which makes unmolding very easy.

Storage: Cover and refrigerate until serving. Serve within 48 hours.

IV-6 MOUSSE AU CHOCOLAT

In 17th century France, an immoderate love for chocolate was considered to be such a typically Spanish "vice" that Marie-Thérèse d'Autriche, a Spanish princess and wife of Louis XIV, was forced to indulge her craving in secret. Her penchant for chocolate was well known, however, since a historian of the day wrote that, "Maria-Thérèse had only two passions: the king and chocolate."

The most classical French dessert is nonetheless one of the most exquisite. Serve it with crème chantilly as a dessert, in a Pudding St. Martin, a rolled cake...

(IV-6)
Mousse au Chocolat
(Chocolate Mousse)

Ingredients: (for about 3 cups mousse)

5	ounces semi-sweet chocolate
2	tablespoons heavy cream
1	teaspoon lemon or orange juice
4	egg yolks
4	egg whites
	pinch salt
1	tablespoon sugar

Over a double boiler, melt chocolate, then remove from heat and beat in cream, juice and egg yolks. Cool.

In a large mixing bowl, beat egg whites and salt at high speed until soft peaks form. Add sugar and continue beating until very stiff but not dry. Beat 1/3 of whites into chocolate mixture, then pour chocolate mixture into rest of whites and, using a large wooden spoon or rubber spatula, fold in carefully. Spoon into individual dessert cups or a large serving dish. Chill at least 1 hour, then serve with chocolate shavings or crème chantilly (II-1).

Storage: Cover tightly and refrigerate up to 48 hours.

IV-7   MOUSSE À LA MANGUE

Young native brides in the French Antilles observe a charming custom: on their wedding day, they present the bridegroom with a hand-woven basket full of tropical fruit, as a symbol of prosperity and fertility.

Here, the mango, among the most appreciated tropical fruits in France, is the basis for a light, tangy mousse. It can be served in individual dessert dishes or, for a special occasion, as a charlotte, in a casing of biscuits à la cuillère.

(IV-7)
Mousse à la Mangue
(Mango Mousse)

Ingredients: (for about 3 cups mousse, serving 6)

1	fresh mango
2	tablespoons sugar
3	tablespoons lemon juice
1	tablespoon gelatin
1 1/2	cups crème chantilly, (whipped cream) (II-1)
1	egg white
	pinch salt
1 1/2	teaspoons sugar

With a paring knife, peel mango, remove stone, and cut in chunks. Whirl in blender with sugar until perfectly smooth. Strain into a large mixing bowl, to remove stray fibers.

In a small saucepan, heat the lemon juice and gelatin over low heat until gelatin is melted. Stir into mango purée and refrigerate.

Prepare crème chantilly and refrigerate until use. In a small mixing bowl, beat egg white and salt at high speed until soft peaks form. Add sugar and continue beating until stiff but not dry. Reserve 1/2 cup of chantilly for decoration.

With a rubber spatula or large spoon, carefully fold the remaining chantilly and all of whites into chilled mango purée. Spoon into 6 individual dessert dishes and decorate with dollops or rosettes of chantilly, and mango slices. Chill 2 hours before serving.

Charlotte à la Mangue (Mango Charlotte) (IV-7a): Prepare charlotte mold (see IV-12), and follow recipe for Pudding St. Martin (IV-17), substituting mousse à la mangue for mousse au chocolat. Before serving, decorate with rosettes of crème chantilly and mango slices. Serve plain or with crème anglaise (II-3).

Storage: Refrigerate until serving. Serve within 24 hours.

IV-8 ILE FLOTTANTE

Up until the 18th century, sugar was synonymous with riches. In 1736, for the wedding of Marie-Thérèse, future queen of Hungary, sugar occupied a respected place on the gift list, alongside gold and precious stones.

This dessert made of whipped egg whites and prâlin poached in caramel, then served on a lake of English custard sauce, is called, literally, "floating island". It's similar to oeufs à la neige, but is more refined.

(IV-8)
Ile Flottante
(Floating Island)

Ingredients: (for about 6 servings)
2/3   cup caramel (II-8a)

6   egg whites
      pinch salt
1/2   cup prâlin (II-9)

3   cups crème anglaise (II-3)

Prepare caramel and pour into unbuttered 6-inch charlotte mold, rotating quickly to coat evenly before it hardens.

Preheat oven to 350-degrees. In a large mixing bowl, beat egg whites and salt at high speed until stiff but not dry. With a rubber spatula, fold in prâlin.

Spoon into prepared mold, pressing gently with a spoon or spatula to eliminate air pockets, and cover with buttered aluminum foil to prevent browning. Place mold in a larger pan half full of hot water, and bake 30 minutes. Don't overbake, as the egg whites would become rubbery.

While egg whites are baking, prepare crème anglaise. Cool to room temperature, then chill. Cool baked whites completely before turning out onto a deep serving plate. Pour chilled crème anglaise around to create the effect of a floating island.

Storage: Refrigerate until serving. Serve within 2 hours.

IV-9 DIPLOMATE CLASSIQUE

The anonymous cook who decided to call this popular family dessert a "diplomat" probably wanted to create an aura of prestige and luxury. A diplomatic way of using up stale French bread, croissants, and brioche, this classical pudding can be served warm or cold, with crème chantilly, crème anglaise, coulis de fruits, or liquid caramel.

(IV-9)

Diplomate Classique
(Classic Diplomat Bread Pudding)

Ingredients: (for one 8-inch diplomate, serving 6)

- 3 cups milk
- 6 egg yolks
- 2/3 cup sugar
- 1/8 teaspoon salt

- 3 cups bread, or a mixture of bread, croissants, and brioche, cut in 1-inch cubes

- 1/4 cup raisins, macerated in rum or kirsch

    butter for mold

Choose one of the following sauces:
    crème chantilly (II-1)
    crème anglaise (II-3)
    coulis de fruits (II-13)
    liquid caramel (II-8b)

In a large mixing bowl, whisk together the milk, egg yolks, sugar and salt, then stir in the bread mixture and raisins with a wooden spoon. Cover with aluminum foil and let stand 1 hour. Preheat oven to 350-degrees.

Stir the mixture, then pour into 8-inch buttered baking dish. Place dish in a larger dish half full of hot water, and bake 30 to 40 minutes, or until a knife blade inserted in the center comes out clean. Cool at least 30 minutes before serving plain, or with the garnish of your choice.

IV-10   DIPLOMATE AUX FRUITS

Author of a culinary dictionary, creator of numerous recipes, and proprietor of a stupendous waistline, Alexander Dumas was almost as famous for his gourmandise as for his novels. He also had a diplomat's talent for putting boors in their places. A pushy journalist once remarked with a sneer, "Well, Monsieur Dumas, you must know a lot about Negroes. After all, if I remember correctly, some of your ancestors were black."

The writer, whose mixed heritage was known to all, nodded solemnly and replied, "Indeed, sir, you are quite right. To be precise, my father was a mulatto, my grandfather a Negro, and my great-grandfather...an ape! So you see, dear sir," he concluded with an amiable smile, "my family began...there where yours left off."

Here's yet another kind of diplomat, which is also called "Aunt Rose's pudding" in some parts of France. Easy to prepare and refreshing, especially during the summer because no cooking is required, it can be made with any kind of fresh fruit sauce.

(IV-10)

Diplomate aux Fruits
(Diplomat Pudding with Fruit-Summer Pudding)

Ingredients: (for one 8-inch gâteau)
40	biscuits à la cuillère (ladyfingers) (I-5)
3	cups coulis de fruits (fresh fruit sauce) (II-13)
3 1/2	cups crème anglaise (II-3) or
	2 or 3 cups crème chantilly (II-1)

In an unbuttered 8-inch soufflé dish mold, layer ladyfingers and fresh fruit sauce, beginning and ending with a layer of ladyfingers. Cover with a plate, place a 2-pound weight on top, and place mold on a second plate to catch any overflow of juice. Refrigerate overnight.

Thirty minutes before unmolding, place in freezer, then place mold in hot water for 1 minute. Dry off mold and invert on serving plate. Serve with crème chantilly or crème anglaise, or if you want a more refined presentation, spoon crème chantilly into a pastry bag with a 5/8-inch fluted nozzle and cover the gâteau with rosettes of chantilly.

Storage: Refrigerate until serving (within 24 hours), after unmolding.

IV-11   BAVAROIS AUX FRUITS

We owe the name of this dessert to a Bavarian prince's Parisian vacation in the early 18th century. Each day, at the ultra-chic Café Procope, he ordered tea sweetened with a special syrup, which immediately became known as a "bavarois". Since then, the drink has changed considerably, and the name has been extended to designate a kind of creamy molded dessert.

The bavarois can be simple or spectacular, depending upon the elaborateness of the mold used to make it.

(IV-11)

Bavarois aux Fruits
(Bavarian Cream with Fresh Fruit Sauce)

Ingredients: (for 1 bavarois, serving 6)
Bavarian Cream:
- 2 2/3   cups crème anglaise (II-3)
- 1   tablespoon unflavored gelatin, softened in 3 tablespoons water and 1 tablespoon kirsch (see Note)
- 2   cups crème chantilly (II-1)

- 1/2   cup crème chantilly (II-1)
- coulis de fruits (II-13)
- fresh fruit and toasted slivered almonds for decoration

Bavarian Cream (IV-11a): Prepare crème anglaise. Remove from heat and whisk in gelatin mixture. Cool to room temperature, then refrigerate, whisking occasionally to speed cooling and check consistency. When the mixture is very thick, remove from refrigerator, then carefully fold in 2 cups crème chantilly.

Spoon into unbuttered 6 to 8-inch decorative mold, pressing gently with a rubber spatula to eliminate unsightly air pockets, and refrigerate several hours, until bavarois is very firm.

To unmold, freeze 30 minutes, then dip mold in hot water for 1 minute. Dry off mold, then place serving plate on top and invert. Spoon 1/2 cup chantilly into a pastry bag with a fluted nozzle, and pipe rosettes of chantilly around the base and on the top.

Decorate with fresh fruit and toasted almonds. Serve with fresh fruit sauce. If you don't have a decorative mold, spoon the soft bavarois (immediately after folding in the chantilly) into individual dessert dishes. Chill, decorate, and serve as above.

Note: -Gelatin in granules must first be softened in liquid, in a metal cup, and then dissolved (or liquefied) over a pan of simmering water.

IV-12 CHARLOTTE RUSSE

England's Queen Charlotte, wife of King George III, lent her name to an originally British dessert made of spiced apples baked in a casing of buttered bread. Later, Antonïn Carême, France's most genial pastry chef, created a much refined version, replacing the apples with whipped cream. It was naturally called "charlotte à la parisienne", but soon became "charlotte à la russe" the Russian style of table service being in vogue at the time.

(IV-12)
Charlotte Russe
(Charlotte Russe - Basic Recipe)

Ingredients: (for one 6-inch charlotte)
Charlotte Cream:

1 1/2	cups crème anglaise (II-3)
2	teaspoons gelatin, softened in 2 tablespoons water, and dissolved over simmering water (see Note IV-11)
2	cups crème chantilly (II-1)
12	biscuits à la cuillère (I-5)
1/2	cup sirop à entremets (dessert syrup) (II-12)
1	teaspoon kirsch
	coulis de fruits (fresh fruit sauce) (II-13)

Charlotte Cream (IV-12a): Prepare crème anglaise, then immediately whisk in gelatin mixture. Cool to room temperature, then chill, stirring occasionally, to speed up cooling and check consistency. While the crème anglaise is cooling, prepare and chill the crème chantilly.

When the crème anglaise is very thick, fold in the chantilly (whipped cream) and spoon into the prepared mold, Chill several hours, until very firm. Before unmolding, freeze 30 minutes, then place mold in hot water for 1 minute. Dry off mold, place serving plate on top and invert charlotte. Serve with coulis de fruits.

To line the 6-inch charlotte mold: Stir together sirop à entremets and kirsch in a shallow dish. Dip in the biscuits one at a time, turning quickly to avoid soaking, and line the unbuttered mold, cutting when necessary to fit and make a solid lining.

Charlotte au Café (Coffee) (IV-12b): Stir 1 teaspoon coffee extract into crème anglaise and proceed as directed for Charlotte Russe. Serve with plain or coffee-flavored crème anglaise (II-3c).

Charlotte au Prâlin (Praline) (IV-12c): Stir 1/3 cup prâlin into hot crème anglaise and proceed as above. This charlotte can also be made in an unlined mold. After unmolding, cover the outside (but not the top) with langues de chat (IX-3), overlapping slightly. Use 1 cup crème chantilly to attach them and decorate the top.

Storage: Cover and refrigerate until serving. Serve within 24 hours.

IV-13 CHARLOTTE AUX FRAISES OU FRAMBOISES

For hundreds of years, strawberries were known in England, but only as a highly prized delicacy reserved for the richer classes. In fact, up until the turn of the century, no one short of a duke was allowed the honor of having strawberry leaves embroidered on his ceremonial robes, or included in his family coat of arms. This refreshing charlotte can be prepared with strawberries or raspberries.

(IV-13)

Charlotte aux Fraises ou Framboises
(Strawberry or Raspberry Charlotte)

Same ingredients as for Charlotte Russe (IV-12), adding:

1/2	pound fresh strawberries or raspberries
1/4	cup sugar
1	teaspoon kirsch
3/4	cup crème chantilly (II-1)

If strawberries are very sandy, dust off with a soft brush, or clean with a wet cloth. Don't wash raspberries. Set aside about a dozen of the most attractive strawberries, then cut the rest in half and mix with the sugar and kirsch. Do not cut raspberries in half.

Prepare mold and charlotte cream as (IV-12). With the cream, fill mold about 1/3 of the way, then spread 1/2 of the berries over the cream. Continue alternating the cream and berries, finishing with a layer of cream. Refrigerate and unmold as described in the basic recipe.

Shortly before serving, spoon the 3/4 cup chantilly into a pastry bag with a small star nozzle. Pipe rosettes of chantilly around the base and on the top, then decorate with the reserved fruit. Serve alone or with a fresh strawberry or raspberry sauce.

Note: For a more elegant touch, the mold can be lined with jelly roll slices. You'll need about 12 to 14 individual sized (about 2 1/2 inches long and 1 1/2 inches in diameter) jellyrolls, available in most bakeries or grocery stores. With a sharp paring knife, cut them in 1/4-inch thick slices (no need to moisten them in sirop and kirsch), butter mold lightly and arrange slices in a solid layer, as with biscuits à la cuillère. Finish recipe as above. Before serving, brush with warm abricotage, then decorate with chantilly and fruit. Serve alone or with fresh fruit sauce.

Storage: Refrigerate until serving. Serve within 12 hours.

Afterword: *Louis XV was particularly fond of strawberries, which he had cultivated in the gardens of the Louvre. By 1766, ten different species were enjoyed by the French court.*

IV-14   CHARLOTTE À LA MELBA

At the height of her career, Nelly Melba, the renowned 19th century Australian cantatrice, gave her name to the latest thing in dresses, hairstyles, gloves…César Ritz, founder of Paris' most luxurious hotel, even named a kind of toast after Miss Melba. Naturally, it didn't take long for a dessert to be created in her honor: pêches melba. This vanilla and peach charlotte served with a fresh raspberry sauce is a variation of the original dessert, which included a swan carved out of a block of ice!

(IV-14)
Charlotte à la Melba
(Peach Charlotte with Raspberry Sauce)

Ingredients: (for one 6-inch charlotte, serving 6)

 2   large, firm, ripe yellow peaches

1 1/2   cups crème anglaise (II-3)
 2   teaspoons gelatin, softened in 3 tablespoons water and dissolved over hot water
 3   cups crème chantilly (II-1)

 18   biscuits à la cuillère (I-5)
1/2   cup sirop à entremets (II-12)
 1   teaspoon kirsch

 coulis de framboises (fresh raspberry sauce) (II-13)

With a sharp paring knife, peel peaches, then cut in thin slices, reserving 1/2 peach for the final decoration.

Prepare crème anglaise, then whisk in gelatin mixture. Cool to room temperature, then chill, stirring occasionally to speed cooling and check consistency. While the crème anglaise is cooling, prepare and chill crème chantilly, reserving 1 cup for decoration.

Prepare a 6-inch charlotte mold as for a charlotte russe (IV-12) basic recipe. You'll have about 6 leftover biscuits.

When the crème anglaise is very thick, fold in 2 cups of chantilly, then spoon 1/3 of this mixture into the prepared mold. With half of the peaches, cover the cream, then cover the peaches with 3 biscuits, dipped quickly in the sirop à entremets. Repeat, ending with a layer of cream mixture. Cover and chill several hours, until very firm.

Before unmolding, freeze 30 minutes, then place mold in hot water 1 minute. Dry off mold, place serving plate on top, and invert charlotte. Spoon reserved chantilly into pastry bag and pipe rosettes around the base and on the top. Decorate the top with a "pinwheel" of peach slices and serve immediately with fresh raspberry sauce..

Storage: Cover and refrigerate until serving. Serve within 24 hours.

IV-15 CHARLOTTE PANÂCHÉE

Gaston Phoebus, one of medieval France's most colorful figures, was as renowned for his romantic poetry and good looks as for his courage on the battlefield. When a jealous rival poisoned his wife, he decided to carry out a diabolical plan of revenge. To everyone's astonishment, he married the guilty lady…then proceeded to make her regret the day she'd laid eyes on Gaston Phoebus, Comte de Foix. The only being never to fall from his good graces? "Panâche", his piebald horse.

In France, "panâche" designates something composed of two colors or flavors, whether a two-toned horse, a mixed drink served in Parisian cafés…or this exquisite chocolate-vanilla charlotte.

(IV-15)
Charlotte Panâchée
(Chocolate & Vanilla Charlotte)

Ingredients: (for one 5-inch charlotte, serving 6)
Charlotte Cream (see IV-12a for technique)

3/4	cup crème anglaise (II-3)	
1	teaspoon gelatin	
2	cups crème chantilly (II-1)	
3	cups mousse au chocolat (IV-6)	

Mold Lining (see IV-12)

16	biscuits à la cuillère (ladyfingers) (I-5)	
3/4	cup sirop à entremets (dessert syrup) (II-12)	
1	teaspoon rum or kirsch	
1/2	cup crème chantilly (II-1)	
	grated chocolate or chocolate sprinkles	
6	candied cherries	

Prepare charlotte cream and line mold with 12 biscuits as in (IV-12). You should have 4 to 5 leftover biscuits. Save them for the top, which will become the base. Spoon all of the charlotte cream into a pastry bag with a large fluted nozzle, and spoon all of the chocolate mousse into another large pastry bag with a large fluted nozzle. Pipe a 1-inch deep layer of charlotte cream in bottom of mold, followed by a 1-inch layer of mousse. Continue alternating with the rest of the two creams. Moisten the remaining ladyfingers with syrup/kirsch mixture and cover the cream. This will form the base, when inverted. Refrigerate at least 6 hours.

Unmold as in charlotte russe basic recipe (IV-12). Shortly before serving, spoon chantilly into a pastry bag with a small star nozzle and pipe rosettes of cream around the base and on the top. Decorate with grated chocolate or chocolate sprinkles, and cherries. Serve alone or with a chilled chocolate sauce (II-15a).

IV-16 CHARLOTTE AUX MARRONS

How an economic crisis gave birth to a regional specialty: In the late 19th century, France's silk industry suffered such a serious setback that in the Ardèche, a region where the situation was particularly alarming, a group of resourceful citizens founded the country's first "marron glacé" factory. Today, the Ardèche is still France's leading producer of chestnut products.

Chocolate sauce is the perfect complement for this charlotte, rich in "marron glacés".

(IV-16)
Charlotte aux Marrons
(Chestnut Charlotte with Chocolate Sauce)

Ingredients: (for one 6-inch charlotte, serving 6)

3	tablespoons rum
2	teaspoons gelatin

2 1/2	cups canned chestnut cream
3 1/4	cups crème chantilly (whipped cream) (II-1)
1/4	cup chopped candied chestnuts

12	biscuits àla cuillère (ladyfingers) (I-5)
1/2	cup sirop à entremets (dessert syrup) (II-12)
1	teaspoon rum

1/2	cup crème chantilly (II-1)
7 to 8	candied chestnuts
	cold chocolate sauce (II-15a)

In a small saucepan, soften gelatin in rum, and heat until gelatin is dissolved. Cover and set aside. In a large mixing bowl, fold together chestnut cream and chantilly. Whisk a spoonful of chestnut mixture into the warm gelatin mixture, then gently fold gelatin into rest of chestnut mixture.

Line mold as in (IV-12). Spoon 1/3 of cream into mold, then sprinkle on half the chopped candied chestnuts. Repeat, then finish with a layer of cream. Refrigerate at least 4 hours. Unmold (see IV-12). Shortly before serving, spoon 1/2 cup chantilly into pastry bag with small star nozzle, and pipe rosettes around the base and top of charlotte. Decorate with whole candied chestnuts. Serve with cold chocolate sauce.

Storage: Refrigerate until serving. Serve within 12 hours.

IV-17   PUDDING ST. MARTIN

In France, our Indian Summer is known as "St. Martin's Summer" because of an old legend. On a freezing November day, a traveling monk by the name of Martin gave his clothes to an old man in rags encountered on the road. The old beggar, who was really none other than Christ in disguise, caused several days of warm weather to follow as compensation for Brother Martin's kindness…and his state of undress.

This rich chocolate dessert was created in the 17th century and traditionally served in French monasteries on St. Martin's day, November 11.

(IV-17)

Pudding St. Martin
(St. Martin's Pudding - Chocolate Mousse Mold with Ladyfingers)

Ingredients: (for one 8-inch pudding)
- 24   biscuits à la cuillère (ladyfingers) (I-5)
- 3/4   cup sirop à entremets (dessert syrup) (II-12)
- 3   cups mousse au chocolate (IV-6)

1 3/4   cups crème anglaise (II-3)

Pour the sirop à entremets into a shallow dish and quickly dip the ladyfingers one by one, to moisten but not soak them, then line the unbuttered charlotte mold, cutting them in pieces and fitting them in when necessary to make an even lining.

Prepare the mousse au chocolat. Spoon 1/3 into the prepared 8-inch charlotte mold and cover mousse with a layer of biscuits. Repeat layering, ending with biscuits. If any of the biscuits rise above the pudding, trim them off with a sharp knife. Cover and refrigerate at least 6 hours, or better yet, overnight.

Thirty minutes before serving, place mold in freezer. To unmold, place mold in hot water for 1 minute, then cover with serving plate and invert. Serve with chilled crème anglaise.

Storage: Refrigerate until serving. Serve within 24 hours of unmolding.

IV-18   BRIOCHE FOURRÉE AU BAVAROIS

Joséphine Bonaparte, notorious for her shocking conduct in the boudoir, may have been a bad wife to Napoléon, but she made up for her years of "libertinage" by being an exemplary grandmother. Her indulgence knew no bounds, even when her unruly grandsons, looking for a sweet treat, got into the hothouse at Malmaison and cut down her prized sugarcane.

A simple brioche can become quite a treat, when garnished with a rich filling, and served with fruit or cream sauce. A slightly dry brioche will be less fragile, and easier to handle.

(IV-18)

Brioche Fourrée au Bavarois
(Filled Brioche with Fruit & Bavarian Cream)

Ingredients: (for one filled brioche, serving 8)
- 1   brioche parisienne (III-13)
- 1   cup sirop à entremets à la vanille or au kirsch (II-12)
- 1   recipe bavarian cream (IV-11a)

With a serrated knife, slice off the "head" of the brioche and set it aside. Then cut down into the brioche, stopping just short of the bottom, and cut all around, leaving a 1/2-inch thick shell. Now, stick the knife through the crust about 1/2-inch from the bottom of the cut brioche. Carefully remove the core. Brush the inside of the brioche, and the cut side of the head, with sirop. Fill with soft bavarian cream, pressing down gently with a rubber spatula to avoid air pockets. Place the top, and refrigerate for several hours. Serve with fresh fruit sauce (II-13), hot or cold chocolate sauce (II-15a), or liquid caramel (II-8b).

Storage: Although best if served the same day, a filled brioche can be kept, covered and refrigerated, for 24 hours.

Brioche Fourrée à la Mousse au Chocolat (Filled Brioche with Chocolate Mousse) (IV-18a): Same as above, replacing the bavarian cream with mousse au chocolat (IV-6). Serve with cold crème anglaise (II-3), or crème chantilly (II-1), or for a double chocolate treat, with hot or cold sauce au chocolat (II-15a).

IV-19 BRIOCHE POLONAISE

In medieval Europe, candied fruit was very popular among the upper classes, who, after meals, enjoyed candied plums, apricots, oranges, and lemons, along with the traditional sugar coated almonds and spiced wine. Even Pope Clement VI was unable to resist this new delicacy, since he ordered large quantities of it from Apt, a French city still known today for its excellent "confiseries".

This meringue-cloaked brioche is filled with a mixture of vanilla pastry cream and chopped candied fruit.

(IV-19)
Brioche Polonaise
(Polish Brioche - Meringue Brioche with Vanilla Cream)

Ingredients: (for one filled brioche, serving 8)

- 1   brioche parisienne (III-13)
- 1   cup sirop à entremets au rhum (II-12)
- 2   cups crème patissière à la vanille (II-2)

- 1/2   cup finely-chopped candied fruit
- 1/2   cup candied whole cherries

- 1   recipe meringue française (I-12)
- 1/2   cup toasted sliced almonds
       powdered sugar

With the serrated knife, cut off the brioche "head", then cut the brioche into 4 equal horizontal layers. Spread a little cream mixture on the cake board, and place the bottom layer of brioche. Brush with sirop, spread with about 1/4 of cream, sprinkle on about 1/4 of candied fruit and cherries. Place second layer, brush with sirop, spread on more cream, sprinkle with fruit, and so on with the rest of brioche. Brush the cut side of head with sirop, and replace.

Preheat oven to 425-degrees. Prepare meringue française, and with a metal spatula, cover the brioche with an even layer of meringue. Sprinkle generously with almonds and dust with powdered sugar. Place on a baking sheet and bake 10 to 15 minutes, or until meringue is an even dark cream color. Serve cold.

Storage: Keep, loosely covered in a cool dry place for up to 24 hours.

IV-20   TIMBALE BELLE HÉLÈNE

In 1864, Jacques Offenbach presented his latest comic opera, "La Belle Hélène", to the Parisian public. The connection between the opera, Helen of Troy, and the Trojan War went no further than the title, but that didn't keep it from becoming an immediate success. Overnight, an impressive array of "Belle Hélène" products were created. Timbale Belle Hélène, of course, was one of them. Delicate vanilla cream and pears are nicely offset by a hot fudge sauce, while crisp meringues add texture. This is a dessert worthy of a fancy dinner party.

(IV-20)
Timbale Belle Hélène

Ingredients: (for one 6-inch gâteau, serving 6)

2	large ripe pears
1 1/2	cups crème anglaise (II-3)
2	teaspoons unflavored gelatin
3	cups crème chantilly (II-1)
12	oval meringues françaises (I-12)
1 1/3	cups sauce au chocolat (II-15)

With a paring knife, peel and core pears, then cut in half, lengthwise. If they're not quite ripe enough, place in a medium saucepan with 1/2 cup water, 1 tablespoon sugar, and 1 teaspoon lemon juice, cover and poach over low heat until tender. Drain well, then set aside one half pear for decoration.

Prepare the crème anglaise, then immediately whisk the gelatin into the hot crème. Cool to room temperature, then chill, stirring occasionally to speed cooling and check consistency.

Meanwhile, prepare crème chantilly. When the crème anglaise is very thick, fold in 1 1/2 cups chantilly. Spoon 1/3 of this mixture into the unbuttered mold, pressing gently with a spoon or rubber spatula to eliminate air pockets. Crumble 3 meringues on top, then cover with half the pears, thinly sliced. Repeat, finishing with a layer of cream mixture. Stack with plates on top to weigh down and refrigerate 4 hours, until very firm.

Before unmolding, place in freezer for 30 minutes, then in hot water for 1 minute. Dry off mold, place serving plate on top, and invert. Spoon remaining 1 1/2 cups chantilly into the pastry bag. Pipe large rosettes on the flat sides of the 6 remaining meringues and attach them to the sides of the gâteau, then pipe rosettes around the bottom, the top, and between the meringues. Decorate the top with a "pinwheel" of thinly sliced pears. Serve with warm sauce au chocolat (II-15).

Storage: Cover and refrigerate until serving. Serve within 12 hours.

Afterword: Centuries ago, this city of Reims was as famous for its pears as for its champagne. Charles X, whose coronation was held in Reims, was presented with champagne and pears. "We offer you our best," the mayor told him solemnly. "Our wines, our pears...and our hearts." Other visiting sovereigns, including Louis XV, Louis XVI, and Napoléon were to receive the same honors.

IV-21   BISCUIT BALZAC

Down through the ages, coffee has had its unconditional supporters...and its arch enemies. Louis XV was so fond of it that he prepared it himself. Napoleon often declared that the burning sensation caused by strong coffee "resuscitated" him. Fontenelle, an 18th century writer and philosopher, drank such prodigious quantities that a friend became concerned for his health.

"Cher ami, permit me to advise you concerning your immoderate consumption of coffee," he warned gravely. "It is, as everyone knows, a slow poison."

Fontenelle looked up from his work table. "I've been drinking it for eighty years," he remarked with a smile. "It must be slow indeed, not to have killed me by now."

Hahnemann, the founder of homeopathic medicine, blamed coffee for heart problems, loquacity, "vacillation" and lustful thoughts! And then there was Honoré de Balzac, who carefully enumerated the frightful infirmities caused by coffee. Irony or paradox? Balzac himself drank forty cups of coffee a day! This quick and easy dessert is reminiscent of a coffee flavored layer cake, but much faster to put together.

(IV-21)

Biscuit Balzac
(Balzac's Cake - Coffee Layer Cake)

Ingredients: (for one 8-inch gâteau)

3/4	cup butter, softened
4	tablespoons powdered sugar
3	egg yolks
4	tablespoons strong black coffee, freshly brewed, then chilled
20	biscuits à la cuillère (ladyfingers) (I-5)
1	cup unflavored sirop à entremets (dessert syrup) (II-12)
1/2	cup strong black coffee
2	cups crème chantilly (whipped cream) (II-1)
1/4	cup toasted slivered almonds

In a medium mixing bowl, cream butter and sugar until light and fluffy. Beat in egg yolks, then coffee, a teaspoon at a time, until mixture is light and creamy. Pour sirop à entremets and coffee into a shallow dish and dip biscuits, turning once.

Line bottom of dish with biscuits, spread on a thin layer of filling, and repeat with the rest of ingredients, ending with a layer of filling. Prepare crème chantilly. Immediately before serving, spoon chantilly into pastry bag and cover top with rosettes or "shells" of crème. Sprinkle with almonds and serve.

Note: If you prefer, this dessert can be unmolded after several hours of refrigeration. Unmold as for a charlotte (IV-12), then cover top and sides with rosettes of crème chantilly.

Storage: Cover and refrigerate until 30 minutes before serving. Serve within 24 hours.

Chapter V

Individual Pastries
(Patisseries Individuelles)

V-I ÉCLAIRS

"Éclair", in everyday French, simply means "thunderbolt". Was the anonymous creator of these pastries inspired into action during a terrible thunderstorm?

Garnish these ever-popular puff pastries with your choice of the following: chocolate filling and icing, coffee filling and icing, or the less common but equally delicious vanilla filling and chocolate or coffee icing.

(V-1)
Éclairs
(Eclairs)

Ingredients: (for 8 éclairs)
1 1/4   cups pate à choux (I-11)
      oil for baking sheet
  1   egg, beaten with a pinch of salt (egg wash)

1 1/8   cups crème patissière au café, au chocolat, or à la vanille (II-2)
1/2   cup plain crème au beurre (II-4) or crème chantilly (II-1)
      (whippped cream) made with 1/4 cup heavy cream

  1   cup fondant au café or au chocolat (II-10)

If you are using crème au beurre, make it a day in advance. To use, heat very gently. Also, it is best to prepare and flavor the fondant at least a day ahead.

Preheat oven to 425-degrees. Prepare pâte à choux and spoon into pastry bag with 5/8-inch nozzle. On a very lightly-oiled baking sheet, pipe out eight 5-inch long éclairs, spacing well to allow for expansion during baking. Brush with beaten egg and bake at 425-degrees for 15 minutes, then lower heat to 400-degrees, prop oven door open with a spoon, and bake another 15 minutes, until golden brown. Don't underbake.

While the choux are baking, prepare and flavor crème patissière. Cool to room temperature, then add the crème au beurre and beat until smooth. If you prefer to use crème chantilly in the filling, make it now and fold carefully into the cooled crème patissière. In either case, chill filling thoroughly before using.

To Garnish: Many pastry chefs garnish their éclairs by splitting the pastry shell lengthwise—somewhat like a hotdog bun—then opening and filling. This method, in my opinion, makes for a rather unattractive presentation, and the exposed filling dries out quickly. The method I use is just as quick and easy, and the finished pastry is more presentable: spoon the chilled filling into a pastry bag with small star-shaped nozzle.

Remember, the smooth, even underside of the shell is generally used as the top of the finished pastry, while the puffed side goes on the bottom. So, using the nozzle, make 2 small holes in the puffed side, about 1/2-inch from the end. Insert the nozzle in one end and squeeze until cream appears in the second hole. Pipe more filling into the second hole, to be sure that the éclair is well filled. Repeat with the rest of the shells.

More→

(Éclairs, Cont.)

In a medium saucepan, heat fondant very gently. Dip the even sides into the warm fondant, then lift up over the pot, and with a spatula smooth the fondant and remove excess. Place, fondant side up, on a wire rack to set.

Storage: Refrigerate until serving, preferably the same day as made. Can be kept for up to 24 hours.

V-2   ÉCLAIRS À LA CHANTILLY

According to the Flammarion dictionary, the word "caramel" comes, not from an Arabic term but from the medieval Latin word "cannamella" which means "sugar cane", or more literally, "honey cane". These sumptuous whipped cream-filled éclairs can be topped with crunchy caramel or semi-sweet chocolate.

(V-2)
Éclairs à la Chantilly
(Whipped Cream Filled Eclairs)

Ingredients: (for 8 éclairs)
- 1 1/4   cups pâte à choux (I-11)
- 1   egg beaten with a pinch of salt (egg wash)

- 2/3   cup caramel (II-8a)

- 2   cups crème chantilly (II-1)

Preheat oven to 425-degrees. Prepare pâte à choux and spoon into pastry bag with 5/8-inch fluted nozzle. On a lightly-greased baking sheet, pipe eight 5-inch long éclairs. Brush with egg wash and bake at 425-degrees for 15 minutes, then turn down heat to 400-degrees and, propping oven door open with a spoon, bake for another 20 minutes, or until golden brown. Cool.

While the éclairs bake, prepare the crème chantilly. Chill. In a large saucepan, prepare an amber-colored caramel. Since the éclair bottoms are generally smoother and more even than the tops, it's better to use them as the top. So, dip the smooth bottoms in the caramel, then place them, caramel side down, on an oiled surface to cool. Repeat the operation as soon as they're cool. (If necessary, keep the caramel liquid by placing over a double boiler). Cool again.

With a large serrated knife, split each éclair down one side, taking care not to touch the caramel, which would show fingerprints. Spoon the crème chantilly into a pastry bag with a 1/2-inch nozzle and fill generously.

Éclairs à la Chantilly au Glacés au Chocolat (with Chocolate Glaze)(V-2a):
Prepare as above, replacing the caramel with 5 ounces of semi-sweet chocolate, melted in a double boiler. Dip each éclair top (that is, the smooth bottom) into

More→

(Éclairs à la Chantilly, Cont.)

the melted chocolate, and cool right side up. Don't re-dip. Be careful not to touch the chocolate when you're opening or filling the éclairs. It would melt upon contact with the warmth of your hands. The amount of chocolate called for here will be more than enough. Save the leftover chocolate for chopping and mixing with fillings, custards, etc.

Storage: Refrigerate until serving. Serve within 2 hours.

V-3 RELIGIEUSES
Curiously enough, "religieuse", in non-culinary French, simply means "nun". Did a clergywoman happen to bustle past the shop of an unknown baker as he set out his latest creation? It's not impossible…these rotund cream-filled pastries certainly could have brought to mind the dark, flowing robes of a stout little nun.

(V-3)
Religieuses
(Iced Cream Puffs)

Ingredients: (for about 6 religieuses)
1 1/4   cups pâte à choux (I-11)
        oil for baking sheet
   1   egg, beaten with a pinch of salt (egg wash)

1 1/8   cups crème patissière au café or au chocolat (II-2)
 1/2   cup plain crème au beurre (II-4) or
        1/2 cup unsweetened crème chantilly (II-1)

1 1/2   cups fondant au café or au chocolat (II-10)
 1/2   cup plain crème au beurre (II-4)

It's best to make the crème au beurre in advance and freeze or refrigerate it until use. Fondant, too, should be prepared and flavored at least a day in advance.

Preheat oven to 425-degrees. Prepare pâte à choux and spoon into a pastry bag with 5/8-inch nozzle. On a very lightly-oiled baking sheet, pipe out six 2 1/4-inch round choux, spacing well to allow for expansion while baking. On another sheet, pipe out six 1 1/4-inch round choux. Brush with beaten egg.

More➤

(Religieuses, cont.)

Bake at 425-degrees for 15 minutes, then lower the heat to 400-degrees, prop open the oven door with a spoon and bake for another 15 to 20 minutes, until golden brown. Don't underbake. The smaller choux will bake more quickly, so watch them closely and remove as soon as they're done. Cool thoroughly before filling.

While the choux are baking, prepare and flavor the crème patissière, and, if you're using it, the crème chantilly. Cool the crème patissière to room temperature, then beat in the crème au beurre (or carefully fold in the crème chantilly). Refrigerate until use.

To garnish: Spoon chilled filling into a pastry bag with a small star-shaped nozzle. With the nozzle, make a small hole in the bottom of each chou and fill.

In a medium saucepan, heat fondant very gently. Turn the large choux over and dip the tops in the warm fondant, using a twisting motion to cover well. Lift the choux up over the saucepan, and with a finger smooth the fondant and remove excess, then place rightside up on a wire rack. Ice the small choux the same way, and place them on top of the large ones.

To decorate: If the crème au beurre is too cold, heat it very gently to just soften, then spoon it into a pastry bag with a small star-shaped nozzle and pipe several teardrop-shaped rosettes at the base of the "head", and one small round rosette on the very top.

Storage: Refrigerate until serving. Serve within 24 hours.

V-4   CYGNES

During the Middle Ages, swan, which was among the most highly prized meats of the time, was prepared in the following way: feathers intact, it was carefully skinned, then cooked, "redressed" with its feathers, and presented on an artificial lake. It may not have tasted very good, but it was always sure to amuse guests at royal dinners.

These charming pâte à chou swans filled with whipped cream are surprisingly easy to make. They could replace the all-too-predictable cupcakes at a children's party, the usual cookies at afternoon tea, or make an excellent dessert after a heavy meal.

(V-4)
Cygnes
(Swan Cream Puffs)

Ingredients: (for 6 swans)

     1 1/4   cups pâte à choux (I-11)
        1   egg, beaten with a pinch of salt (egg wash)

        2   cups crème chantilly (II-1)
            powdered sugar

Preheat oven to 425-degrees. Prepare pâte à choux, spoon into pastry bag with a 5/8-inch fluted nozzle, and on a lightly-greased baking sheet, pipe out six 2 x 3-inch choux. Hold the pastry bag slightly inclined, and draw it out some to make an oval. Stop squeezing, then pull the nozzle back and up to form a small point. Replace the nozzle with a 1/4-inch round nozzle and pipe out six 3-inch long candy cane shaped choux for the swans' necks.

Brush all pâte à choux with beaten egg and bake at 425-degrees for 15 minutes, then lower the heat to 400-degrees, prop the oven door open with a spoon, and bake for another 15 to 20 minutes. The smaller choux will bake more quickly than the larger, so remove them and finish baking the others. Don't underbake. The choux would fall or be soggy when filled. Cool.

While the choux are baking, prepare and chill chantilly.

To garnish: With a serrated knife, cut the top off of each chou, about 1/3 of the way down. Cut each top in half, lengthwise. Remove any fragments of undercooked dough from the bottom half. Spoon the crème chantilly into a pastry bag with a 1/8-inch star nozzle and fill the bottoms. Place the "candy cane" at the wider end, well anchored in the chantilly. Place the 2 halves of the top, cut side down, in the chantilly to form wings. Pipe rosettes of chantilly down the back, between the wings, and immediately before serving, dust wings lightly with powdered sugar.

Storage: Refrigerate until serving. Serve within 2 hours.

V-5   SALAMBOS AU GRAND MARNIER

Salambos were created in Paris in 1862, shortly after the publication of Gustave Flaubert's popular novel entitled **Salambô.** *The pastry cream filling for these individual choux can be flavored with rum or kirsch, as well as Grand Marnier.*

(V-5)
Salambos au Grand Marnier
(Cream Puffs with Grand Marnier)

Ingredients: (for 8 salambos)

1 1/4	cups pâte à choux (I-11)
1	egg, beaten with a pinch of salt (egg wash)

1 1/8	cups crème patissière (II-2)
3	tablespoons Grand Marnier

1	cup plain fondant (II-10)
1	drop red food coloring
	silver or red balls for decoration

Preheat oven to 425-degrees. Prepare pâte à choux. Spoon into pastry bag with a 5/8-inch fluted nozzle, and on a lightly-greased baking sheet, pipe out eight 2 x 3 inch ovals. Brush with beaten egg, and bake at 425-degrees for 15 minutes, then lower heat to 400-degrees, prop oven door open with a spoon, and bake for another 15 to 20 minutes, until golden brown. Be careful not to underbake. Cool.

While the choux are baking, prepare crème patissière. Remove from heat and beat in Grand Marnier. Cool to room temperature, then refrigerate until use.

To garnish: Spoon chilled filling into a pastry bag with a 1/8-inch star nozzle. With the nozzle, make a small hole in the bottom of each chou, and fill.

In a medium saucepan, heat fondant, then beat in food coloring. The fondant should be pale pink. Turn the choux over and dip the tops into the warm fondant, then lift them up over the saucepan. With a spatula, smooth fondant and remove excess, then place right side up on a rack to set. Top each chou with a silver or red ball.

Salambos au Kirsch (Kirsch) (V-5a): Flavor crème patissière with 3 tablespoons kirsch, color plain fondant with 1 drop green food coloring to make it pale green, and decorate with silver pearls or mimosa balls.

Salambos au Rhum (Rum) (V-5b): Flavor crème patissière with 3 tablespoons rum, top with plain white fondant, and decorate with chocolate sprinkles by dipping one end of fondant-covered top.

Storage: Refrigerate until serving. Serve within 24 hours.

V-6 CHOUX PRÂLINÉS

"No, nothing can replace butter!" Those were said to be the last words murmured, ironically enough, by Hippolyte Mège-Mouriès. He died in 1880, only eleven years after having invented margarine, a substitute for butter which was barely accepted at the time, but widely-used today.

Prâlin filling enriched with butter (the real thing, please!) makes these individual puffs irresistibly creamy.

(V-6)

Choux Prâlinés
(Cream Puffs Praline)

Ingredients: (for 8 large choux)
1 1/4	cups pâte à choux (I-11)
1	egg beaten with a pinch of salt (egg wash)
1/3	cup finely-chopped almonds
1 1/8	cups crème patissière (II-2)
1/3	cup prâlin (II-9)
1/2	cup butter

powdered sugar

Preheat oven to 425-degrees. Prepare pâte à choux and spoon into a pastry bag with a 5/8-inch fluted nozzle. On a lightly-greased baking sheet, pipe out 8 large choux about 2 1/2-inches in diameter. Brush with egg wash and sprinkle with almonds. Bake for 15 minutes at 425-degrees, then lower heat to 400-degrees and, propping the oven door open with a spoon, bake for another 15 minutes, or until the choux are puffed up and golden brown. Cool.

While the choux are baking, prepare crème patissière. Stir in prâlin and cool to room temperature, then chill.

In a medium mixing bowl, beat together the crème patissière and butter until light and creamy. Spoon into a pastry bag with a 1/8-inch star nozzle, and, making a hole in the bottom of each chou with the nozzle, fill. Immediately before serving, dust the choux with powdered sugar.

Storage: Refrigerate until serving. Serve within 2 hours.

V-7 PROFITEROLES AU CHOCOLAT

Profiteroles probably got their name from the French verb "profiter", which means "to profit" or, as in this case, "to enjoy". So..."profitez"!

These small choux traditionally presented in a pyramid and served with hot fudge sauce can also be filled with vanilla ice cream.

(V-7)
Profiteroles au Chocolat
(Cream Puffs with Chocolate Sauce)

Ingredients: (for about 30 profiteroles)
- 1 1/4 cups pâte à choux (I-11)
- 1 egg, beaten with a pinch of salt (egg wash)

- 2 cups crème chantilly (II-1)

- 1 1/3 cups sauce au chocolat (II-15a)

Preheat oven to 425-degrees. Prepare pâte à choux and spoon into a pastry bag with a fluted 1/2-inch nozzle. On a lightly-greased baking sheet, pipe out about 30 small choux, about 1 1/4-inches wide. Brush with beaten egg, then bake about 10 minutes at 425-degrees. Lower heat to 400-degrees, and, propping the oven door open with a spoon, bake for another 10 minutes, until golden brown. Cool.

While the choux are baking, prepare a very firm crème chantilly. Refrigerate until use.

Spoon crème chantilly into a pastry bag with a 1/8-inch star nozzle, and, making a hole in the bottom of each chou with the nozzle, fill. Refrigerate until serving.

To serve, stack the profiteroles in a pyramid on a serving plate. Prepare the sauce au chocolat, pour some over the choux, and serve the rest in a small pitcher. Serve immediately.

V-8 "FIGUES" À LA CRÈME

The fig has accompanied mankind down through the ages: Adam and Eve dressed with its leaves, the ancient Greeks gave it as a New Year's present, and Tantalus was said to have been condemned to see—but never to eat—it.

In his mémoires, the French playwright Marcel Pagnol spoke fondly of after-school snacks with classmates, and of these cream-filled "figs", a specialty of his native Provence.

(V-8)

"Figues" à la Crème
(Cream-Filled "Figs")

Ingredients: (for about 10 "figs")

1 1/4	cups pâte à choux (I-11)
	oil for baking sheet
1	egg, beaten with a pinch of salt (egg wash)
1 1/8	cups crème patissière (II-2) (flavor of your choice)
1/2	cup plain crème au beurre (II-4) or
	1/2 cup unsweetened crème chantilly (II-1)
8	ounces pâte d'amandes (almond paste) (II-18)
2-3	drops green food coloring
	powdered sugar for rolling out
	caramel (II-8a) or brown food coloring (optional)

Preheat oven to 425-degrees. Prepare pâte à choux and spoon into pastry bag with 5/8-inch fluted nozzle. On a very lightly-oiled baking sheet, pipe out about 10 round 2-inch wide choux. Brush with beaten egg and bake at 425-degrees for 15 minutes, then lower heat to 400-degrees, prop open oven door with a wooden spoon, and bake another 15 to 20 minutes, until golden brown. Don't underbake. Cool completely before filling.

While the choux are baking, prepare and flavor the crème patissière, and, if you're using it, the crème chantilly. (If you prefer to use crème au beurre, it can be prepared a day ahead. Remove it from the refrigerator 1 hour before using, and if necessary, heat very gently.) Cool the crème patissière to room temperature, then beat in the crème au beurre (or carefully fold in the crème chantilly). Refrigerate until used.

To garnish: Spoon chilled filling into a pastry bag with a 1/8-inch star nozzle, make a small hole in the bottom of each chou, and fill.

Dust work surface lightly with powdered sugar, and knead the pâte d'amandes until it's workable. Shake on a few drops green food coloring and knead it until color is uniform. Dust surface with more sugar, then roll out pâte to about 1/8-

More→

("Figues" à la Crème, cont.)

inch thick. With a sharp paring knife or chef's knife, cut bands about 4 inches wide. Place a filled chou on its side, on the pâte, and roll up. Make a 1/4-inch seam, then cut. Set the chou on its base, bunch the excess pâte on the top, pressing it together with the fingers to resemble a fig. With the paring knife, trim off at about 1/2 to 3/4-inch above, to form a "stem".

If you're feeling really artistic, you can give the "fig" a more realistic look by brushing it lightly here and there with a small paintbrush dipped in caramel food coloring (available in specialty shops) or in slightly diluted brown food coloring. It's best to practice some on a scrap of pâte d'amandes before doing the "figs".

V-9   PUITS D' AMOUR

"Puits d'Amour", a comic opera written in 1843, gave its name to these caramelized pâte à choux "wells of love". Actually, they're just an updated version of cinnamon-flavored "darioles", a popular medieval pastry.

(V-9)
Puits d'Amour
(Wells of Love - Cream Puffs in Muffins)

Ingredients: (for 10 puits)
- 1/2   cup (generous) pâte à choux (I-11)
     butter for muffin tin

- 1 1/8   cups crème patissière (II-2)

- 2/3   cup caramel (II-8a)
     granulated sugar for glazing

Prepare pâte à choux, using half the quantities given for 1 1/4 cups (I-11). Cover and set aside to cool. While the pâte is cooling, prepare the crème patissière. (To save time, it can be made the day before). Cover and set aside to cool.

Preheat oven to 375-degrees. Brush a muffin tin with cups for 10 muffins with melted butter. Drop one heaping teaspoon pâte à chou into each cup, and with a finger (wet it occasionally if pâte sticks to it) spread pâte around to line cups. Take care to line the cups as evenly as possible, as the resulting pastries' even, attractive shape depends on this. Place in oven, crack oven door immediately with a spoon (no need to wait 10 to 15 minutes, as for most other pâte à choux pastries) and bake for about 20 minutes, until golden brown. During baking, watch pastry carefully. If it browns too quickly, lower heat. Remove from oven

More➤

(Puits d' Amour, cont.)

and cool. Some of the shells may have a domed center. Don't worry, the dome can easily be pushed down with the fingers, and will stay down once filled.

In a medium saucepan, prepare caramel. Holding the shells upside down, dip the rims in the hot caramel. Turn right side up and cool.

With a wooden spoon or wire whisk, beat crème patissière until smooth. Spoon into pastry bag and fill shells, using a swirling motion. Sprinkle filled pastries with sugar and place on a baking sheet under the broiler for about 1 minute, or until the sugar is caramelized. Refrigerate until serving. Serve the same day.

Afterword: *A comic opera, a pastry…there was yet another kind of "Puits d'Amour". In the heart of 12th century Paris, a young woman, abandoned by the man she loved, drowned herself in one of the town's wells…a well which the romantic Parisians immediately dubbed "Puits d'Amour".*

V-10   MERINGUES À LA CHANTILLY

Who's never heard of Chantilly lace? It's just one of the things that have made the French town of Chantilly famous. The others? Thoroughbred race horses, porcelain, and a sumptuous Renaissance château, the walls of which echo with memories of Vatel, the château's unfortunate head cook who commited suicide in the name of honor. These crisp meringues with a filling of whipped cream can be assembled in no time at all for unexpected guests, if the meringue shells are made in advance.

(V-10)
Meringues à la Chantilly
(Meringues with Whipped Cream and Fruit)

Ingredients: (for 6 meringues)
- 12   oval meringues (I-12)
- 2   cups crème chantilly (II-1)
   decorations (fresh raspberries or strawberries, candied cherries, sugar coated violets, silver pearls, etc.)

Place 2 meringues, flat sides facing each other, in each of 6 fluted paper pastry cups. Spoon chantilly into a pastry bag with 1/2-inch fluted nozzle and fill the space between the meringues. Top each with a fresh raspberry or strawberry, or another chosen decoration.

Storage: Refrigerate until serving. Serve within 2 hours.

V-11 TÊTES DE NÈGRE

In the 17th century, European noblewomen were so fond of chocolate that they had it delivered to the church by their domestics and served to them during overlong religious services. Scandalized, the officiating priests threatened the offenders with excommunication. Their answer? A change of churches, of course.

These meringue and crème au beurre "heads" are most often chocolate flavored, but can also be made with prâlin, coffee, or even coconut.

(V-11)
Têtes de Nègre
(Meringue Heads)

Ingredients: (for 6 têtes)

12	round or oval meringues (I-12)
1 1/4	cups crème au beurre au chocolat (II-4a)

4	ounces grated semi-sweet chocolate or
	1 1/2 cups chocolate sprinkles or
	1 1/2 cups finely chopped walnuts

With a small metal spatula, spread a 1/2-inch layer of crème au beurre on the flat side of one meringue, then press the flat side of a second meringue into it to form a ball. Assemble rest of meringues the same way, place on baking sheet or tray, and refrigerate 30 minutes.

Place grated chocolate or walnuts in a shallow dish. With a pastry brush, cover each ball with a thin layer of crème au beurre. This procedure is messy and delicate, so be sure to wear an apron, and to handle the meringues gently, or they could crumble or break in your hands. Place in dish and coat with chocolate or walnuts by gently shaking the bowl from side to side. Place in fluted paper pastry cups and refrigerate until serving.

A la Noix de Coco (Coconut) (V-11a): Prepare as above, using 1 1/4 cups plain or vanilla flavored crème au beurre and 1 1/2 cups unsweetened flaked cocount.

Au Prâlin (Praline) (V-11b): Prepare as above, using 1 1/4 cups crème au beurre pralinée and 1 1/2 cups sliced toasted almonds. Place the almonds in a shallow dish and crush with hands, to facilitate coating.

Au Café (Coffee) (V-11c): Prepare as above, using 1 1/4 cups crème au beurre au café and 1 1/2 cups sliced toasted almonds.

Storage: Cover and refrigerate until serving. Serve within 48 hours.

V-12 SUCCÈS INDIVIDUEL

In France's southern region of Provence, many restaurants, auberges, and pastry shops are named in honor of "Good King René". This little known 15th century monarque was dethroned before he could influence the country's political history, but left the indelible mark of a fine gastronomist. Particularly concerned about quality, he never went anywhere without enormous supplies of wine and fresh butter.

These almond and chocolate buttercream cakes are worthy of even King René's table.

(V-12)
Succès Individuel
(Almond Cream Cakes)

Ingredients: (for 10 individual pastries)

20	2 1/2-inch round succès shells (I-4a)
1 2/3	cups prâlin crème au beurre (II-4c)
1	cup finely chopped toasted almonds or finely crushed, lightly toasted cookie crumbs
1/2	cup powdered sugar

In each of 10 round metal rings, 2 1/2 inches wide, and 1 inch high, place 1 succès shell. With a spoon, fill almost to the top with buttercream and top with another succès shell. Place on a tray or baking sheet and refrigerate 1 hour. Remove from refrigerator, dip sponge in hot water, and rub outside of rings to loosen. Remove rings. Place almonds or cookie crumbs in a shallow dish and roll each succès, wheel-fashion, to coat the sides. Refrigerate. Thirty minutes before serving, remove to allow buttercream to soften. Immediately before serving, dust tops generously with powdered sugar.

Individual Delicieux (V-12a): Replace plain succès shells with chocolate succès shells (I-4b). Dust tops with unsweetened cocoa instead of powdered sugar and substitute almonds or cookie crumbs with chocolate sprinkles. Prepare and serve as directed above.

Storage: Cover and refrigerate until serving. Serve within 24 hours.

V-13 CHOCOLATINES INDIVIDUELLES

"Happy chocolate! Who, after having gone around the world on women's smiles, passes away in their mouths, as a tender, flavorful 'kiss'..."—Brillat-Savarin

These individual chocolate cream cakes can be served with afternoon coffee, or as a dessert.

(V-13)
Chocolatines Individuelles
(Individual Chocolate Cream Cakes)

Ingredients: (for 10 chocolatines)

20	2 1/2 inch round succès shells (I-4a)
2	cups chilled chocolate mousse (IV-6)
1/4	cup powdered sugar
2	tablespoons unsweetened cocoa

In each 10 round metal rings, 2 1/2 inches wide and 1 inch high, place 1 succès shell. With a spoon, fill almost to the top with chocolate mousse, then top with another succès shell. Place on a baking sheet or tray and refrigerate at least 3 hours. Remove from refrigerator, dip sponge in hot water, and rub outside of rings to loosen. Remove rings. Return to refrigerator. In the small bowl, mix together powdered sugar and cocoa powder. Immediately before serving, remove from refrigerator and dust generously with the mixture.

Storage: Cover and refrigerate until ready to serve. Serve within 24 hours.

V-14   ST. HONORÉS INDIVIDUEL

After her divorce from Napoléon, Joséphine Bonaparte retired to her domain in Malmaison, and devoted her time to entertaining. Malmaison soon became famous for its fine cuisine, its pastries, and especially for the succulent tropical fruits shipped from Joséphine's native Martinique and raised in hothouses.

The elegant presentation of these individual cream-filled pastries makes them perfect for afternoon or evening entertaining.

(V-14)
St. Honorés Individuel
(Individual St. Honorés)

Use same ingredients as for large St. Honoré (VI-16), replacing 10-inch cutting guide with a round 4-inch cookie cutter.

On a lightly-floured surface, roll out pâte feuilletée or rognures to 1/8-inch thick. With a fork or rolling pastry piercer, prick well, then cut out ten 4-inch disks. Place on lightly-oiled baking sheets and refrigerate.

Preheat oven to 425-degrees. Prepare pâte à choux, spoon into pastry bag with a 5/8-inch nozzle, and pipe a band of dough around the rims of the disks, about 1/4-inch from the edge. On another lightly-oiled baking sheet, pipe thirty 3/4-inch choux. Brush the pâte à choux with beaten egg. Bake pastry base and pâte à choux at 425-degrees for 10 minutes, then lower heat to 400-degrees, prop oven door open with a spoon, and bake for another 10 to 15 minutes, until the pâte à choux is puffed up and golden brown. The small choux will bake more quickly, so you'll need to remove them sooner. Cool.

While the pastry is baking, prepare the crème chantilly (II-1) or crème chiboust (II-5). Refrigerate until use.

To garnish: Spoon a little filling into a pastry bag with a 1/8-inch star nozzle. Make a small hole in the bottom of the choux, and fill.

Prepare caramel. When it's reached a deep amber color, remove from heat and dip the tops of the choux and place them, caramel side up, on a wire rack to cool. If the caramel has thickened too much, return it to very low heat (so it won't burn), dip the bases of the cooled choux, and place 3 choux, regularly spaced, on each disk.

Spoon the rest of filling into pastry bag and fill the shells, piping decorative rosettes on the surface and between the choux. Decorate each St. Honoré with a candied violet or a candied cherry half.

Storage: Refrigerate until serving. Serve within 2 hours.

V-15   SAVARINS INDIVIDUEL

Gastronomical history has retained the famous last words of ninety-nine year old Aurore Brillat, murmured toward the end of a heavy meal: "I think I'm going to die...quick, serve the dessert!"

Later, Mme. Brillat's brother remarked with a smile, "She arrived in the hereafter just in time for coffee..."

How could her son Anthelme, known to us as "Brillat-Savarin", be anything but one of 19th century France's great gastronomists?

These attractive individual savarins can be decorated with crème chantilly, crème patissière, or fresh fruit.

(V-15)
Savarins Individuel
(Individual Savarins)

Ingredients: (for about 10 savarins)
    8   ounces baba dough (VI-18) (1/2 recipe)
       butter for molds

Syrup:
  2 1/2 cups water
    2 cups sugar
    3 tablespoons rum (or other alcohol) or 1 teaspoon vanilla
        extract

  1/2 cup abricotage (II-11a)

    1 cup crème chantilly (II-1)
  10 candied cherry halves (or 10 whole raspberries or
        whole small strawberries) or
      1 cup crème patissière à la vanille (II-2) or
      2 cups fresh fruit salad

Brush 10 individual ring-shaped baba molds with melted butter. Place 1 tablespoon dough in each mold and spread it evenly with a wet finger. (Don't use flour to avoid sticking). Place molds on a baking sheet and let rise 30 minutes at room temperature or until dough just reaches the edge of pan. (Don't allow to overrise, as the cakes would be too delicate).

Preheat oven to 375-degrees. Bake 15 minutes, or until golden brown. Cool, then turn out. It's best to leave babas in a dry place for 24 hours before soaking, but they can be soaked once they're completely cooled. Bring the sugar and water to a boil, remove from heat and add flavoring.

More→

(Savarins Individuel, Cont.)

Drop the cakes, one by one, into the warm syrup and hold them under with a skimmer for several seconds, until the bubbles stop rising to the surface. (this indicates that they're completely soaked). With the skimmer, lift out cakes and place on a wire rack to drain. In a small saucepan, heat abricotage and brush the cakes, then place them in 10 round plastic baba containers (this is optional but highly recommended, since some syrup would run out and quickly fill the bottom of a serving plate).

Decorate in one of the following ways:
Spoon the crème chantilly into pastry bag with a star-shaped nozzle and pipe a generous rosette in the centers. Top with a candied cherry half or a whole raspberry or strawberry.

In a mixing bowl, whisk together crème patissière and crème chantilly, then use the cream to fill and decorate as above.

Fill the centers with fruit salad and top with a candied cherry half. Brush lightly with more abricotage.

Storage: Refrigerate until serving. Serve preferably the same day, but in any case, within 24 hours. The baked, undecorated savarins can be frozen and stored in a plastic bag for 1 month. No need to thaw, soak and decorate as above.

V-16 INDIVIDUAL VAL D'ISÈRES

Beginning in ancient times, and up until the late 19th century, French peasants believed that it was unwise to fall asleep under any kind of tree. For some reason—and no one can say why, for sure—the shade of the walnut tree was considered to be particularly dangerous for unwary slumberers.

For an afternoon get-together, serve these chocolate-iced walnut tartlets with an assortment of individual pastries.

(V-16)
Individual Val d'Isères
(Walnut Tartlets with Chocolate Icing)

Same ingredients as for large Val d'Isère (VII-21), replacing the 10-inch pie plate with twelve 4-inch tartlet pans, and adding a 6-inch round pastry cutter, and 2 baking sheets.

On a lightly-floured surface, roll out pastry to 1/8-inch thick. With a fork or rolling pastry piercer, prick well, then cut out twelve 6-inch disks. Brush tartlet pans with melted butter and line with pastry. Place on baking sheet and refrigerate 1 hour.

Preheat oven to 350-degrees. Line the tartlets with foil and fill halfway with rice or dried peas. Remove the foil and peas after 8 to 10 minutes, then continue baking until pastry is golden brown. Cool completely, then tip shell gently into hand, to avoid breakage during unmolding.

Prepare filling and biscuits à la cuillère (ladyfingers) (I-5) dipped in syrup. With a teaspoon, spread a thin layer of filling in the bottom of each tartlet shell, then place on top a dipped biscuit à la cuillère. (The biscuits will probably be too long. Trim them with a paring knife, and use the trimmings for filling the last shells). Cover with the remaining filling, smoothed with a small metal spatula into a domed shape.

Place on a tray or baking sheet and refrigerate 15 minutes. While the tartlets are chilling, prepare the icing. Dip the tartlets into the warm icing, holding them up over the pan and smoothing off the excess icing with a spoon or metal spatula. Top each tartlet with 2 or 3 walnut halves. Return to the refrigerator until ready to serve.

Storage: Cover and refrigerate up to 48 hours.

V-17 AMANDINES

Ragueneau, a celebrated 17th century pastry chef, was, at heart, a frustrated poet whose dreams of literary glory—and mediocre poetry—brought on financial disaster. Edmond Rostand immortalizes him in "Cyrano de Bergerac", in which he gives his recipe for amandines. In verse, of course!

Although these rich almond tartlets were originally made presented with a sprinkle of sliced almonds, fruits can be added for variety.

(V-17)
Amandines
(Almond Cream Tartlets)

Ingredients: (for 8 amandines)
-   8   ounces pâte sablée (I-7) or pâte brisée (I-6)
        butter for pans

-   1   cup frangipane (almond pastrycream) (II-7)
-   1/2   cup blanched, sliced toasted almonds
-   1/3   cup abricotage (apricot glaze) (II-11a)

On a lightly-floured surface, roll out pastry to about 1/8-inch thick. With a fork or rolling pastry piercer, prick well, then cut out eight 6-inch disks. Brush eight 4-inch round tartlet pans with melted butter and line with pastry. Place on a baking sheet and refrigerate 1 hour.

Preheat oven to 350-degrees. With a fork or electric beater, beat frangipane until smooth, then spread a heaping tablespoon in each unbaked pastry shell. Sprinkle generously with sliced almonds and bake about 20 minutes, or until frangipane is puffed and golden brown. Cool 5 minutes, then turn out carefully onto wire rack and finish cooling, right side up.

In a small saucepan, gently heat abricotage, and brush over cooled pastries. Serve the same day.

Storage: Refrigerate until serving. Can be frozen, unglazed, for up to 2 months. To serve, thaw for several hours in the refrigerator, then heat for 5 minutes in a 300-degrees oven. Glaze as directed above.

Cherry Amandines (V-17a): Same ingredients as for plain amandines, adding:
-   48   fresh or canned cherries in unsweetened juice

Fresh cherries must be washed and pitted. No need to poach them, since they will be baked in the amandine. Canned cherries need only be drained.

More➤

Follow directions for basic recipe. On each filled, unbaked amandine, place 6 cherries. Bake and glaze as directed. All fruit amandines, including those made with red fruits, should be glazed with abricotage, since the frangipane predominates. (Leave off sliced almonds).

Blueberry Amandines (V-17b): Same ingredients as in basic recipe, adding:
    1/2   cup fresh or canned blueberries in unsweetened juice

Wash fresh blueberries, or drain canned. Follow directions for basic recipe. On filled, unbaked pastry shells, place about 1 teaspoon blueberries, spreading slightly. Bake and glaze as directed above. (Leave off sliced almonds).

Pineapple Amandines (V-17c): Same ingredients as for basic amandines, adding:
    4   slices pineapple in unsweetened juice

Drain pineapple, then with a sharp paring knife, cut each slice into 12 equal pieces. Follow directions for basic recipe, then place 6 pineapple chunks on frangipane-filled unbaked shells. Bake and glaze as directed above. (Leave off sliced almonds).

Raisin Amandines (V-17d): Same ingredients as for basic recipe, adding:
    1/2   cup raisins
    1/2   cup water
    1   teaspoon lemon juice

In a small saucepan, heat water and lemon juice to boiling, then add raisins, cover and simmer 10 minutes, until raisins are plump. Drain. Follow directions in basic recipe, then divide the raisins between the filled, unbaked shells. Leave off sliced almonds. Bake and glaze as directed above.

Raspberry Amandines/Blackberry Amandines (V-17e): Same ingredients as in basic recipe, adding:
    1/4   pound fresh raspberries or frozen raspberries or
            same amount of fresh or frozen blackberries

Wash fruit and divide between filled, unbaked pastry shells. Bake and glaze as directed above. (Leave off sliced almonds).

Apricot Amandines (V-17f): Same ingredients as for basic recipe, adding:
    8   canned apricot halves in light syrup

Drain and dice apricots. Follow directions in basic recipe, then divide diced apricots between filled, unbaked shells. Bake and glaze as directed above.

V-18   TARTELETTES AUX FRUITS

In the 17th and 18th centuries, when it became fashionable for noble ladies to prepare and serve pastries to guests, multicolored fruits were used to transform modest tarts and tartlets into family coats of arms.

Impress your guests with a colorful array of fruit tartlets! Pastry shells baked and frozen in advance make it possible to prepare them on short notice.

(V-18)
Tartelettes aux Fruits
(Fruit Tartlets)

Ingredients: (for 8 tartlets)
- 8   ounces pâte sablée (I-7) or pâte brisée (I-6)
       butter for pans

- 1/3   cup frangipane (II-7) (optional)
- 1 1/8   cups crème patissière (II-2)

- 1 1/2-2   cups fruit (fresh, canned, or frozen)
- 1/3   cup nappage (II-11) (apricot or raspberry/currant)

On a lightly-floured surface, roll out pastry to about 1/8-inch thick. With a fork or rolling pastry piercer, prick well, then cut out eight 6-inch disks. Brush eight 4-inch round tartlet pans with melted butter and line with pastry. Using a teaspoon, spread a very thin layer of frangipane over bottom of pastry. This step can be eliminated, if you wish, although the frangipane adds richness and flavor. Place lined pans on a baking sheet and refrigerate 1 hour, to reduce shrinkage during baking.

Preheat oven to 375-degrees. If you've left out the frangipane, you can line the pastry with foil and fill the molds halfway with rice or dried peas. Remove the foil and peas after 8 to 10 minutes, then return to the oven for another 5 minutes, or until pastry is golden brown. For frangipane-lined shells, bake 10 to 15 minutes. Cool thoroughly, then tip shell out into hand, to avoid breakage.

Beat crème patissière until smooth and spreadable, then fill each shell, smoothing with a spoon or metal spatula. Cover garnished shell with fruit. In a small saucepan, heat nappage, then brush over fruit.

Storage: Refrigerate until serving. Serve the same day. Pastry shells can be baked and frozen for up to 2 months. To use, heat unthawed shells in 300-degrees oven for 5 minutes. Cool, then garnish as directed above.

More➤

(Tartelettes aux Fruits, cont.)

Cherry Tartlets (V-18a):

1/3	pound fresh cherries
1/2	cup water
1	tablespoon sugar
1	teaspoon lemon juice or
1/3	pound canned cherries in unsweetened juice
	(not prepared cherry pie filling)

1/3	cup raspberry/currant nappage (II-11b)

Follow directions in basic recipe. If you're using fresh cherries, wash and pit them, then place them in a medium saucepan with water, sugar and lemon juice. Cover and poach 10 minutes. Drain. Canned cherries need simply be drained. Garnish cream-filled shells with cherries, and brush with warm nappage.

Raspberry Tartlets (V-18b):

1/2	pound fresh or frozen, whole unsweetened raspberries
1/3	cup raspberry/currant nappage (II-11b)

Follow directions in basic recipe. Don't wash fresh fruit. Arrange whole, **unthawed** raspberries on cream-filled shells. Brush with warm nappage.

Strawberry Tartlets (V-18c):

1/2	**pound fresh strawberries (not canned or frozen) small to medium**
1/3	cup raspberry/currant nappage (II-11b)

Follow directions in basic recipe. Don't wash fruit. If it's dusty, clean it off with a soft pastry brush. To garnish, place one small strawberry in center of cream-filled shell, then arrange strawberry halves around the central one, leaning them up against it as for the large strawberry pie (VII-2). Brush with warm nappage.

Apricot Tartlets (V-18d):

12	fresh apricots
1/2	cup water
1	tablespoon sugar
1	teaspoon lemon juice
	or
24	canned apricot halves in light syrup

1/3	cup abricotage (II-11a)
8	candied cherry halves

More➤

(Tartelettes aux Fruits, cont.)

Follow directions in basic recipe. If you're using fresh apricots, wash them, cut in half, and place in a medium saucepan with water, sugar and lemon juice. Cover and poach 10 minutes. Drain. Canned fruit need only be drained. Place 3 apricot halves on each cream-filled shell, overlapping fruit for good coverage. Brush with warm abricotage. For a nice finishing touch, place a candied cherry half in the center of each tartlet.

Blueberry Tartlets (V-18e):
    12   ounces canned blueberries in light syrup or
             12-ounces stewed, drained blueberries
    1/3   cup abricotage (apricot glaze) (II-11a)

Follow directions in basic recipe. Drain canned or stewed fruit and cover cream-filled shells. Brush with warm glaze.

Pineapple Tartlets (V-18f):
    8   slices canned pineapple in unsweetened juice
    1/3 cup abricotage (II-11a)
    8   candied cherry halves

Follow directions in basic recipe. Drain pineapple, and, with a sharp paring knife, cut each slice in half. Cut each half into 6 equal fan-shaped pieces. On each cream-filled shell, arrange 5 pieces of fruit along the rim, in a fan-like pattern. Place 4 more pieces in the same way, just underneath, overlapping the first row. End with the last 3 pieces. Brush with warm abricotage and place a candied cherry half at the base of the pineapple fan.

V-19 MIRLITONS

In 1885, Aristide Bruant opened a café in Montmartre called "Le Mirliton". The specialty of the house was "l'engueulade", which consisted of being singled out of the audience and insulted by the famous singer. People came from miles around to enjoy this dubious privilege.

Originally used to designate a soldier's cap, the word "mirliton" was later given to a kind of musical instrument. Were the first mirlitons shaped like a hat or a flute, or were they simply served for the first time in Aristide Bruant's café, between "engueulades"…?

(V-19)
Mirlitons
(Almond Tartlets)

Ingredients: (for 8 mirlitons)

    8   ounces pâte brisée (I-6) or
            pâte feuilletée rognures (I-8a))
         butter for pans

    1/3 cup ground almonds
    3   tablespoons sugar
    1/4 cup heavy cream
    1   egg
         pinch salt
    1/2 teaspoon coffee extract

         powdered sugar

On a lightly-floured surface, roll out pastry to about 1/8-inch thick. With a fork or rolling pastry piercer, prick dough, then cut out eight 6-inch disks. Brush eight 4-inch round tartlet pans lightly with melted butter and line with pastry. Place on a baking sheet and refrigerate 1 hour.

Preheat oven to 350-degrees. In a mixing bowl, whisk together filling ingredients. Spoon the filling into the prepared pans, dust generously with powdered sugar, and bake 25 to 30 minutes, or until pastry is golden brown and filling is set. Remove from oven, cool a few minutes, then tip tartlets out of pans.

Storage: Can be stored, tightly covered, in a cool, dry place for 2 to 3 days. Can be placed in a plastic bag and frozen for 1 month. Thaw in the refrigerator for 1 hour, then heat 10 minutes in a 275-degrees oven.

V-20 BARQUETTES AUX MARRONS

Although these chestnut tartlets iced with two-toned fondant are usually given the shape of a small boat, or "barquette", they can also be prepared round, iced with a chocolate glaze, and topped with a candied chestnut.

(V-20)
Barquettes aux Marrons
(Chestnut "Barquettes")

Ingredients: (for 8 to 10 barquettes)

8	ounces pâte sablée (I-7) or pâte brisée (I-6)
	melted butter for pans
15	candied chestnuts, finely chopped
1 1/4	cups crème au beurre à la vanille (II-4)
1	cup fondant au café (II-10b)
1	cup fondant au chocolat (II-10a)
1/2	cup crème au beurre à la vanille (II-4f)

Brush ten 4-inch long barquette pans (or eight 4-inch round tartlet pans) with melted butter and place, closely grouped but not touching, on counter top. On a lightly-floured surface, roll out pastry to about 1/8-inch thick. With a fork or rolling pastry piercer, prick well, then lift up the whole sheet of dough and place on top of pans. Gently press the dough into the pans, then roll a rolling pin across the dough, to cut it.

(This is the quickest way to line the oblong barquette pans, but may take a little practice. If you have trouble handling large pieces of dough, you can use smaller pieces and a few pans at a time, or simply cut out oblongs slightly larger than the pans, and line them one at a time). Place on a baking sheet and refrigerate 1 hour.

Preheat oven to 350-degrees. Line pans with foil and place a spoonful of rice or dried beans in each pan and bake about 10 minutes, then remove the foil and beans and bake until shells are golden brown. Cool 5 minutes, then carefully tip out of pans and finish cooling.

In a medium mixing bowl, beat or whisk crème au beurre until light, then stir in chopped chestnuts. With a small metal spatula, fill the pastry shells, building up and shaping the filling to create a high ridge in the center, which slopes steeply to the sides. (A cross-section of the pastry would be triangular). Place on a baking sheet or tray and freeze 1 hour.

More➔

(Barquettes aux Marrons, cont.)

In 2 medium saucepans, heat the two fondants very gently. (Take care not to overheat it. Aside from losing its shine, the too-hot fondant would melt the crème au beurre and slide right off).

Remove from heat and ice the barquettes in the following way: Dip one side onto the coffee fondant, hold up over the saucepan, and with a spatula, remove excess fondant. Dip the other side into the chocolate fondant and remove excess. When all the barquettes are iced, spoon the remaining crème au beurre (beaten until creamy, if necessary) into the pastry bag and pipe a "chain" of "shells" along the central ridge, from end to end.

Variation: If you don't have barquette pans, or if you just prefer a round shape, prepare eight to ten 4-inch round tartlet shells (as directed above), and fill them, giving them a domed shape. Ice with chocolate glaze (II-16) and top each tartlet with a candied chestnut.

Storage: Refrigerate until serving. Serve same day as prepared.

V-21 NONNETTES DE REIMS

"Sunshine in a jar" was the pretty name given to orange marmalade by Mary Stuart, Queen of Scots. It and honey give these oblong tea cakes their sunny taste.

A religious order's white robes are imitated by the white icing on these "little nuns", a specialty from Reims dating back to the Middle Ages.

(V-21)
Nonnettes de Reims
(Iced Honey Cakes)

Ingredients: (for about 36 nonnettes)

1 1/2	cups flour
1/4	teaspoon salt
1	teaspoon baking powder
1/4	teaspoon cinnamon
	pinch nutmeg
1/3	cup honey
1/3	cup sugar
1/4	cup water
3/4	cup orange marmalade
1	egg
1/2	cup oil
	butter and flour for pan
1	egg white
1 1/3	cups powdered sugar

Preheat oven to 325-degrees. In a small mixing bowl, stir together dry ingredients. In a large saucepan, heat honey, sugar, and water very gently, stirring occasionally, until sugar is dissolved. Remove from heat and whisk in marmalade, egg, oil, then beat in the dry ingredients. Stop beating as soon as batter is completely mixed.

Pour into buttered and floured 9 x 12-inch cake pan and bake for 30 to 40 minutes, or until a cake tester inserted in the middle comes out clean. Cool 5 minutes, then turn out onto a cooling rack or directly onto a cutting board.

In a small mixing bowl, beat egg white and powdered sugar with a fork until the mixture is thick and smooth. Pour into middle of completely cooled cake and spread evenly with a metal spatula. Allow to set for 10 minutes. With a chef's knife, cut into thirty-six 1 1/2 x 2-inch pieces.

Storage: Can be kept 2 to 3 days, if tightly covered. Can also be frozen, uniced, for one month. Ice before serving.

Note: The egg white in the icing can be replaced by butter. The icing won't be quite as white, but will be more moist.

V-22   BAGUETTES AU CITRON

In Ancient Greece, two criminals condemned to be thrown in the snake pit had waited all day for their sentence to be carried out. Shortly before sundown, one of them drew a small yellow object from his tunic and began to eat it. His cell mate, an incredibly fat, greasy little man, sidled up to him.

"Dimitri Stefanos", he introduced himself with a toothless grimace meant to be a smile.

The other man paused and glared at him. "Petros Davidos", he finally offered, his eyes narrowing with suspicion. He swallowed with difficulty and took another bite.

Dimitri nodded at the yellow object. "Mind if I have some?"

Petros just looked straight ahead and continued chewing. He obviously didn't think the question deserved an answer.

"I'll give you a hundred pieces of silver for half your lemon," Dimitri said.

Petros grunted. "What do you think this is? The town marketplace?"

"Two hundred."

"No."

"Five hundred," he insisted.

"Sorry."

"A thousand!" Dimitri made a grab for the lemon.

Petros jerked his hand away. "Not for a thousand. Not for a million." He put his face close to Dimitri's. "I wouldn't trade half this lemon for the Golden Fleece!"

Dimitri had begun to sweat. "Ah, come on..."

"I told you, it's not for sale. Besides, any idiot knows that a half a lemon won't work against snake bite. You have to eat a whole one."

"Have a heart! Without any antidote, I don't stand a chance!"

A mean smile stole across Petros' scarred face. "Well, now, isn't that a crying shame!"

Dimitri ignored the sarcasm. "Listen, tell me where you got it, at least." His eyes darted around the ill-lit cell, as though he expected to discover a fruit vendor comfortably installed in one corner.

More→

(Baguettes au Citron, cont.)

"Where I got it? What's it to you?" Petros stuffed the rest of the lemon into his mouth and shrugged. "Lady friend who came to see me yesterday," he said, his voice muffled by the chunk of lemon. "Tavern keeper's wife. Sometimes pays to be nice to the ladies, eh?" he added with a leer as he licked the lemon juice off his fingers.

The fat man stiffened. "A tavern keeper's wife?"

"Hummm." Petros belched and rubbed his stomach. The lemon, rind and all, had given him a terrible case of heartburn, but knowing that he was now protected from the serpents' venom, he felt ready for anything.

"Buxom? Blond? Name of Cornucopia?" Dimitri persisted hoarsely. He'd forgotten completely about the lemon and even the snake pit.

Petros shot him a surprised glance. "Yeah. And real accommodating, if you know what I mean!"

Dimitri had become pale as a mushroom. "My wife! My Cornucopia!"

"Hey!" Petros laughed, "Small world."
"...with a pig like you!"

"Now wait a minute, Dimi. No need to get personal. You aren't exactly Heracles yourself."

"Don't you call me Dimi, you swine!" Dimitri's face had gone from white to an angry purple. It was barely visible in the darkening cell.

"Settle down, will you?" Petros said, feeling mildly irritated. He'd never seen a husband put up such a fuss. "Coco gave me something for you, just in case I saw you..."

Dimitri wasn't listening anymore. "Coco? You dirty, rotten——"

With the grace of a toreador, Petros sidestepped the tavern keeper's sudden lunge. The captain of the guards who had just entered the cell wasn't as fast.

"In a fiesty mood, eh?" He snarled, picking himself up. "The snakes love that. Especially the cobras. Take him away!" The guards dragged Dimitri out.

Petros watched the iron clad door grate shut, then sat down in the straw and pulled another lemon from his tunic. "Well, Dimi old boy," he said with a little smile as he tossed it in the air and caught it, "What do they always say? Win a few, lose a few!"

More→

(Baguettes au Citron, Cont.)

This updated version of a story told by Atheneus, a Greek grammarian, in his "Banquet of the Sophists", illustrates the Ancients' belief that lemons could effectively counteract poison. This iced lemon cake may not have the virtues attributed by Atheneus. It is, however, very good with tea or coffee.

(V-22)
Baguettes au Citron
(Lemon Bars with Lemon Icing)

Ingredients: (for one 9 x 12-inch cake)
Cake:
2/3	cup flour
1	cup finely ground blanched almonds
1/3	cup butter, softened
3/4	cup sugar
4	egg yolks
	juice and finely-grated rind of 2 lemons (about 1/2 cup juice)
3	egg whites
1/8	teaspoon salt
3	tablespoons sugar

Lemon Icing:
1	cup powdered sugar
1/4	cup butter, softened
2	tablespoons lemon juice
1	lemon, thinly sliced for decoration

Preheat oven to 350-degrees. In a small mixing bowl, stir together flour and ground almonds. In a large mixing bowl, beat butter and sugar until light and creamy, then beat in egg yolks, followed by lemon juice and rind. Beat in dry ingredients. Stop beating as soon as batter is well blended.

In a deep mixing bowl, beat egg whites and salt at high speed until soft peaks form. Add sugar and continue beating until stiff but not dry. Beat 1/3 of whites into batter to soften it. With a rubber spatula, carefully fold in rest of whites.

Spread batter in buttered and floured 9 x 12-inch pan, and bake about 20 minutes, or until golden brown. Cool 5 minutes, then turn out onto wire rack. Cool thoroughly.

In a medium mixing bowl, beat together icing ingredients until smooth and creamy. With a metal spatula, spread over top of cake. Let set 15 minutes. With a serrated knife, trim edges and cut cake into twelve 4 1/2 x 2-inch pieces. Decorate each piece with a half lemon slice and serve on an oblong plate.

Storage: Iced cake can be tightly covered and kept, unrefrigerated, for 48 hours. Uniced cake can be wrapped in plastic or aluminum foil and frozen for 2 months. Thaw several hours in the refrigerator, then ice and decorate as directed above.

V-23 NIDS DE PÂQUES

Beginning with the Middle Ages and continuing up until the 19th century, it was customary, especially among aristocrats, to exchange painted eggs at Easter time. Invariably the traditional red, they were often decorated with pictures which symbolized the wishes conveyed by the giver. For example, a sun stood for wealth, a stag was the symbol for good health, a hen or rooster meant happiness in general, and flowers of all kinds symbolized love. These tiny nests filled with candy eggs and topped by a fluffy yellow chick will delight guests at a children's Easter egg hunt, or coffee guests during the Easter season.

(V-23)
Nids de Pâques
(Easter Nests)

Ingredients: (for 12 individual nests)

1	recipe for 1 génoise (I-1)
	butter and flour for muffin tin
2 1/2	cups crème au beurre (your choice of flavors) (II-4)
1	cup sirop à entremets (II-12)
	(flavor to go with crème au beurre)
1	cup finely chopped toasted almonds or
	prâlin (II-9) or chocolate sprinkles
	small candy eggs (number depending on size)
12	tiny chicks

The cake can be prepared a day ahead or the same day as served. Preheat oven to 325-degrees. Butter and flour 12 muffin tins. Prepare génoise batter and spoon into tins. Place on a baking sheet and bake about 15 minutes, then remove from tin and cool, right side up, on a wire rack.

During baking, the batter will rise up and stick to the rims of the tin, then fall a little to form a slight dip in the center of the cakes. This is just what we want, since it creates a "nest" effect.

While the cakes are baking, prepare crème au beurre and sirop à entremets, or make them ahead and freeze or refrigerate. To use cold crème au beurre, heat gently.

To garnish: Reserve 1 cup crème au beurre for decoration. With a serrated knife, split the cakes in half. Brush bottoms with sirop, turn over and brush again, then spread with crème au beurre. Place tops, brush with sirop, and with a small metal spatula, cover sides and tops with crème au beurre. Place chopped almonds, prâlin, or chocolate sprinkles in a shallow dish and roll cakes, wheel fashion, to cover sides completely. Beat a little more flavoring or coloring into the reserved crème au beurre so that the decoration will stand out more, then spoon it into the pastry bag. Holding the bag over the cake, pipe a squiggly "string" of crème au beurre around the edge, going around several times and building up to form the sides of a nest. Fill with candy eggs and top with chicks.

Storage: Cover and refrigerate for up to 48 hours. Remove from refrigerator 30 minutes before serving to allow crème au beurre to soften.

Note: A decorating tip with a flat, many-holed end would achieve the same "nest" effect, and would be easier to use.

V-24 JÉSUITES

These triangular cream-filled pastries were named, long ago, for the three-cornered hat which was once a rigorous part of the Jesuit priest's official dress.

(V-24)
Jésuites
(Cream Filled Puff Pastry Triangles)

Ingredients: (for 6 Jésuites)

11   ounces pâte feuilletée classique (I-8) or
   pâte demi-feuilletée (I-9) or rognures (I-8a)

1 1/8   cups crème patissière (II-2) or
   1 cup frangipane (II-7) or
   1 cup frangipane and crème patissière, mixed

1   whole egg, beaten with pinch salt (egg wash)
1/3   cup untoasted, sliced almonds

   powdered sugar (optional)

On a lightly-floured surface, roll out pastry to 1/8-inch thick. Prick with a fork or rolling pastry piercer. Using a ruler and chef's knife, cut a 12 x 12-inch square.

Beat cold crème patissière or frangipane until creamy, and with a metal spatula, spread it evenly over half the pastry in a 6 x 12-inch band. Fold the ungarnished pastry over the garnished half, to form a 6 x 12-inch rectangle. Place on an ungreased baking sheet and refrigerate 1 hour.

Preheat oven to 375-degrees. Transfer pastry to a work surface. Brush with egg wash and sprinkle on almonds. With a chef's knife, cut into 6 triangles, 4 inches wide at the base. Place on ungreased baking sheet and bake 30 to 40 minutes, until golden brown. Serve warm or cold, dusted, if you like, with powdered sugar.

Storage: Can be frozen, unbaked, for up to 1 month. Prepare and cut into triangles as above, but leave off egg wash and almonds. Freeze on a baking sheet or tray, then store in plastic bag. Bake, unthawed, as directed above (after having brushed with egg wash and sprinkled on almonds) about 10 minutes longer.

V-25   PETITS FOURS "FRAIS"

"Petit four", roughly translated as "small oven" was probably applied, as early as the Middle Ages, to small, bite-sized pastries because bakers made them at the end of the baking day, when their ovens had begun to cool off. These tiny éclairs, religieuses, caramel puffs, and salambos are particularly elegant when served on a silver tea tray.

(V-25)

Petits Fours "Frais"
(Cream Puff Pastry Petit Fours)

Ingredients: (for about 60 to 70 pastries)
   1 1/4   cups pâte à choux (I-11)
   1   whole egg, beaten with a pinch of salt (egg wash)

(fillings and toppings depending upon kind of pastry)

Preheat oven to 425-degrees. Prepare pâte à choux, spoon into pastry bag with 1/2-inch fluted nozzle, and on lightly-greased baking sheets, pipe out your choice of shapes:

Carolines (Miniature `Eclairs): 1 1/2-inch long "sticks"
Cream Puffs and Caramel Almond Puffs: 1 inch "balls" of dough
Salambos: 1 1/4-inch long ovals
Religieuses: Same number of 1/2-inch and 1 inch "balls"

Brush dough with egg wash and bake 10 minutes at 425-degrees. Reduce heat to 400-degrees, prop open oven door with a spoon, and bake another 10 minutes, until golden brown. Cool.

Icing and Filling:
Carolines (V-25a):   (for about 15 pastries)
   2/3   cup coffee or chocolate pastrycream (II-2a)
   1   tablespoon butter, softened
   1/2   cup coffee or chocolate flavored fondant (II-10a)

In a small mixing bowl, whisk together pastrycream and butter until smooth and creamy. Spoon into a pastry bag with a small star shaped nozzle. With the nozzle (or the tip of a small sharp knife) make a small hole in the bottom of each éclair and fill.

In a small saucepan, heat fondant very gently. Remove from heat and dip éclair tops. Lift up over saucepan. With a finger, remove excess fondant and smooth. Place, fondant side up, on a wire rack to set. Refrigerate until serving.

Cream Puffs with Grand Marnier (V-25b):
   2/3   cup vanilla pastrycream (II-2)
   1   tablespoon Grand Marnier
   1/2   cup plain fondant (II-10)
   1   drop red food coloring
      cinnamon candies (optional)

More→

(Petits Fours "Frais", Cont.)

In a small mixing bowl, whisk together pastrycream and Grand Marnier until smooth and creamy. Fill pastries same way as carolines. In small saucepan, heat fondant very gently, then remove from heat and beat in food coloring. Ice same way as carolines. Top each pastry, if you wish, with a cinnamon candy.

Cream Puffs with Kirsch (V-25c): (for about 15 pastries)
2/3 cup vanilla pastrycream (II-2)
1 tablespoon kirsch
1/2 cup plain fondant (II-10)
1 drop green food coloring
mimosa balls (optional)

Fill and ice as cream puffs with Grand Marnier. Top each pastry, optionally, with a mimosa ball.

Salambos (V-25d): (for about 15 pastries)
2/3 cup vanilla pastrycream (II-2)
1 tablespoon rum
1/2 cup plain fondant (II-10)
1/4 cup chocolate sprinkles

Fill and ice as cream puffs. Place the chocolate sprinkles in a shallow dish, and dip one end of iced tops.

Caramel Almond Puffs (V-25e): (for about 15 pastries)
1 1/2 tablespoons finely chopped almonds

1/2 cup vanilla pastrycream (II-2)
1/4 cup prâlin (ground caramelized almonds) (II-9)
1 tablespoon butter

powdered sugar

After brushing unbaked dough with egg wash, sprinkle with chopped almonds, then bake as directed. Prepare vanilla pastrycream, then whisk in caramelized almonds. Cover and allow to cool to room temperature, then whisk in softened butter until mixture is smooth and creamy. Chill. Fill puffs as above. Refrigerate until serving. Immediately before serving, dust with powdered sugar.

Religieuses: (V-25f): (for about 15 pastries)
3/4 cup coffee or chocolate pastrycream (II-2a or 2b)
1 1/2 tablespoons butter, softened
2/3 cup coffee or chocolate flavored fondant (II-9)
1/3 cup vanilla buttercream (II-4)

Fill and ice as above. Atop each large chou, set a small chou. Spoon buttercream into pastry bag with small star shaped nozzle, and pipe a tiny rosette on each top, and several buttercream "candles" around the base of each "head".

V-26   MINI-TARTELETTES AUX FRUITS

At King Stanislas' court, nobles and servants shook their heads and, for once, agreed with each other. Even the king had to admit it: Bébé the midget might have been great entertainment, but he had every imaginable vice. To name a few: Laziness—the most patient tutors threw up their hands in disgust and declared him uneducable; Lechery— ladies either doubled over with laughter or fled, screaming, when they found him hiding in their skirts; Jealousy—an unsuspecting rival narrowly escaped being roasted alive when, in a sudden rage, Bébé pushed him into a blazing fireplace. Incorrigible Bébé! The career of this famous midget, one of 18th century France's greatest "stars", was destined to be short-lived. Bébé died of old age...just a few months short of his 22nd birthday.

The French have always delighted in miniatures, be they portraits of a loved one, court midgets...or these bite-sized fruit tartlets.

(V-26)
Mini-Tartelettes aux Fruits
(Miniature Fruit Tartlets)

Ingredients: (for 20 miniature tartlets)
- 8   ounces pâte sablée (I-7) or pâte brisée (I-6)
- 1   cup frangipane (II-7)

Fruit: (your choice of the following):
- 10   apricots (fresh: washed and cut in twenty 1-inch wedges; canned: drained and cut)
- 4   peach or pear halves (fresh: peeled, cored, and cut in 1-inch wedges; canned: drained and cut)
- 3   pineapple slices (fresh or canned: drained and cut in twenty 1-inch wedges)
- 40   raspberries (fresh or frozen)
- 40   blackberries (fresh or frozen)
- 40   cherries (fresh: washed and pitted; canned: drained)
-     abricotage (II-11a)

Preheat oven at 375-degrees. On a lightly-floured surface, roll out pastry to about 1/8-inch thick. With a fork or rolling pastry piercer, prick well. Cut out circles of pastry and line pans. Spoon frangipane into pastry bag and fill lined pans halfway. Place fruit—apricots, peaches, pears, or pineapples—1 wedge per pan. Raspberries, blackberries, or cherries can go 2 per pan. Place on a baking sheet and bake 8 to 10 minutes, or until golden brown. Remove from oven and allow to cool a few minutes, then tip out of pans. In a small saucepan, heat abricotage, then brush over tartlets. Refrigerate until serving. Serve within 2 hours.

Chapter VI

Large Pastries
(Gros Gâteaux)

VI-1   LE MAINTENON

Françoise d'Aubigné often remarked with a smile, "My life has been a veritable miracle!" And she was right. Born to parents with aristocratic origins but no fortune to show for it, she was forced to beg in the streets as a child. How she was named Marquise de Maintenon, secretly married to King Louis XIV, and became "almost queen" of France has filled countless volumes.

This copious layer cake filled with frangipane under a covering of crisp meringue was named in honor of the amazing marquise.

(VI-1)
Le Maintenon
(Layered Cake with Meringue & Frangipane)

Ingredients: (for one 10-inch gâteau)
- 1   8-inch génoise (I-1)
- 1   cup frangipane (II-7)
- 1   cup sirop à entremets au rhum (II-12a)
- 1   recipe (about 3 cups) meringue française (I-12)
- 1   cup blanched, chopped almonds for decoration

Prepare génoise, frangipane, and sirop à entremets a day ahead.

To garnish: Preheat oven to lowest setting. With a serrated knife, cut génoise into 3 layers. Turn over bottom layer, brush copiously with sirop à entremets, then turn back over and place on a 10-inch cake board. Brush with more sirop, then, with a metal spatula, spread on half the frangipane. Place second layer on top, brush with sirop, and spread with rest of frangipane. Place last layer on top and brush with sirop.

Prepare the meringue française and with a metal spatula, spread top and sides of cake with meringue. Save about 1 cup for the decoration. Place almonds in a shallow dish. Slide a metal spatula under the cake board, lift it up off work surface, and place in the palm of one hand. With the other, scoop up a handful of almonds and press into the sides of cake, turning it little by little and repeating process until sides are completely covered. Spoon rest of meringue into pastry bag with 1/8-inch star nozzle and cover the top of gâteau with little peaks of meringue. Sprinkle on leftover almonds.

Place in oven, prop door open with a wooden spoon, and bake 1 to 1 1/2 hours, or until meringue is dry and very lightly browned. If it colors too rapidly, turn off oven.

Storage: Refrigerate until serving. Serve within 24 hours.

VI-2   LA FORÊT NOIRE

The Germans call it "Schwartzwald", the French "la Forêt Noire", and the Americans, the "Black Forest". This hauntingly beautiful region of Germany, directly across the border from the French province of Alsace, is famous among world travelers for its extensive forests of evergreens, and for the cake which bears its name.

This cake, a delicious combination of Germany's and Alsace's regional products—cherries, chocolate, and cream—was enthusiastically adopted long ago by France.

(VI-2)

La Forêt Noire
(Black Forest Cake)

Ingredients: (for one 8-inch gâteau)

1	8-inch génoise au chocolat (I-1a)

1/2	cup water
1/4	cup sugar
1	pound sour cherries

3	cups crème chantilly (whipped cream) (II-1)
1/3	cup ganâche aux kirsch (II-17b)
1/2	cup sirop à entremets au kirsch (dessert syrup) (II-12a)

1	cup chocolate sprinkles
	chocolate shavings (optional)

Prepare the génoise au chocolat a day ahead, so it will be easier to handle. Prepare sirop (II-12a) ahead.

Reserve 8 to 10 fresh cherries for the decoration, then wash and pit the rest. Place in a medium saucepan with sugar and water, cover and poach about 10 minutes, until tender. To drain, turn into a collander or strainer over a large bowl. Reserve this syrup for another use, or discard. Cool.

Prepare chantilly, reserving 2/3 to 1 cup for the decoration. Refrigerate until use.

To garnish: With a serrated knife, cut cake horizontally into 3 layers. Place the bottom layer on an 8-inch cake board, brush with sirop, and, with a small metal spatula, spread on all of ganâche. Place second layer on top, brush with sirop, and spread on about 1/2 cup chantilly. On top of chantilly, arrange the cherries in an even layer.

More➤

(La Forêt Noire, cont.)

Spread 1/2 cup chantilly on top of cherries. Place last layer on top and press lightly. Brush with sirop, and with a metal spatula fill in space left on the sides with more chantilly. Spread the top and sides evenly with the rest of chantilly, smoothing top well.

Place chocolate sprinkles in a shallow dish. Slide a metal spatula under the cake board, lift it up off work surface, and place in the palm of one hand. With the other hand, scoop up a handful of sprinkles and press gently into the sides, working around little by little and repeating until sides are completely covered. Spoon reserved chantilly into pastry bag and pipe out a pattern of swirls and rosettes on top. Decorate with reserved cherries, and, if you wish, with chocolate shavings.

Storage: Cover and refrigerate until serving. Serve within 24 hours.

VI-3   LE RÉGENT
In its entire history, France has had only three regents: Philippe d'Orleans, who ruled from 1715 to 1723, when Louis XV came of age; the "Régent", a 132-carat diamond bought by Phillipe d'Orleans for the French crown;…and this exquisite chocolate layer cake, probably created in Paris during the Belle Epoque, the late 19th century. This cake is a chocolate-lover's special: chocolate cake, chocolate whipped cream, chocolate icing garnished with chocolate sprinkles.

(VI-3)
Le Régent
(Chocolate Cake with Chocolate Icing and Cream)

Ingredients: (for one 8-inch gâteau)
- 1 8-inch génoise au chocolat (I-1a)
- 1 cup sirop à entremets à la vanille (II-12b)
- 2 cups crème chantilly au chocolat (II-1a)
- 1 1/2 cups crème au beurre au chocolat (II-4a)
- 1 cup chocolate sprinkles

Prepare génoise, crème au beurre, and sirop à entremets a day ahead.

Prepare crème chantilly. To garnish: With a serrated knife, cut génoise into 3 layers. Turn over bottom layer, brush with sirop, then turn back over and place on an 8-inch cake board. Brush with more sirop, then, using a metal spatula, spread on half of chantilly. Place second layer on top, brush with sirop and spread on rest of chantilly. Place last layer on top and brush with sirop.

More➤

(Le Régent, cont.)

Reserve 1/2 cup crème au beurre for decoration. With a metal spatula, spread rest of crème au beurre on sides and top of cake. Smooth top well. Place chocolate sprinkles in a shallow dish. Slide a metal spatula under the cake, lift it up off work surface, and place in the palm of one hand. With the other, scoop up a handful of sprinkles and press into the side to form a half moon. Turn little by little, repeating until a pattern of arcs is formed around the bottom. Spoon reserved crème au beurre into a pastry bag with a 1/8-inch star nozzle and pipe out a pattern of swirls and rosettes on top.

Storage: Refrigerate until serving. Serve within 24 hours.

VI-4 FRAISIER

Dijon may be famed for its mustard, Toulouse for its sausage, and Reims for its champagne, but Plougastel is just as renowned for its strawberries. Every year on the third Sunday in June, thousands of visitors gather in this small town in Brittany for the traditional Strawberry Festival. This refreshing and attractive strawberry cream cake is just as delicious when made with fresh raspberries, in which case, it's called a "framboisier".

(VI-4)

Fraisier

(Strawberry Cream Cake)

Ingredients: (for one 8-inch gâteau)

1 8-inch génoise (I-1)
1 cup sirop à entremets au kirsch (II-12a)
1 pound fresh strawberries
1 1/8 cups crème patissière (II-2)
3 cups crème chantilly (II-1)

Prepare génoise and sirop à entremets a day ahead.

Remove strawberry stems and dust fruit with a soft brush, or clean with a wet cloth. Set aside 8 to 10 for the decoration.

Prepare crème patissière, cool to room temperature, then chill until use.

Prepare crème chantilly, reserving about 2/3 cup for decoration. Beat 1/2 cup of remaining chantilly into chilled crème patissière until smooth, then fold in another 1/2 cup chantilly.

More→

(Fraisier, cont.)

To garnish: With a serrated knife, cut the génoise into 3 layers. Turn over the bottom layer, brush with sirop, then turn back over and place on an 8-inch cake board. Brush again with sirop, and with a large metal spatula spread on half of cream filling. With a paring knife, cut half the strawberries into 1/4-inch slices, and arrange on the bed of cream, overlapping them slightly for good coverage.

Repeat with the second layer, then place the last layer on top and brush with sirop. With a metal spatula, spread remaining chantilly over top and sides of cake, smoothing well. Leave the sides plain, or drag a small metal spatula blade through the chantilly in a repeated vertical or diagonal motion to form a rippled pattern. Spoon reserved chantilly into pastry bag and, if you like, pipe a pattern of rosettes on top, then decorate with strawberries.

"Framboisier" (Raspberry Cream Cake) (VI-4a): Prepare as fraisier, replacing strawberries with 1 pound fresh raspberries. Don't wash raspberries. Reserve several for the decoration, then cut the rest in half, and place them as you would the strawberries. Finish the cake as above, decorating with rosettes of crème chantilly and raspberries.

aux Ananas (Pineapple Cream Cake) (VI-4b): Prepare as above, replacing the strawberries with about 2 cups fresh, diced pineapple. (The sirop à entremets can be flavored with kirsch, as for the fraisier and the framboisier, or, if you prefer, the kirsch can be replaced with rum). Save a dozen or so wedges of pineapple for the decoration, then use the rest as above.

Storage: Cover and refrigerate until serving. Serve within 2 hours.

VI-5   MOKA AU CAFÉ

Over a thousand years ago, a Yemenite goat herder noticed that an unusual animation reigned among his goats. Intrigued, he chewed a few of the berries the animals had been eating, and felt an immediate surge of energy. Coffee had just been discovered! For centuries, Middle Eastern connoisseurs considered moka to be the most superior variety of coffee, so much so that the hot beverage prepared with the roasted and ground moka beans was strictly reserved for the sultan and his harem.

The moka was originally a coffee flavored layer cake, but the name gradually came to designate layer cakes of any flavor. In this recipe, therefore, the coffee buttercream and filling can be replaced by the flavors of your choice.

(VI-5)
Moka au Café
(Coffee Flavored Layer Cake)

Ingredients: (for one 8-inch moka)

1	8-inch génoise (I-1)
1 1/4	cups crème patissière au café (II-2b)
1/2	cup crème au beurre au café (II-4b)
1	cup sirop à entremets au café (II-12c)
1 1/2	cups crème au beurre au café (II-4b)
1	cup toasted sliced almonds
8 to 10	candy coffee beans

Prepare génoise, crème au beurre (you will need 2 cups, divided), and sirop à entremets a day ahead.

Prepare crème patissière, cool to room temperature, then chill. Beat in 1/2 cup crème au beurre au café to make "crème légère". Beat until smooth.

To garnish: With a large serrated knife, cut génoise into 3 layers. Spread a little crème au beurre on an 8-inch cake board to help anchor the cake. Turn over the bottom layer, brush copiously with sirop, then turn back over and place on cake board. Brush with more sirop, then, using a metal spatula, spread on 1/3 of the crème légère.

Place second layer on top, brush with sirop, and spread on 1/3 of crème légère. Reserve 1/2 cup crème au beurre au café, for decoration. Beat remaining 1/3 of crème légère into 1 cup crème au beurre. With a metal spatula, spread crème au beurre over top and sides of cake. Place almonds in a shallow dish. Slide a

More➤

(Moka au Café, cont.)

metal spatula under cake board, lift it up off the work surface, and place in the palm of one hand. With the other, scoop up a handful of almonds and press into sides, turning cake little by little and repeating until sides are covered. Spoon reserved 1/2 cup crème au beurre into pastry bag and pipe out a pattern of swirls and rosettes on top. Decorate with candy coffee beans.

Storage: Cover and refrigerate until 30 minutes before serving. Serve within 24 hours.

Afterword: *The 19th century Larousse dictionary commented that coffee drinking was particularly recommended for "men of letters, soldiers, sailors, all laborers who work in elevated temperatures, and finally for all inhabitants of countries where cretinism reigns!"*

VI-6 LE PÉRIGOURDIN

The fruit of the walnut tree, which probably originated somewhere on the banks of the Caspian Sea, was prized by the ancient Romans for two reasons: its agreeable taste, and its supposed power to cure migraines. The brain-like shape of the shelled nut is the most likely explanation for this old belief. This moist cake from Périgord, one of France's most important walnut-producing regions, is nicely set off by chocolate icing.

(VI-6)

Le Périgourdin
(Chocolate-Iced Walnut Cake)

Ingredients: (for one 10-inch gâteau)

2	tablespoons butter
4	eggs
1/2	cup sugar
1/3	cup flour
1/8	teaspoon salt
1	cup coarsely-ground walnuts
1/2	teaspoon baking powder, sifted if lumpy
	butter and flour for pan
2	cups crème au beurre au chocolat (II-4a)
1/2	cup sirop à entremets (II-12)
1	cup chopped walnuts
8 to 10	walnut halves

Preheat oven to 350-degrees. In a small saucepan, melt butter, then clarify and set aside to cool. In a large mixing bowl over a pot of hot water, beat whole eggs and sugar at medium speed until barely warm, then remove from heat and beat at high speed until the mixture forms a ribbon. In a small bowl, stir together flour, salt, ground walnuts, and baking powder. Fold carefully into egg mixture, then fold in warm butter.

Pour into a buttered and floured 10-inch manqué pan and bake about 30 minutes, or until cake is light brown and pulls away from sides of pan. Remove from oven, cool 5 minutes, then turn out onto a cooling rack.

To garnish: Reserve 1/2 cup crème au beurre for decoration. With a long serrated knife, cut cake horizontally into 3 layers. Spread a spoonful of crème on a 10-inch cake board, place bottom layer, brush lightly with sirop à entremets, and using a metal spatula, spread evenly with about 1/3 cup crème au beurre. Repeat with second layer, then place last layer on top, brush with sirop and cover sides and top with remaining crème. Place walnuts in a shallow dish, and, holding gâteau in the palm of one hand, with the other, scoop up a handful of walnuts and press gently into the sides, turning the cake little by little and working around until sides are completely covered. Spoon reserved crème into pastry bag and pipe out a pattern of swirls and rosettes on the top. Decorate with walnut halves.

Storage: Refrigerate until 30 minutes before serving. Serve within 48 hours.

VI-7 GÂTEAU MOUSSELINE AU CITRON

Queen Marie-Antoinette's frivolous behavior may not have been a direct cause of the French Revolution, but it certainly helped bring about her own downfall and precipitate the nation into one of its most nightmarish periods. Among the very few survivors of the royal family: Princess Marie-Thérèse, affectionately nicknamed "Mousseline" by her mother.

Tender génoise and light lemon mousse make this the perfect dessert after a heavy meal.

(VI-7)
Gâteau Mousseline au Citron
(Lemon Mousse Cake)

Ingredients: (for one 8-inch gâteau)

1	8-inch génoise (I-1)

1 1/3	cups crème au citron (II-6)
1	tablespoon lemon juice
1/4	cup sirop à entremets (II-12)
1	teaspoon gelatin
2	cups crème chantilly (II-1)
2	lemons, sliced thin
2/3	cup sirop à entremets (II-12)

Prepare génoise and crème au citron a day ahead.

In a small saucepan, whisk together lemon juice, sirop, and gelatin. Heat gently, stirring occasionally until gelatin is dissolved. Beat into crème au citron until smooth, then refrigerate.

Prepare crème chantilly and, with a rubber spatula, fold carefully into cooled lemon mixture.

Line bottom of unbuttered 8-inch manqué or soufflé pan (ceramic or glass, not metal) with lemon slices. With a serrated knife, cut génoise into 3 horizontal layers. Spread 1/3 of lemon mousse into prepared pan, then place 1 layer of cake on top, trimming some, if necessary, to make it fit. Brush generously with sirop and repeat the process, finishing with a layer of cake. Place 2 dinner plates on top and refrigerate at least 2 hours. A half hour before unmolding, place in freezer, then dip the pan in hot water for 1 minute. Dry the mold, place serving plate on top and invert. Refrigerate until serving. Serve within 24 hours.

Afterword: *Just as modern-day women carry lipstick in their handbags, elegant 18th century ladies wouldn't have dreamt of going anywhere without a supply of lemons, since frequent bites taken from them kept their lips red.*

VI-8 OPÉRA

In 1860, when the French Emperor Napoléon III chose Charles Garnier to design Paris' new opera house, the architect hardly suspected that his most vehement adversary would be...the Empress herself.

"But it's no particular style," she exclaimed, waving dramatically at the series of blueprints spread out in front of her. "It's not Greek, it's not Louis XIV," she threw up her hands and shot an accusing look at Monsieur Garnier. "It's not even Louis XV!"

Garnier stiffened, but forced himself to answer calmly. "No, Your Majesty. Those styles have come and gone. This style," he pointed at the drawings, "is Napoléon III."

The Empress pursed her lips. "The stage is too big," she insisted with a frown, "and the hall itself is too small."

Garnier felt his patience slipping away. "There must be enough room on the stage for the sets and the actors," he retorted, "and if the hall were bigger, whose voice could possibly carry enough to be heard by the audience? And then, who would bother to come to the new opera house?"

Before the Empress could continue, Napoléon leaned forward, a knowing look playing across his face. "Don't worry", he murmured with a wry smile. "I realize that she doesn't even know what she's talking about!" The subject was obviously closed. Garnier had won.

A few months later, when the Empress saw the architect at an official reception, she blushed and said, "You must admit, Monsieur, that I was somewhat disagreeable with you..."

"Quite so," he answered, bowing ceremoniously. "Your Majesty was perfectly odious!"

More➤

(Opéra, cont.)

The richness and elegance of this layered pastry matches that of the architectual masterpiece which gave it its name.

(VI-8)

Opéra
(Chocolate Glazed Cake with Praline Buttercream)

Ingredients: (for one 3 1/2 x 10-inch Opéra)
- 1   10 x 15-inch biscuit joconde (I-3)
- 1/2   cup sirop à entremets à la vanille or au rhum (II-12)
- 1   cup crème au beurre au prâlin (II-4c)
- 1/3   cup ganâche au rhum or à la vanille (II-17)
- 5/8   cup glaçage au chocolat (II-16)

Using a long serrated knife and a ruler, cut biscuit joconde into 4 equal rectangles, about 3 1/2 x 10 inches. Spread a little crème au beurre on a 3 x 10-inch rectangular cake board and place first layer. Brush with sirop, then with a metal spatula, spread on 1/3 of crème au beurre. Place second layer, brush with sirop, spread on all of ganâche. Place third layer, brush with sirop, spread on 1/3 of crème au beurre. Place fourth layer, brush with sirop, spread with rest of crème au beurre. Refrigerate for at least 1 hour, to harden crème au beurre.

Prepare glaçage au chocolat, cool to room temperature (it should be thick but easy to pour). Pour over the gâteau. With a large metal spatula, smooth the top in one stroke, letting the excess glaçage run down over the sides. Return to refrigerator.

A half hour before serving, remove the gâteau from refrigerator. Dip a sharp serrated knife blade in hot water, then wipe quickly. Trim the sides to remove the uneven patches of glaçage and reveal the layers of cake and crème.

La Joconde (IV-8a): Replace crème au beurre prâlinée with crème au beurre au café, and sirop au rhum or à la vanille with sirop au café. Prepare as above.

Storage: Refrigerate until 30 minutes before serving. Serve the same day as prepared.

VI-9 MARJOLAINE

Although romantic-minded pastrychefs say that this mousse-filled layer cake was named in honor of a lady named "Marjolaine", more practical ones insist that the original recipe simply called for marjolaine (French for "marjoram"), a sweet tasting spice still used in cooking, but rarely in modern-day pastry making.

(VI-9)
Marjolaine
(Chocolate & Caramel-Almond Filled Cake)

Ingredients: (for one 5 x 10-inch gâteau)
- 1   10 x 15-inch biscuit joconde (I-3)
- 1/3   cup sirop à entremets au rhum (II-12a)
- 1/3   cup ganâche au rhum (II-17a)

Chocolate Mousse:
- 3   ounces semi-sweet chocolate
- 3   tablespoons butter

Praline Mousse:
- 1/4   cup prâlin (II-9)
- 4   tablespoons butter, softened

- 6   egg whites
- 1/8   teaspoon salt
- 3   tablespoons sugar

     powdered sugar for topping

In a small saucepan over very low heat, melt chocolate and butter. With a fork, beat until smooth, then set aside to cool.

In a small mixing bowl, beat together prâlin and butter until creamy. In a deep mixing bowl, beat egg whites and salt at high speed until soft peaks form. Add sugar and continue beating until very stiff. Divide whites between 2 medium mixing bowls.

Add a spoonful of whites to chocolate mixture, then beat until smooth. Fold this lightened mixture into half the whites. Do the same with the prâlin/butter mixture. Refrigerate both mousses at least 1 hour, or until firm.

Using a serrated knife and a ruler, cut biscuit joconde into 3 equal rectangles, about 5 x 10 inches. Spread a little ganâche on a 4 x 10-inch rectangular cake board and place first layer. Brush with sirop, then spread on half the ganâche. Over the ganâche, spread on all the chocolate mousse. Place second layer, brush with sirop, spread on rest of ganâche, then all of prâlin mousse. Place last layer and brush with sirop. Refrigerate 2 hours. Immediately before serving, trim sides and ends with a serrated knife, dipped in hot water and dried. Dust generously with powdered sugar.

Storage: Refrigerate undusted gâteau until serving. Serve same day as prepared.

VI-10 DAMIER CHOCORANGE

Colette, famed author of the "Claudine" series, and of "Gigi" once wrote about the preparation of chocolate in her childhood home: "In those days, we made chocolate with cocoa, sugar and vanilla. At the top of the house, soft plaques of chocolate were set out on the terrace to cool. And every morning, five-petaled flowers pressed into the plaques revealed cats' nocturnal passage..."

Almost as renowned for her gourmandise as for her books, Colette would have loved this attractive and delicious orange-chocolate "checkerboard" cake.

(VI-10)
Damier Chocorange
(Orange & Chocolate Checkerboard Cake)

Ingredients: (for one 9 x 9-inch cake)

2/3	cup flour
1/2	cup cornstarch
1	teaspoon baking powder

1/2	cup butter, softened
3/4	cup sugar
3	egg yolks

1/3	cup fresh orange juice
	finely grated rind of 1 orange
2	tablespoons Grand Marnier

3	egg whites
1/4	teaspoon salt
1	tablespoon sugar
	butter and flour for cake pan

Garnish:

2/3	cup orange marmalade
3	tablespoons Grand Marnier

1 1/4	cups chocolate glaze (II-16)

18	1 1/2-inch squares of candied orange peel

Preheat oven to 350-degrees. Butter and flour a 9 x 9-inch square cake pan. In a small mixing bowl, stir together dry ingredients. In a large mixing bowl, beat butter and sugar until creamy, then beat in egg yolks and orange rind. Lower speed and beat in dry ingredients and juice, alternately. Stop beating as soon as well mixed.

More➤

(Damier Chocorange, cont.)

In a deep mixing bowl, beat egg whites and salt at high speed until soft peaks form. Add the sugar and continue beating until stiff but not dry. Beat a big spoonful of whites into batter, then carefully fold in rest of whites. Spread in prepared 3 x 3-inch square cake pan and bake 25 to 30 minutes, or until a cake tester inserted in the middle comes out clean. Cool 2 or 3 minutes, then turn out onto wire rack.

In a small saucepan, heat orange marmalade until warm and smooth, then remove from heat and stir in Grand Marnier. If the top of cake is domed, even it off with a serrated knife, then cut cake into 3 horizontal layers. Place the bottom layer on a 9 x 9-inch cake board, spread on half the marmalade, place the second layer and spread on rest of marmalade. Place the last layer and set the cake on a wire rack.

Prepare chocolate glaze, and allow to cool 10 minutes. Pour glaze over center of cake, spreading carefully with a metal spatula for perfect coverage. Arrange candied orange squares in a checkerboard pattern.

Storage: Cover tightly and store in a cool, dry place (preferably not in the refrigerator, because the glaze would become dull), for 48 hours.

VI-11 GÂTEAU AUX MARRONS

General Brutus Motus always found something to complain about. Always. And this time, Paolus the cook realized, was no exception. Why should it be? The Gauls—may Jupiter's lightening bolt strike off their toes!—had begun their seige almost a year before and the long-awaited convoy from Rome had yet to arrive. No, Motus couldn't really be blamed. Even the greatest general—and he was among Rome's best—would have become testy by now.

Paolus hesitated a moment at the commanding officer's open door. "General Motus?" He hoped vaguely that his superior wouldn't hear him. Maybe if he held his breath and crept away...

General Motus looked up from the report he was writing. "What are you waiting for, Paolus?" he growled, throwing down his stylus, "An engraved invitation to come in?"

"Definitely in a foul mood," Paolus thought as he came into the room and saluted.

Motus came right to the point. "Well, what do you have to say for yourself?"

"Say for myself?" A surprised look came over the cook's face.

"Oh, knock it off," Motus said. "You know perfectly well what I'm talking about."

Paolus shook his head slowly. "Sir, I assure you..."

"The food around this place is atrocious!" Motus cut in. "A pig wouldn't eat the slop you serve!"

Paolus had been waiting for it. Still, it was hard to take. "I do my best, General..."

"Your best, my eye!" Motus said. "What did we have for lunch today?"

"Roasted chestnuts, General."

"And for dinner last night?"

The cook pretended to think back. "Uh...boiled chestnuts, I believe."
"For breakfast a month ago?"

"Chestnut purée," Paolus said firmly. "We always have chestnut purée for breakfast."

Motus rose and came dangerously close. "And would you mind telling me," he said, articulating slowly, "what you plan to serve this evening?"

Paolus' gaze flitted around the room, as if looking for an answer written on the wall. He didn't find one. "Chestnuts au gratin, General," he finally said.

More ➤

(Gâteau aux Marrons, Cont.)

"And you wonder why I'm dissatisfied!" Motus thundered, *striking his work table with a ham-sized fist.*

Paolus took a step backward. "But for Saturday night," he offered quickly, "I've planned a surprise."

"Really?" Motus *looked hopeful.*

"Chestnut soufflé!"

The general closed his eyes and took a deep breath. "Paolus, do you realize just how close my troops are to a full-scale rebellion?"

Paolus fidgeted and looked at his feet. He knew better than to answer.

"And I can't say I blame them much," Motus continued. "It's hard enough being under seige. But with your chestnut soup, your chestnut cream, your oh so memorable 'chestnut surprise'...that was the last straw!" He began to pace the floor.

Paolus shrugged. "But what can I do? All we have is chestnuts..."

A sentinal burst into the room. "General Motus!" he cried, forgetting to salute, "The convoy from Rome..."

"Arms?" the general asked automatically.

"No, General. Food!"

"How many wagons?"

"Forty-three, General." This time, the soldier remembered to salute. Motus dismissed the two men with a nod. Paolus rushed out to the loaded wagons. The head of the convoy, a fat, condescending sergeant, handed a scroll to him. Feverishly, he unrolled it.

"Please acknowledge receipt of 43 wagons fresh chestnuts..."

Paolus gave the scroll back to the Sergeant. "Take this to General Motus," he said faintly, "You'll receive a fitting reward." The sergeant hurried away.

Paolus looked at the receeding figure and shook his head. "Sometimes," he murmured with a sigh, "it just doesn't pay to get up in the morning."

Although the Romans were doubtless responsible for introducing the chestnut tree to ancient Gaul, no one really knows for sure if the Roman army managed to survive a long seige thanks to its reserve of chestnuts.

More➔

(Gâteau aux Marrons, Cont.)

This moist chestnut cake might have been one of "Paolus'" more appreciated specialties. You can serve it plain, with a simple chocolate glaze, fill it with chestnut purée, or make it into a cream-filled roll.

(VI-11)
Gâteau aux Marrons
(Chocolate-Glazed Chestnut Cake)

Ingredients: (for one 9-inch cake)

1/2	cup flour
1 1/2	teaspoons baking powder

1/3	cup butter, softened
1/2	cup sugar
1/2	cup canned chestnut purée
3	egg yolks
1/2	teaspoon vanilla extract

3	egg whites
1/4	teaspoon salt
1	tablespoon sugar
	butter and flour for pan

Garnish:

5/8	cup chocolate glaze (II-16)
9	candied chestnuts

Preheat oven to 350-degrees. In a small bowl, stir together flour and baking powder.

In a medium mixing bowl, beat together butter and sugar until creamy, then beat in chestnut purée, egg yolks and vanilla.

In a deep mixing bowl, beat egg whites and salt at high speed until soft peaks form, then add the sugar and continue beating until stiff but not dry. Beat 1/2 of whites into batter, to make it softer, then fold all of softened batter into rest of whites. Spread in buttered and floured 9-inch round cake or manqué pan, and bake 20 to 30 minutes, or until cake is browned and pulls away from sides of pan. Cool 5 minutes, then turn out onto wire rack.

To garnish: Pour barely warm chocolate glaze over cooled cake (placed on wire rack over large plate or bowl) and spread carefully with a metal spatula for perfect coverage. Allow glaze to set 15 minutes. With a long serrated knife blade (preferably longer than the cake is wide), make a wavy pattern in the glaze by dragging it across almost flat (at a very slight angle) in a back and forth, or "zigzag", motion. Smooth sides well with a small metal spatula, place 8 candied chestnuts around edge of cake, at regular intervals, with one in the center. Cover (no need to refrigerate unless weather is very hot) until serving. Serve within 24 hours.

More➔

(Gâteau aux Marrons, Cont.)

Storage: Uniced cake can be wrapped in plastic or foil and frozen up to 2 months. Thaw in refrigerator several hours, then garnish as directed above.

Variation:
- 2/3   **cup canned chestnut purée**
- 5/8   **cup chocolate glaze (II-16)**
- 9   **candied chestnuts**

Prepare cake as above, decreasing sugar from 1/2 cup to 1/3 cup. With a long serrated knife, cut cooled cake into 3 equal layers. Spread a spoonful of chestnut purée on a 9-inch cake board and place bottom layer. Spread on half the chestnut purée, place second layer, and spread with rest of purée. Top with last layer. Glaze and decorate as above.

Rolled Chestnut Cake (VI-11a):
- 1/3   **cup sirop à entremets au rhum (II-12a)**
- 2   **cups crème chantilly (II-1)**
  - **powdered sugar for dusting**
  - **grated lemon peel or grated fresh orange peel or**
    - **chopped candied orange peel**

Preheat oven to 350-degrees. Prepare batter for original recipe. Butter and flour a 10 x 12-inch baking sheet and spread on batter, being careful to avoid thick or thin spots. Bake about 8 to 10 minutes. A cake tester, inserted in the center, should come out clean. Remove from oven, and, with a chef's knife, trim off uneven or brittle edges. Place hot cake on a sheet of waxed or parchment paper and roll up tightly. Cool.

Unroll cake and generously brush both sides with sirop. Reserve about 1/2 cup crème chantilly for decoration, and spread on rest. Roll cake tightly and refrigerate until serving. Immediately before serving, place cake seam-side down on a work surface, and dust with powdered sugar. With a chef's knife, trim off ends, using one clean, sharp motion. Place cake on serving plate. Spoon remaining 1/2 cup crème chantilly into a pastry bag with a 1/4-inch unfluted round nozzle, and pipe a fat squiggle of chantilly down the center of cake. Sprinkle fresh or candied orange peel over chantilly and serve immediately.

Note: This rolled cake can also be covered entirely with chantilly. You'll need about 2 additional cups chantilly, which can be spread on with a knife or spatula, then "scratched" with a fork to resemble tree bark. It can also be piped on in small rosettes, shells, or peaks, depending upon the nozzle used. In any case, decorate with orange peel or candied chestnuts.

Storage: Refrigerate until serving. Serve within 24 hours. Ungarnished cake can be frozen, rolled in paper, for up to 2 months. Thaw wrapped cake 12 hours in refrigerator.

VI-12   GÂTEAU ROULÉ À LA CONFITURE

In 1555, the world's first book devoted solely to jams and preserves or "confitures" was published in Lyon. The author, Michel de Nostre-dame, alias "Nostradamus" was better known for his books in which strangely accurate predictions for the future still disconcert modern readers. This classical jelly roll is very easy and quick to make. It's equally good with crème au citron.

(VI-12)
Gâteau Roulé à la Confiture
(Jelly-Roll)

Ingredients: (for one 10-inch roll)
    1   biscuit roulé (I-2)
    1/3   cup sirop à entremets (II-12)
    1   cup tart seedless jam or
        crème au citron (lemon curd) (II-6)
        powdered sugar

Prepare biscuit roulé. Place on the work surface, waxed paper side down, and cover with a cloth to trap steam and help soften the cake as it cools. When cooled, turn over and carefully peel off paper, then brush lightly with sirop à entremets. With a metal spatula, spread on jam or lemon curd. Roll up tightly, trim off ends with a chef's knife, and dust with powdered sugar.

Storage: This cake is best when eaten the same day, but can be refrigerated up to 48 hours, wrapped in plastic. Dust with powdered sugar immediately before serving.

VI-13   BÛCHE DE NOËL

The "bûche de Noël" was, in days gone by, an enormous log which burned in farmhouse fireplaces during Christmas Eve gatherings. It could be from any kind of tree, but had to be big enough to burn from the moment that nine stars appeared in the sky, in memory of the nine months during which the Virgin Mary awaited the birth of Jesus, until sunrise on Christmas morning. At midnight, when the log was struck, gifts were said to spring from it like sparks.
In French cities, this rolled cake decorated like a log replaced the traditional "bûche" long ago. If you want it to look realistic, make it with coffee, chocolate, or prâlin-flavored crème au beurre. For a touch of "fantaisie", surprise your Christmas dinner guests with a pink or green bûche, flavored, respectively, with Grand Marnier or kirsch.

(VI-13)
Bûche de Noël
(Yule Log)

Ingredients: (for one 12-inch bûche)
    1   biscuit roulé (I-2)
    1   cup sirop à entremets à la vanille or
        flavored according to the flavor of crème au beurre (II-12)
    1 1/4   cups crème au beurre à la vanille (II-4f)
    1 1/4   cups crème au beurre, your choice of flavors (II-4)

More➔

(Bûche de Noël, cont.)

Decorations: Silver pearls, mimosa balls, chocolate sprinkles, miniature pine cones, flowers, artificial mushrooms, toy Santas, reindeer, Christmas trees, almond paste cutouts, etc.

Assembly time is minimal, when the components for this recipe are prepared ahead of time.

To assemble: Unroll biscuit roulé, remove paper from top, then turn over and carefully peel paper off underside. Brush both sides generously with sirop à entremets. If crème au beurre is very cold, heat gently. With a metal spatula, spread about 3/4 cup crème au beurre à la vanille evenly over the cake. Roll up tightly.

With a chef's knife, cut off the ends at an angle, to obtain 2 wedge-shaped pieces of cake. Place the rolled cake, seam-side down, on an oblong serving plate. Put a dollop of vanilla crème au beurre in 2 different places on the cake, and stick on the 2 wedges, to resemble cut branches. Put more dollops of vanilla crème au beurre on the flat ends of the branches, and on the ends of the log. Flatten them some with a knife or spatula, but there's no need to smooth carefully.

Spoon all of the flavored crème au beurre into the pastry bag with ribbon nozzle, and cover the roll with long strips of icing, to resemble the bark on a log. When you come to the branches, go right over them, vanilla crème au beurre and all. Do the same with the ends. Hold a sharp knife under hot water for a few seconds, then, with one clean motion, trim off about half the crème au beurre on the ends. The white center will be revealed, surrounded by colored "bark". Decorate with silver pearls, artificial mushrooms, etc.

Storage: Cover and refrigerate for up to 48 hours. Remove 1 hour before serving. Garnished but undecorated log can be wrapped in plastic and frozen for up to 1 month. Thaw 24 hours in refrigerator, then garnish and decorate as above.

VI-14   MILLEFEUILLE

The millefeuille may have been named after the "Feuillantines", a religious order for women founded in the 16th century by the Abbé de Feuillans. The whiteness of the powdered sugar topping was reminiscent of the white robes worn by the members of the religious community. Both Carême and La Varenne gave recipes for this classical pastry.

The millefeuille, which literally means "a thousand layers" is more commonly known as the "napoleon" in the United States. This is an excellent way of using up a large amount of pâte feuilletée rognures.

More→

(Millefeuille, Cont.)

(VI-14)
Millefeuille
(Napoleons)

Ingredients: (for 6 servings)
- 1   pound, 7 ounces pâte feuilletée rognures (I-8)

- 2 1/4   cups crème patissière (pastrycream) (II-2)
- 1   cup crème chantilly (whipped cream) (II-1), **unsweetened**

      powdered sugar

On a lightly-floured surface, roll out rognures to about 1/8-inch thick, then, using a ruler and a chef's knife, cut three 8 x 12-inch rectangles. Place on ungreased baking sheets, prick all over with a fork, then refrigerate 1 hour.

While the pastry is "resting", prepare crème chantilly. Then prepare crème patissière and cool to room temperature. Beat in about 1/2 cup of chantilly, then with a rubber spatula, fold in the rest of chantilly. Chill.

Preheat oven to 425-degrees and bake pastry about 20 minutes, until golden brown and crisp. Don't underbake, as it would get soggy after being filled. Cool, then stack the 3 layers on top of each other, and with a serrated knife, trim about 1/2-inch off edges, to give the pastry perfectly clean lines.

Select and set aside the most even rectangle, which will go on top. Place bottom rectangle on a wire rack, and, with a metal spatula, spread evenly with about 1/3 of crème. Repeat with the second rectangle, then place the third rectangle on top. With a metal spatula, use the rest of crème to fill in the spaces on the sides. Smooth well. Dust the top with powdered sugar.

If you want to give the millefeuille a professional look, hold a skewer or other long, narrow metal object over a gas flame until red hot, then press firmly into the powdered sugar surface to form a diagonal caramelized stripe. Repeat at 2-inch intervals, then turn pastry around and repeat the whole procedure, until a crisscross pattern is formed. Serve whole or cut into individual servings.

Note: Although the millefeuille is best when made with rognures, it can also be made with fresh pâte demi-feuilletée. Be sure to prick it well, then after refrigeration, bake with another baking sheet the same size placed on top to keep it from puffing up too much. After removing the baking sheet, watch closely and prick more, if necessary.

au Chocolat (VI-14a): Use crème patissière au chocolat instead of crème patissière à la vanille. That is, stir about 4 ounces semi-sweet chocolate, or 1/2 cup chocolate chips into hot crème patissière. Stir occasionally to speed up melting. Prepare as above.

Storage: Refrigerate until serving. Serve within 2 hours.

VI-15   MILLEFEUILLE AUX FRUITS ROUGES

Raymond Lulle, a 14th century alchemist, declared in his writing that a drink made of strawberries and ground pearls would cure leprosy. His colleagues were less ambitious. They were convinced that the strawberry's healing powers were limited to dysentery, tuberculosis, and gout...

Strawberries or raspberries and whipped cream make this variation of the classical millefeuille a refreshing summer dessert.

(VI-15)
Millefeuille aux Fruits Rouges
(Strawberry or Raspberry Napoleons)

Ingredients: (for one 8 x 12-inch pastry, serving 6)

1	pound, 7 ounces pâte demi-feuilletée (I-8) or pâte feuilletée rognures (I-8a)
1 1/8	cups crème patissière (II-2)
3	cups crème chantilly (II-1)
1	pound fresh strawberries or raspberries, cleaned

Prepare and trim 3 rectangles of pastry 8x12-inches (see VI-14). While pastry is baking, prepare crème patissière and crème chantilly. Chill. Set aside about 1/3 of the fruit for decoration.

Place bottom layer of pastry on wire rack and, with a metal spatula, spread on the cold crème patissière. Set the second layer of pastry on top, then spread on about 1/3 of the crème chantilly. Arrange the fruit on the crème (if you're using strawberries, cut them in half) in an even layer. Spoon the remaining 2 cups of crème chantilly into the pastry bag and pipe large rosettes over the fruit, especially around the edges, for an attractive presentation. Place the last layer of pastry on top and decorate with remaining fruit and rosettes of crème chantilly.

Storage: Refrigerate until serving. Serve within 2 hours.

VI-16   ST. HONORÉ

Saint Honoré, Bishop of Amiens around 660 A.D., was said to have received the holy sacrament directly from the hand of God one day as he celebrated mass. This legend easily explains why he subsequently became the patron saint of bakers.

This elaborate-looking pastry is rich but light, so it makes a perfect "company" dessert.

(VI-16)
St. Honoré

Ingredients: (for one 10-inch gâteau)
    7   ounces pâte demi-feuilletée (I-8) or rognures (I-8a)
         oil for baking sheets

1 1/4   cups pâte à choux (I-11)
    1   egg, beaten with a pinch of salt (egg wash)

    4   cups crème chantilly (II-1)
  2/3   cup hard caramel (II-8a)

         candied violets or cherries for decoration

Preheat oven to 450-degrees. On a lightly-floured surface, roll out pâte feuilletèe or rognures to 1/8-inch thick. With a paring knife, and using a 10-inch plate or cake board for a guide, cut out a 10-inch disk. Place on a lightly-oiled baking sheet, prick well with a fork, and refrigerate until used.

Prepare pâte à choux, spoon into pastry bag with a 5/8-inch fluted nozzle, and pipe a band of dough around the rim of the disk, about 1/4-inch away from the edge. On another lightly-oiled baking sheet, pipe out twelve 1 1/4-inch choux. You'll probably have some leftover dough. A small amount can simply be piped in a spiral in the center of the pastry shell. A larger amount can be used to make a few larger choux, which could be frozen for later use.

Brush the pâte à choux with beaten egg and bake pastry base and choux at 450-degrees for 10 minutes, then lower heat to 400-degrees, prop oven door open with a spoon, and bake for another 15 minutes, until the pâte à choux is puffed up and golden brown. The small choux will bake more quickly, so keep an eye on them and remove them after about 15 minutes. Cool completely.

While the pastry is baking, prepare the crème chantilly. Refrigerate until use.

To garnish choux: Reserve about 1 1/2 cups crème chantilly for decoration. Spoon 1/2 cup of it into a pastry bag with a 1/8-inch fluted nozzle, making a hole in the bottom of each chou with the nozzle. Fill.

Prepare caramel. When it's a deep amber color, remove from heat and dip the tops of the choux in, then place them, caramel side up, on waxed paper or a

More➜

(St. Honoré, cont.)

lightly-oiled baking sheet to cool. Dip the bases of the cooled choux in the caramel and place them at regular intervals around the rings of pâte à choux.

Spoon 2 1/2 cups crème chantilly into pastry shell, smoothing well to make an even surface. Spoon remaining 1 cup of chantilly into pastry bag with a 5/8-inch fluted nozzle, and pipe large rosettes over the surface and between the choux. Decorate with candied violets or cherry halves.

A La Crème Chiboust (VI-16a): Replace crème chantilly with 4 cups crème chiboust (II-5). Prepare as above.

Storage: Refrigerate until serving. Serve within 2 hours.

VI-17   SUCCÈS

The succès, which simply means "success", was aptly named. Tender disks of almond-rich pastry filled with prâlin-flavored buttercream are sure to be a big success, whether served at tea time, or for dessert after Sunday dinner. The "chocolatine" calls for the same pastry base, filled with chocolate mousse, and the "délicieux", yet another possibility, is just as true to its name as the succès.

(VI-17)

Succès
(Almond Cake with Praline Buttercream)

Ingredients: (for one 8-inch gâteau)
Pastry Base:

1	cup blanched ground almonds
1/3	cup granulated sugar
1/3	cup powdered sugar
4	egg whites
	pinch salt
1	tablespoon granulated sugar
1/4	cup sliced untoasted almonds

Filling:

1 2/3	cups crème au beurre pralinée (II-4c)
1/4	cup powdered sugar
1	cup chopped toasted almonds

Preheat oven to 350-degrees. In a medium mixing bowl, stir together dry ingredients. In a large mixing bowl, beat egg whites and salt at high speed until soft peaks form. Add the tablespoon of sugar and continue beating until very stiff. Dust whites generously with part of dry ingredients and fold in carefully with a rubber spatula. Repeat until all dry ingredients are mixed in.

More➔

Butter and flour baking sheets, or line them with waxed paper, using a dot of batter in the corners and center to make it stick. With a pencil and using an 8-inch cake board as a guide, trace a circle in the middle of each baking sheet. Spoon batter into pastry bag and pipe two 8-inch disks, beginning in the center and piping in a closed spiral, ending just inside the traced circle. Sprinkle one of the disks with the sliced almonds. Bake about 10 minutes, then switch the sheets around so the pastry will brown evenly, and bake for another 10 minutes, until the disks are golden brown.

With a metal spatula, remove immediately from baking sheets and cool on wire racks. While the pastry bakes, prepare the crème au beurre, or better yet, make it in advance. To use, heat gently.

To assemble: Stack the disks on the cake board and trim them with a serrated knife to make them exactly the same size. Reserve the one with almonds for the top. Drop a big dollop of crème au beurre on the cake board, place the bottom layer, and press gently to make it stick.

With a metal spatula, spread on about 3/4 of the crème au beurre, then place top layer. Spread the rest of the crème au beurre on the sides, smoothing well. Dust top generously with powdered sugar. Place almonds in a shallow dish. Slide a metal spatula under the cake board, lift it off the work surface, and place it in the palm of one hand. With the other hand, scoop up a handful of almonds and press into sides, working around little by little until sides are completely covered.

An alternative for dressing up this gâteau, especially nice for a holiday table: Leave off the toasted almonds and wrap a brightly colored ribbon around it. I like to use gold ribbon because it's the most striking, but any bright color will be fine. You'll need about 3 1/2 feet of 1-inch wide ribbons.

La Chocolatine (VI-17a): Use the same pastry base as for the succès. Garnish with 3 cups of mousse au chocolat (IV-6), chilled at least 2 hours before using, and dust top of gâteau with unsweetened cocoa powder. Chill until serving. Leave sides plain or tie up, as with the succès, with a bright ribbon.

Le Délicieux (VI-17b): Add 2 tablespoons sifted cocoa powder to the succès batter. Fill with crème au beurre pralinée, and dust with unsweetened cocoa powder. Cover sides with chocolate sprinkles or tie up with a ribbon.

Storage: Refrigerate finished gâteau until shortly before serving. Remove from refrigerator about 1 hour ahead of time, to allow the crème au beurre to soften. The pastry base can be wrapped in plastic and frozen for up to 2 months. Allow to thaw in refrigerator 12 hours before using.

VI-18   BABA AU RHUM

*King Stanislas of Poland happened to be reading **1001 Arabian Nights** when his cook served him a new pastry, a kind of rum-soaked sponge cake. Enthused, the sovereign immediately called it the "Ali Baba" in honor of his favorite story, but with popular use, the first part of the name eventually dropped off.*

(VI-18)

Baba au Rhum
(Rum-soaked Sponge Cake)

Ingredients: (for one 9-inch baba)

2	eggs
1 3/4	cups flour
1	teaspoon salt
2	teaspoons sugar
1/2	cake compressed yeast
7	tablespoons hot tap water
1/4	cup butter, softened
	butter for mold
2 1/2	cups water
2	cups sugar
3	tablespoons rum (or if you prefer: kirsch, Grand Marnier, Cointreau, etc.)
1/2	cup abricotage (apricot glaze) (II-11a)
	several candied cherry halves
	angélique (optional)

In a large mixing bowl, place eggs, then without stirring, place flour. In 3 different places, put salt, sugar, and crumbled yeast. Stir with the hand until partially mixed, add 3 tablespoons water, and knead as for brioche dough; that is, with a lifting motion of the cupped hand, until the dough becomes elastic, for about 10 to 15 minutes.

Add the rest of the water, a tablespoon at a time, kneading well between each addition. The secret of a good baba lies in sufficient kneading, so don't be afraid of overhandling the dough. Add the butter and continue kneading until the dough pulls away from the sides of the bowl, about another 10 minutes. The dough should be very soft and rather elastic, but not runny.

Clean sides of bowl with a rubber spatula, cover and let rise in a warm place for 15 minutes. Punch down. Butter baba mold or 9-inch tube pan and spread dough evenly in bottom. Let rise in a warm place for 30 to 40 minutes, but not until doubled in volume, as it would be too fragile and would tend to fall apart even with careful handling. Preheat oven to 375-degrees, and bake 20 minutes, or until golden brown. Immediately turn baba out onto a cooling rack.

More➤

(Baba au Rhum, cont.)

Syrup: In a medium saucepan, heat water and sugar to a boil. Remove from heat and stir in flavoring. You can soak the baba as soon as it's cool, but it's better to leave it, uncovered, for 24 hours before soaking.

Pour the syrup into a large flat-bottomed pan. Turn the baba over and place it carefully in the warm syrup, leaving it to soak for about 10 minutes. Carefully pick it up, turn it back over and place on a wire rack over a plate. Pour any excess syrup over it and leave it on the rack until it stops dripping. The baba should be thoroughly soaked. Before serving, brush with warm apricot glaze and decorate with cherry halves and angélique.

Storage: Refrigerate, covered, until serving. Serve within 48 hours. Can be frozen, unsoaked, while still warm. Thaw several hours before soaking and decorating.

VI-19   SAVARIN
Although the baba au rhum was invented in the early 18th century, the Julien brothers further refined it in 1825, and named the new dessert after Brillat-Savarin, one of France's great culinary masters.

(VI-19)
Savarin

Ingredients:
>   1   soaked baba (VI-18)
>
> Choose from one of the following:
>   2   cups crème chantilly (II-1)
>   2   cups crème patissière (II-2)
>   2   cups crème légère (II-2c)
>   2   cups fresh fruit salad

Place the baba on a serving plate and garnish the middle with the filling of your choice. If you're using one of the crèmes, fill with 3/4 of filling, then spoon the rest into a pastry bag with a small star-shaped nozzle and cover the surface of the cake with rosettes.

Storage: Refrigerate until serving. Serve within 2 hours.

VI-20   GALETTE DES ROIS

In ancient Rome and Roman-occupied Gaul, Saturn, god of peace and prosperity, was honored once a year with festivities called Saturnales. A drawing was held to choose a "king", who presided over the celebrations...celebrations which usually degenerated into drunken orgies.

Needless to say, the priests who brought Christianity to Gaul had a dim view of these pagan festivities, but realized that trying to eliminate the Saturnales altogether wouldn't have worked. So they found a way to make everyone happy; the celebration continued, but the pagan god was replaced by the Christ child, and the king—one of the three magi—was chosen by hiding a dried bean in a kind of brioche.

Ever since the 15th century, the Feast of the Three Kings has been celebrated on Twelfth Night—that is, January 6. Traditionally, the youngest guest crawls under the table and calls out the name, at random, of each guest to be served, but not before reserving one portion for God, one for the Blessed Virgin, and one for the first of the Three Kings: servings which are set aside for the poor.

During the French Revolution, it was extremely unhealthful to celebrate anything even vaguely connected with religion or royalty...so everyone who wanted to hang onto his head was forced to celebrate the "Feast of Neighborliness" by eating "liberty cake"...and even the dried bean was replaced by a tiny ceramic liberty cap! To Parisians' general satisfaction, the original brioche has been replaced in recent years by a luscious medley of pâte feuilletée and frangipane.

(VI-20)
Galette des Rois
(King's Cake)

Ingredients: (for one 12-inch galette)

- 1   pound, 6 ounces pâte feuilletée classique (I-8) or
      pâte demi-feuilletée (I-9)
- 1   egg, beaten with a pinch of salt (egg wash)
- 1 3/4   cups frangipane (II-7)
- 1   whole almond or 1 dried bean
      (or, if available, a small ceramic token)
      powdered sugar (optional)

The frangipane, which can be prepared several days ahead, should be removed from the refrigerator 1 hour before use. Pâte feuilletée can be prepared up to 3 days in advance, but if you're using pâte demi-feuilletée, prepare it immediately before using.

More➤

(Galette des Rois, cont.)

Cut pâte into 2 equal pieces. On a lightly-floured surface, roll out one of them to 1/8-inch thick and using a 12-inch plate or cake board as a guide, cut out a 12-inch disk. Place on an ungreased baking sheet and brush the rim with a 1 1/2-inch band of beaten egg.

With a whisk or wooden spoon, beat the frangipane until creamy, then spread it over the pastry, taking care not to touch the band of egg. Place the whole almond or dried bean on the frangipane, close to the edge (this reduces the risk of cutting into it at serving time). Roll out and cut the rest of the pâte like the first and place it on top, pressing edges firmly to seal. Refrigerate 1 hour.

Before baking, brush the whole surface with beaten egg, and with a paring knife, mark firmly with a diamond or spiral design. Preheat oven to 450-degrees. Bake galette 10 minutes, then lower heat to 375-degrees and bake for another 35 to 40 minutes, until golden brown. If you want a glazed finish, dust with powdered sugar 15 minutes before the end of baking. If the sugar isn't melted by the time the galette has finished baking, put it under the broiler for a minute or two, watching closely to prevent burning. Serve warm.

Storage: The galette can be frozen before baking. Freeze on a baking sheet, then wrap in plastic and store in the freezer for up to 2 months. To bake, thaw 2 hours on a baking sheet in the refrigerator, then brush with egg, decorate with a knife, and bake as directed above.

Afterword: *Serve it with well-chilled champagne and, if children are among your guests, don't forget to provide a jewel-studded aluminum foil crown in honor of the "king".*

VI-21 CONVERSATION

Created in 1871, the conversation was probably named after **Les**
Conversations d'Emilie, *a very popular novel published the same year.*

(VI-21)
Conversation

Ingredients: (for one 10-inch gâteau)

14   ounces pâte feuilletée rognures (I-8a) or
       pâte brisée (I-6)

1 3/4   cups frangipane (II-7)

1   tablespoon egg white
2/3   cup powdered sugar

butter for pie plate

On a lightly-floured surface, roll out half the pastry to about 1/8-inch thick. Line buttered 10-inch pie plate and prick lightly with a fork but don't trim. With a rubber spatula or large spoon, spread on frangipane. Roll out rest of pastry and cover frangipane. Press edges firmly to seal, then trim without fluting. Save trimmings.

In a small bowl, beat together egg white and powdered sugar with a fork until creamy and smooth. If the icing is too runny, beat in a little more sugar. With a pastry brush, dust top of gâteau to remove any traces of flour and, with a metal spatula, spread icing evenly on top.

Knead the pastry trimmings a little to make them smooth, then roll out and cut into 1/2-inch wide strips. Arrange them on top of the icing in a diagonal crisscross pattern. Press edges well to make them stick, then trim off excess. Refrigerate 15 minutes, while oven is being preheated to 350-degrees, then bake for about 40 minutes, or until the crust is golden brown and the icing a deep ivory shade. If the top browns too quickly, cover it loosely with aluminum foil. Let cool 20 minutes before serving.

VI-22 PARIS-BREST

Some pastry chefs say that this big ring of pâte à choux filled with prâlin cream was created around the turn of the century in honor of a bicycle race from Paris to the Britanny port of Brest. Others affirm that it was invented by the cook in charge of the first-class dining car in the Paris-Brest train. The second explanation is probably the more likely: it used to be called the "Paris-Nice" as well.

(VI-22)
Paris-Brest
(Cream Puff Pastry filled with Praline Cream)

Ingredients: (for one 10-inch pastry)

1 1/4	cups crème patissière (II-2)
1/2	cup prâlin (II-9)
2/3	cup pâte à choux (I-11)
1	egg, beaten with a pinch of salt (egg wash)
1	cup untoasted sliced almonds
2/3	cup butter, softened
	powdered sugar

Prepare crème patissière, then stir in prâlin. Cool to room temperature, then refrigerate.

Preheat oven to 425-degrees. Prepare pâte à chou and spoon into a pastry bag with a fluted 3/4-inch nozzle. On a very lightly-greased baking sheet, pipe out a 9-inch circle. Pipe another circle just inside and touching the first. Then pipe a third circle, on top of the first two, in the middle. (This can be done without a pastry bag, although it's quite a bit more work. Carefully spoon dough in a 2 1/2-inch wide band to form a 9-inch circle.)

Brush with beaten egg and cover completely with almonds, then turn over the baking sheet and tap gently to remove excess almonds. Bake 15 minutes at 425-degrees, then lower heat to 400-degrees, prop oven door open with a spoon, and bake another 20 to 25 minutes, until pastry shell is puffed up and golden brown. Remove from oven and cool.

In a medium mixing bowl, beat together butter and chilled crème patissiére until light. The filling should be creamy but firm. If it's too soft, refrigerate until firm.

To garnish: With a serrated knife, split the pastry shell in half, horizontally. Spoon filling into pastry bag and pipe into shell, making large rosettes or "shells" around the outer rim. As with the pastry shell, this can be done with a spoon, but the pastry won't be as attractive. Place the top half over filling, and just before serving, dust generously with powdered sugar.

Storage: Cover and refrigerate until serving. Serve within 12 hours.

VI-23 CROQUEMBOUCHE

Solidity was the main characteristic of the Middle Ages' party cakes, and for an excellent reason: they generally contained a surprise, like ladies—dressed or not (you see, that one was around long before bachelor parties came into vogue)—or enough exotic animals to fill a zoo, or even a 28-member orchestra.

Next to its ancestors, the croquembouche may seem modest. It isn't! In France, no wedding reception or christening party would be complete without this pyramid of cream-filled puff pastry and caramel. It's one of the most spectacular French pastries, but, paradoxically, one of the easiest to prepare. This recipe makes a small gâteau which will serve fifteen, but you can double or triple the quantities to fit your guest list.

(VI-23)

Croquembouche
(French Wedding Cake)

Ingredients: (for one gâteau serving 15)
Base:
1 1/2	cups flour
1	tablespoon sugar
1/4	teaspoon salt
1/3	cup butter, softened
3/4 to 1	cup water

Choux:
2 1/2	cups pâte à choux (I-11)

Filling:
2 1/4	cups crème patissière (II-2) plain or flavored
1	cup crème chantilly (II-1)

Assembly:
2/3	cup caramel (II-8a)

Decoration:
2/3	cup caramel (II-8a)
	Jordan almonds

Base: It can be prepared a few days ahead of time. Preheat oven to 350-degrees. In a medium mixing bowl, stir together dry ingredients, then mix in the butter and enough water to make a stiff dough. Roll out to 1/2-inch thick, and, using a plate or a 10-inch cake board, cut out a 10-inch disk. Prick all over and bake on a lightly-oiled baking sheet for 20 minutes, or until golden brown.

You needn't worry about handling the dough too much and ending up with a tough crust, since the base serves only to hold up the cake, and is never eaten.

More➜

(Croquembouche, cont.)

You may feel, in that case, that the sugar and butter in the recipe are superfluous. They aren't: dough made without them would crack and fall to pieces.

Choux: Preheat oven to 425-degrees. Prepare pâte à choux, spoon into a pastry bag with a 1/2-inch fluted nozzle, and on a lightly-oiled baking sheets, pipe out about sixty 1 1/4-inch choux, then pipe out 4 or 5 2-inch long "s" shapes. Bake at 425-degrees for 10 minutes, then lower heat to 400-degrees and, propping the oven door open with a spoon, bake another 10 minutes, or until golden brown. Remove from oven and cool.

Filling: While choux are baking, prepare crème patissière. Cool. Prepare crème chantilly. Beat half the chantilly into the cooled crème patissière, then, with a rubber spatula, fold in the rest. Chill.

Assembly: Spoon the chilled filling into a pastry bag with a 1/8-inch star nozzle, and making a hole in the bottoms of the choux with the nozzle, fill. Place the pastry base on a wire rack, and the filled choux on a large plate beside it.

Prepare the caramel. When it turns a light amber color, remove it from the heat, where it will continue to cook and darken. Here, the time element is important. You must work quickly, before the caramel hardens.

Dip one side of each chou into the caramel, and attach them to the rim of the base, side by side, until a ring is formed. Hot caramel can cause painful burns, so be careful to hold the choux with the fingertips or use a long fork. Using fewer choux, make a slightly smaller ring on top of the first one, and continue with the rest of the choux until you have a hollow, cone-shaped pastry. If you see, toward the end, that you'll have some leftover choux, put them in the hollow part before sealing. Guests who can't eat crunchy caramel will appreciate it.

To decorate: Make more caramel, but this time, wait until it turns a deep amber color, it will look prettier and taste better. Drizzle most of it over the pastry, then use the remainder to attach the "s"-shaped choux at regular intervals around the base, and Jordan almonds all over. You could also decorate with candied violets, candied cherry halves, rosettes of crème au beurre, silver balls, etc.

Storage: The croquembouche must be eaten within several hours, especially if the weather is humid or stormy. Don't refrigerate it, as the caramel would melt and you'd end up with a large pile of choux to show for your work.

VI-24 DÉLICE AUX MARRONS

The Roman army, which was doubtless responsible for introducing the chestnut tree to ancient Gaul, was said to have survived a long siege thanks to its reserve of chestnuts. During the Middle Ages, chestnuts became such an important part of the French peasant's diet that the tree was nick-named "arbre à pain": "bread tree".

This unusual pastry made of creamy chestnuts hidden by a rich chocolate icing is sometimes surprising to the American palate. It will quickly become a favorite, especially among the children in the family.

(VI-24)
Délice aux Marrons

Ingredients: (for one 10-inch gâteau)

1	pound fresh chestnuts
2/3	cup heavy cream
1/2	cup (1 stick) butter, softened
2/3	cup sugar
1/4	teaspoon vanilla extract
	butter for loaf pan

With a sharp paring knife, peel off the tough outer skin of the chestnuts. In a large saucepan, cook chestnuts in just enough water to cover, for 30 minutes. Drain, and while they are still hot, peel off the thin inner skin. Reserve several chestnuts for the decoration, and grind the rest in a food mill. In a medium mixing bowl, beat together chestnuts and heavy cream until smooth.

In a large mixing bowl, beat together butter and sugar until creamy, beat in vanilla extract, then chestnuts. Line buttered 10-inch loaf pan with waxed paper, and spoon chestnut purée into it, pressing gently with a rubber spatula to eliminate air pockets. Refrigerate 1 hour.

Icing:

8	ounces semi-sweet chocolate
2	tablespoons water
2/3	cup heavy cream

While the gâteau is chilling, make the icing: In a medium saucepan, melt chocolate in water over very low heat. With a wooden spoon, stir in cream, then beat until smooth. Set aside to cool.

To assemble: Remove loaf pan from refrigerator and invert onto an oblong serving plate. Remove paper and chill 30 minutes. With a metal spatula, spread icing. Smooth well, or draw a fork across the icing to imitate tree bark. Decorate with chestnut halves. Refrigerate until serving.

Storage: This gâteau will keep well, covered and refrigerated, for 3 to 4 days.

VI-25 NÉGRE EN CHEMISE

Chocolate: a remedy or a poison? Madame de Sévigné believed first one, then the other. "If you are not feeling well," she wrote confidently to her daughter, "drink some chocolate. It will cure you." Later, she warned, "It is the source of vapors, palpitations…it soothes you for a time, then causes sudden fevers which lead to death." Apothecaries of the time obviously didn't agree: they recommended it to their clients as a purgative, a treatment for tuberculosis, and…an aphrodisiac!

A luscious cross between a cake and a steamed pudding, this rich chocolate dessert "dressed" with whipped cream ("chemise" means shirt) is particularly appreciated by children.

(VI-25)
Négre en Chemise

Ingredients: (for one 6-inch gâteau)
- 2/3 cup sugar
- 5 tablespoons flour
- 1/8 teaspoon salt

- 4 ounces semi-sweet chocolate
- 1/3 cup butter, softened
- 3 egg yolks
- 1/2 teaspoon vanilla extract

- 3 egg whites
- pinch salt
- 1 tablespoon sugar

- butter for mold

- 3 cups créme chantilly (II-1)

Preheat oven to 350-degrees. In a small bowl, combine dry ingredients. Over a double boiler, melt chocolate, then remove from heat and beat in butter, egg yolks, and vanilla, followed by dry ingredients. Stop beating as soon as blended.

In a large mixing bowl, beat egg whites and salt at high speed until soft peaks form. Add sugar and continue beating until very stiff but not dry. Beat a big spoonful of whites into chocolate mixture to soften it, then carefully fold chocolate mixture into rest of whites.

Spread batter in a generously buttered 6-inch charlotte mold or soufflé dish, place in a larger pan half full of hot water and bake, uncovered, for 40 to 50 minutes, or until a knife blade, inserted in the center, comes out clean. Cool 10 minutes, then invert onto a serving plate and chill at least 2 hours before serving. Immediately before serving, prepare créme chantilly, spoon into pastry bag, and cover the entire gâteau with rosettes or peaks of chantilly.

Storage: Refrigerate until serving—within 2 hours.

Chapter VII

Pies and Tarts
(Tartes)

VII-1   TARTE AUX POIRES AUX AMANDES

An ancient manuscript tells us about an unusual payment: The Pharaoh Cheops, one of the honored few to repose in Egypt's Great Pyramids, presented a thousand pears to his favorite magician as a reward for his extraordinary magic tricks.

This simple but exquisite almond-pear pie is just as good when made with fresh cherries, blackberries, peaches...

(VII-1)
Tarte aux Poires aux Amandes
(Almond-Pear Pie)

Ingedients: (for one 10-inch pie)
Crust:
> 14   ounces pâte sablée (I-7)
>   butter for pie plate

Filling:
> 4   medium pears or 1 (28-ounce) can of pears in light syrup
> 1 3/4   cups frangipane (II-7)
>   abricotage (II-11a))

Poaching Sugar Water:
> 1   cup water
> 1/3   cup sugar
> 1   teaspoon lemon juice

If you're using fresh pears, peel and core them, cut in half, and poach in sugar water until tender. Drain well. Canned pears must also be drained.

Preheat oven to 375-degrees. On a lightly-floured surface, roll out pastry to 1/8-inch thick, line a 10-inch buttered pie plate, and prick lightly. Spread frangipane evenly in the bottom, and with a sharp paring knife, trim pastry to 1/2-inch above the frangipane. Don't flute.

Cut the pears in thin slices, crosswise, without changing their shape, and arrange them on the bed of frangipane in a star-shaped pattern, leaving some space between them to allow the frangipane to rise around the fruit during baking. Press the pears to flatten slightly. Bake 30 to 40 minutes, or until crust and frangipane are well- browned. Don't underbake, as the frangipane would get soggy with cooling. Brush with nappage and serve warm.

Aux Pêches (Peach) (VII-1a): Replace pears with 7 or 8 ripe peach halves, or one large can yellow peaches. If you're using fresh peach halves, peel, remove stone, cut in half, and poach 10 minutes in sugar water (1 cup water, 1/3 cup sugar, and 1 teaspoon lemon juice), then drain. If you're using canned peaches, simply drain well. As above, prepare pastry and garnish with frangipane. Place

More→

(Tarte aux Poires, Cont.)

peach halves, flat side down, on work surface and cut into thin slices, as you would cut the pears (see above). Place peach halves on the unbaked frangipane, with one peach half in the center and the rest around it, in a star pattern. Press gently to flatten peaches slightly. Bake and glaze as above.

Aux Cerises (Cherries) (VII-1b): Replace pears with 8 to 10 ounces fresh cherries, or canned cherries in light syrup (not prepared pie filling). Wash and pit fresh cherries, then poach 10 minutes in sugar water (1 cup water, 1/3 cup sugar, and 1 teaspoon lemon juice), then drain. If you're using canned cherries, drain well. Prepare pastry and frangipane as above, then arrange cherries on unbaked frangipane. Bake and glaze as above.

Aux Mûres ou Myrtilles (Blackberry or Blueberry) (VII-1c): Replace pears with 8 to 10 ounces fresh or frozen blackberries or blueberries. Wash fresh berries. If you're using frozen berries, don't thaw them. Prepare and garnish pastry as above, then scatter berries evenly over frangipane. Bake and glaze as above.

Storage: The unbaked pie can be frozen. Bake unthawed pie as directed above, allowing about 10 minutes more.

VII-2 TARTE AUX FRAISES

For many centuries, only diminutive wild strawberries were known to Europeans, although attempts to "domesticate" them were made by the Dukes de Bourgogne, as witnessed by one of their accounts books dating from the 14th century. It mentions forty days of labor paid to gardeners for transplanting wild strawberries from the nearby forest to the ducal gardens. In the 18th century, a French officer returning from a military engagement in South America brought back a Chilean plant, heavy with large, succulent fruit. The officer's name? "Frézier". And that's why strawberries, in French, are now called "fraises".

An exciting combination of flavors and textures, this pie is so good that it's well worth the time and effort spent making the different components.

(VII-2)
Tarte aux Fraises
(Strawberry Pie)

Ingredients: (for one 10-inch pie)
Crust:

11	ounces pâte sablée (I-7)
1	heaping tablespoon frangipane (II-7)
	butter for pie plate

Filling:

1	layer génoise (I-1)
2	tablespoons sirop à entremets au kirsch (II-12a)
1/2	cup crème patissière (II-2)
1	tablespoon kirsch
1	pound strawberries
1/2	cup nappage (II-11b)
1	teaspoon kirsch

Preheat oven to 350-degrees. On a lightly-floured surface, roll out pastry to 1/8-inch thick, and line a 10-inch buttered pie plate. Trim to 1/2-inch high. Spread the frangipane evenly in the bottom and bake 30 minutes, or until the crust and frangipane are golden brown and completely baked. Cool.

With a damp cloth clean strawberries. Don't wash. Remove stems and set aside.

Using a serrated knife, cut a very thin (1/8-inch thick) slice of génoise and place it in the bottom of the pastry shell. Don't worry if it breaks or crumbles some. It won't be visible, and can consequently be patched together. Brush lightly (don't soak) with sirop à entremets. In a small bowl, beat together the crème patissière and kirsch until smooth and spreadable, then spread over the génoise, using a metal spatula and working carefully to avoid tearing up the delicate

More➤

(Tarte aux Fraises, Cont.)

cake. This may not seem like enough crème. It is, though, as more would overpower the other ingredients.

Over the bed of cake and crème patissière, arrange the strawberries in the following way: Place 1 whole strawberry in the center of the pie, then cut the others in half and lean them up against the central one at a 45-degree angle, continuing around in a spiral pattern until the whole pie is filled. This method probably sounds complicated when described, but you'll see that it's really very easy. It's much better than simply placing the whole strawberries side by side, because the pie is evenly garnished, rather than full of unsightly holes.

Gently heat the nappage and kirsch until smooth and thin enough to spread, and brush over the strawberries. Serve immediately.

aux Ananas (Pineapple) (VII-2a): Prepare tart as above, replacing strawberries with 1 to 1 1/2 pounds fresh or canned pineapple. Drain thoroughly and cut into wedges, then arrange on a cream-filled pastry shell the same way as strawberries. That is, place a small wedge in the center, then place concentric rings of pineapple wedges around it, with the smaller end of the wedges slightly raised (just as the smaller ends of the strawberries are raised). Glaze with warm abricotage (II-11a) and, if you wish, decorate with candied cherry halves or quarters.

Aux Framboises (Raspberry) (VII-2b): Prepare as above, replacing strawberries with same weight of fresh raspberries. Place whole berries very close together to form a solid, attractive layer of fruit. Brush with warm raspberry/currant nappage (II-11b).

Afterword: *Fontenelle, an enlightened 18th century philosopher, believed that the secret to good health and longevity lay in the modest strawberry. According to him, it even offered protection from the terrible epidemics that raged during his lifetime, which explains his enormous year-round consumption. One minor fact seems to add weight to his theory: Fontenelle lived to be 100 years old.*

VII-3 TARTE POLONAISE AU FROMAGE

George Sand, a 19th century French author, is better known for her turbulent love affair with Frédéric Chopin than for her novels. During an extended stay in Majorca, the composer insisted that his mistress frequently prepare his favorite pastry: a cheese pie which he'd grown to love as a child in his native Poland. Fluffy cream cheese and raisins in a tender shortcrust pastry shell make this pie similar to cheesecake.

(VII-3)
Tarte Polonaise au Fromage
(Polish Cheese Pie)

Ingredients: (for one 10-inch pie)
Crust:
- **14** ounces pâte sablée (I-7) or 11 ounces pâte brisée (I-6)

Filling:
- **1/3** cup raisins
  juice and finely-grated rind of one lemon

- **1** 8-ounce package cream cheese, softened
- **1** 3-ounce package cream cheese, softened
- **1/3** cup sugar
- **2** egg yolks

- **2** egg whites
  pinch salt
- **1** tablespoon sugar

In a small bowl, macerate the raisins, lemon juice, and rind for 1 hour.

Preheat oven to 350-degrees. On a lightly-floured surface, roll out pastry to 1/8-inch thick, line a 10-inch buttered pie plate, and prick. Trim and flute edges. Bake for 15 minutes, or until half-baked. Cool.

In a large mixing bowl, beat the cream cheese and sugar until light and fluffy, then beat in the egg yolks. Stir in the undrained raisins.

In another large mixing bowl, beat the egg whites and salt at high speed until soft peaks form. Add a tablespoon of sugar and continue beating until the whites are stiff but not dry. Beat 1/3 of whites into cream cheese mixture until smooth, then fold in the rest of whites. Spread filling in half-baked crust, and return pie to oven for 20 minutes, or until the filling is set and lightly browned. Cool 2 hours before removing from pie plate, and serve well-chilled.

Afterword: *During the Middle Ages, butter in pastries was often replaced by "fromage blanc", which spoiled less quickly. This unctuous dairy product, a kind of light cream cheese, was also a popular dessert. France's King Philippe Auguste was so fond of it, in fact, that while he was away on military campaigns, the queen sent him a regular supply as far as the battlefield.*

VII-4   GÂTEAU DE FROMAGE I

Most historians agree that the origin of yogurt can be traced back to the mists of antiquity, to the shores of the Balkan Sea. Proof that it has always been prized for its nutritional value: Its name, which was derived from a Bulgarian word meaning "long life".

A touch of yogurt lends its unique flavor to this light cheesecake, which can be made with or without fruit.

(VII-4)
Gâteau de Fromage I
(Cheesecake I)

Ingredients: (for one 8 or 9-inch cheesecake)

11	ounces pâte brisée (I-6) or pâte feuilletée rognures (I-8a) or 14 ounces pâte sablée (I-7)
	butter for pan

6	ounces cream cheese, softened
1	cup farmer's cheese
1/2	cup yogurt

3/4	cup sugar
3	egg yolks
1	tablespoon lemon juice
	finely-grated rind or 1/2 lemon

3	egg whites
1/8	teaspoon salt
3	tablespoons sugar

On a lightly-floured surface, roll out pastry to about 1/8-inch thick. Line an 8 or 9-inch springform buttered pan with 2-inch high sides, trim, and prick. Bake at 350-degrees for 15 minutes.

In a large mixing bowl, beat cream cheese until smooth and light. Beat in farmer's cheese and yogurt, followed by sugar, egg yolks, lemon juice, and rind.

In a deep mixing bowl, beat egg whites and salt at high speed until soft peaks form. Add sugar and continue beating until stiff but not dry. Beat a big spoonful of whites into cheese mixture, then carefully fold in rest of whites. Spread filling in lined pan and bake 40 minutes, or until filling is lightly-browned and set. To test, shake the pan gently. If baked, the center won't "tremble". Cool thoroughly before removing sides of springform pan. Serve chilled.

More→

(Gâteau de Fromage I, Cont.)

Gâteau de Fromage aux Ananas (Pineapple) (VII-4a): Replace lemon juice and rind with 1 tablespoon rum. Spread half the filling in lined pan, then sprinkle on 1/2 cup small pineapple chunks. Spread on rest of filling, bake and serve as above.

Gâteau de Fromage aux Cerises (Cherry) (VII-4b): Replace lemon juice and rind with 1 tablespoon kirsch. Spread 1/2 the filling in lined pan, then sprinkle on 1/2 cup pitted, poached (or canned, drained) red cherries. Spread on rest of filling, bake and serve as above.

Storage: Cover with plastic or aluminum foil and refrigerate up to 48 hours.

Afterword: *A health enthusiast before his time, France's King François I drank very little wine, ate moderately, and, at his doctor's urging, consumed a daily portion of yogurt.*

VII-5   GÂTEAU DE FROMAGE II

In medieval France, "flaons" made with white cheese, eggs, and honey were popular desserts, and up until the late 19th century, the "talmouse", a similar pastry, was a favorite among royalty and commoners.

The French still love cheesecake! As proven by this easy recipe, which can be changed to fit anyone's taste.

(VII-5)

Gâteau de Fromage II
(Cheesecake II)

Ingredients: (for one 9 or 10-inch cheesecake)

14	ounces pâte sablée (I-7) or 11 ounces pâte brisée (I-6) or pâte feuilletée rognures (I-8a)
	butter for pie plate
16	ounces cream cheese (two 8-ounce packages), softened
2/3	cup sugar
1	whole egg
1	egg yolk
	pinch salt
1/2	teaspoon vanilla extract

Preheat oven to 350-degrees. Butter a 10-inch pie plate with straight sides or an 9-inch springform pan. On a lightly-floured surface, roll out pastry to about 1/8—inch thick. Line prepared pan. Prick lightly and trim. Line with foil and fill crust with rice or dried beans, taking care to push them up against the edges so they won't slide down during baking, and bake about 15 minutes, until half done. Remove foil and rice or beans.

In a large mixing bowl, beat cream cheese and sugar until light, then beat in egg, yolk, salt, and vanilla extract. Turn into half-baked shell and return to the oven for 20 to 30 minutes, or until the filling is set and very lightly browned on top. Serve chilled.

Gâteau de Fromage à l'Orange (Orange) (VII-5a): Replace vanilla extract with 2 tablespoons finely grated orange rind, 1 tablespoon Grand Marnier or Cointreau, and 2 tablespoons orange juice. Bake as directed above. Place fresh or canned mandarin slices around the rim and brush the whole gâteau with warm abricotage (II-11a).

More➤

(Gâteau de Fromage II, Cont.)

Gâteau de Fromage aux Cerises (Cherry) (VII-5b): Replace vanilla extract with 2 tablespoons kirsch or 1 teaspoon almond extract. Wash and pit 1/2 pound fresh cherries (or simply use canned cherries; you'll need about 1 cup) and cut them in half. Prepare crust and filling as above. Blend cherries into filling just before pouring it into crust. Bake and serve as above.

Gâteau de Fromage Plombières (with Candied Fruit) (VII-5c): Omit vanilla extract. Macerate 1/2 cup chopped candied fruit with 2 tablespoons rum or cognac, for 1 hour. Blend into unbaked filling. Bake and serve as above.

Gâteau de Fromage Marbré au Chocolat (Chocolate Marble) (VII-5d): Prepare filling as above, reserving 1/3 cup. Beat 2 teaspoons unsweetened cocoa into reserved filling. Spread vanilla filling in a partially baked pastry shell, then drop dollops of chocolate filling here and there. With a knife, swirl to form a marbled pattern. Bake and serve as above.

VII-6   PAVLOVA AUX ANANAS

A 19th-century world traveler was responsible for the kiwi's "immigration" from China, where it was called the "fruit of health" (not surprisingly, since it contains ten times as much vitamin C as lemons), to New Zealand. Brown and slightly hairy, the kiwi resembles the New Zealand bird which lent it its name. This light, refined pie of kiwi fruit and pineapple in a meringue crust was named in honor of Russia's great ballerina, Anna Pavlova.

(VII-6)

Pavlova aux Ananas
(Pineapple-Kiwi Pie)

Ingredients: (for one 10-inch pie)
Crust: same as for tarte meringuée (VII-7)

Nappage: abricotage (apricot glaze) (II-11a)

Filling:

2	cups crème chantilly (whipped cream) (II-1)
1/2	small fresh pineapple
3	tablespoons kirsch
3	kiwis

Prepare crust. While it's baking, with a sharp knife, peel pineapple, cut in 1/4-inch thick slices, then cut in 1 1/2-inch wide "fans". Remove fibrous center. In a medium mixing bowl, macerate with kirsch, stirring occasionally, for 1 hour. Drain, reserving 2 tablespoons juice.

More➤

(Pavlova aux Ananas, Cont.)

Prepare crème chantilly, and carefully fold in juice. Peel kiwis and slice thin. Spread chantilly in pie crust. Starting on the outer rim, make a ring of overlapping kiwis, then make a triple ring of pineapple, overlapping well. Finish with a ring of kiwis, and one kiwi slice in the center. Brush with apricot glaze.

Storage: Refrigerate until serving. Serve within 2 hours.

Pavlova aux Fraises (Strawberry) (VII-6a): Replace pineapple and kiwis with about 1 pound fresh and cleaned strawberries. As above, prepare meringue shell and fill with crème chantilly. Cut the strawberries in half, lengthwise, and arrange on chantilly in a decorative fashion. Brush with currant/raspberry glaze (II-11b). Refrigerate until serving. Serve within 2 hours.

Pavlova à la Macédoine de Fruits (Mixed Fruit) (VII-6b): Replace fruit in original recipe with about 2 pounds, total weight, assorted fresh (or in some cases canned) fruit. Strawberries, peaches, pineapple, cherries, raspberries, kiwis, and bananas are possibilities. Prepare the meringue crust and fill with chantilly, as above, then prepare the fruit:

Bananas: Peel, cut in 1/4-inch slices, and sprinkle liberally with lemon juice.

Strawberries: Rinse quickly and pat dry. Cut in half, lengthwise, leaving a few whole, if you wish.

Raspberries: Use whole, unwashed fruit.

Pineapple: Use canned, sliced pineapple, well drained and cut in 1 inch "fans". Or use fresh pineapple, cut the same size.

Cherries: Wash, dry, and pit.

Peaches: Peel, remove stone, and cut in thin slices.

Kiwis: Peel and cut in thin slices.

Arrange the fruit on chantilly in a "disorderly" way, mixing colors and shapes as much as possible. This goes somewhat against the traditional, symetrical arrangement but can look surprisingly elegant. However, if you're afraid of making a mess the first time you prepare this tart, you can do it in a more orderly fashion.

For instance, place a whole strawberry in the center, around it, place an overlapping ring of banana slices, then a double row of cherries, a ring of kiwi slices, and so on, alternating colors, shapes and sizes to produce an attractive arrangement. Brush finished tart with warm abricotage (II-11a), then refrigerate until serving. Serve within 2 hours.

VII-7   TARTE MERINGUÉE AU CHOCOLAT

Some historians affirm that meringue wasn't invented in Poland, but in Germany, by a pastry cook named Mehr. Wherever it was created, Marie Leszczynski still gets the credit for introducing it to France.

The meringue crust enriched with chopped almonds can be made several days ahead of time, and garnished at the last minute with chocolate chantilly.

(VII-7)
Tarte Meringuée au Chocolat
(Meringue Tart with Chocolate)

Ingredients: (for one 10-inch pie)
Crust:

3	egg whites (about 1/2 cup)
3/4	cup sugar
1/2	cup finely-chopped (not ground) almonds
	butter and flour for pan

Filling:

3	cups crème chantilly au chocolat (II-1a)
	chocolate sprinkles for decoration

Preheat oven to lowest setting. Prepare the crust like a meringue suisse. That is, in a double boiler, beat egg whites and sugar at high speed until hot, for about 5 minutes. Place pan in cold water to accelerate cooling, and beat for another 5 minutes, or until cool. Stir in almonds. Spoon meringue into a buttered and floured 10-inch pie plate (with removable bottom), and spread around with a spoon to form a shell with well- defined sides.

Bake, the oven door propped open with a spoon, for about 45 minutes, until the shell is a uniform deep cream color. It should be dry and crusty on the outside, but slightly chewy on the inside. Cool thoroughly, then remove from pie plate.

While the pie shell is baking, prepare the crème chantilly au chocolat. Chill.

To garnish: Place meringue shell on a serving plate, and spread in about 2/3 of the chantilly, smoothing with a spoon to make an even surface. Spoon the rest of chantilly into a pastry bag with a 5/8-inch fluted nozzle and cover the surface with rosettes or "shells" of chantilly. If you don't have a pastry bag, spread on all the chantilly at once, making little peaks or swirls with the back of the spoon. Decorate with chocolate sprinkles. Serve the same day.

Storage: Meringue shell can be kept in a cool, dry place, wrapped in plastic, for several days. Refrigerate garnished pie until serving.

VII-8   TARTE DE LINZE

According to an old legend, the world's first raspberries came from the very spot on Mount Ida where the judgement of Paris, one of Greek mythology's most renowned episodes, took place.

This specialty, in which a sweet raspberry filling is offset by tart apples and cinnamon, was originally from the Austrian town of Linz.

(VII-8)
Tarte de Linze
(Linzer Pie)

Ingredients: (for one 10-inch pie)
Crust:

14	ounces pâte sablée (I-7)
	butter for pie plate

Filling:

2	large apples
1/2	cup water
1 1/4	cups raspberry preserves
1/2	teaspoon cinnamon
1	tablespoon cornstarch
2	teaspoons rum

Cut off 1/4 of pâte sablée and set aside. On a lightly-floured surface, roll out the rest to 1/8-inch thick and line a buttered 10-inch pie plate. Prick lightly with a fork. Bake at 350-degrees for 20 minutes, or until crust is just beginning to take on color.

Meanwhile, peel and core apples, quarter them, and place in the saucepan with water. Cover and cook until tender. Drain, whirl in the blender (or mash with a fork) and mix with the rest of filling ingredients. Pour into prepared crust.

Lightly knead rest of dough to make it easier to handle, then roll it out, and, with a pastry cutter or paring knife, cut long strips about 3/4-inch wide. Arrange them over the filling in a diamond-shaped lattice-work pattern. Press the ends of the strips into the pastry. Bake 30 to 40 minutes, until the crust is golden brown and the filling bubbly and thick. Serve warm.

Variation: Omit the crisscross top. Before serving, pipe or spoon crème chantilly (II-1) over the top, and garnish with semi-sweet chocolate shavings.

Note: Use a tart variety of apple (for example, Pippins or Granny Smiths) for the filling. Milder apples are acceptable but contrast less with the preserves.

Storage: Can be frozen, baked, for up to 2 months. Allow to thaw, then heat at 350-degrees for 15 minutes to recrisp.

VII-9   TARTE PAYSANNE À LA RHUBARBE

Of Asiatic origin, rhubarb was well known in western Europe by the 7th century. It was principally used by monks in their pharmaceutical preparations, and didn't come into wide use as a fruit until a relatively recent period. This classical "peasant pie", which is especially popular in Normandy and Alsace, can also be prepared with apples, pears, or peaches.

(VII-9)

Tarte Paysanne à la Rhubarbe
(Country-Style Rhubarb Pie)

Ingredients: (for one 10-inch pie)
Crust:

11	ounces pâte brisée (I-6) or pâte feuilletée rognures (I-8a)
	butter for pie plate

Filling:

12	ounces (3/4 pound) rhubarb
1/2	cup sugar
1/4	cup (1/2 stick) butter
1/4	cup sugar
1/3	cup heavy cream
1	whole egg
1	egg yolk
1/2	teaspoon vanilla extract

Wash and scrape the rhubarb, then cut into 1-inch pieces. Place in a collander over a large plate and sprinkle on sugar. Stir, then cover and let stand several hours, to allow the excess juice and acidity to drain off. Pat dry with paper towels.

Preheat oven to 350-degrees. On a lightly-floured surface, roll out pastry to 1/8-inch thick. Line a buttered 10-inch pie plate, prick, and trim. (If you're using rognures, refrigerate untrimmed, for 1 hour before baking, to reduce the risk of excessive shrinkage in the oven). Line with foil and half fill with beans or rice. Bake 15 to 20 minutes, until half done. Remove foil and beans or rice.

In a medium saucepan, melt butter, then whisk in rest of filling ingredients until frothy. Arrange rhubarb in the half baked pie shell, to form an even layer, then pour filling over it. Bake for another 20 minutes, or until the custard is golden brown and set. Serve warm or cold, dusted with powdered sugar.

Tarte Paysanne aux Pommes (Apple) (VII-9a): Prepare as above, with 4 medium-sized tart cooking apples. Peel and core apples, cut in half, then cut each half into 9 pieces. Arrange apple chunks in unbaked pastry shell, bake 20 minutes, then pour on custard mixture and finish baking.

More→

(Tarte Paysanne, Cont.)

Tarte Bérgère (Peach) (VII-9b): Prepare this prettily-named "shepherdess pie" as above, with 4 medium-sized, ripe yellow peaches. Peel and cut like apples, then place in partially baked pastry shell, pour on custard mixture, and finish baking.

Can also be made with an equal number of fresh tart pears. If they're not totally ripe, prebake partially as apples.

Storage: Cover and refrigerate until serving. Serve within 24 hours.

VII-10   DARTOIS AUX PÊCHES

The ancient Chinese believed that the peach had the power to preserve the body after death. This old belief explains why this highly esteemed fruit, cultivated in China since the 5th century B.C., is the symbol of prosperity, health, and friendship. Even modern-day Chinese exchange peaches—real ones, or porcelain reproductions thereof—as a token of mutual esteem.

This large pâte feuilletée and peach pastry was probably named for the 19th century vaudevillist Dartois.

(VII-10)

Dartois aux Pêches
(Peach Dartois)

Ingredients: (for one 8 x 12-inch dartois)
Crust:

1	pound 6 ounces pâte feuilletée classique (I-8) or
	pâte demi-feuilletée (I-9)

Filling:

1 1/2	pounds fresh ripe peaches or 2 medium cans (1-pound, each) peaches in light syrup, drained
1	tablespoon butter
1/3	cup sugar
3	tablespoons cornstarch
1/4	teaspoon almond extract
	pinch salt
1	egg, beaten with a pinch of salt
	powdered sugar (optional)

More➤

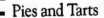

(Dartois aux Pêches, Cont.)

Pâte feuilletée classique can be prepared ahead of time, but if you're using pâte demi-feuilletée, make it immediately before using.

Peel and slice peaches, or drain canned peaches well, and slice. In a medium saucepan, melt butter, then whisk in rest of filling ingredients. Add peaches and cook, stirring constantly, over medium heat until thick. Cool.

Preheat oven to 475-degrees. On a lightly-floured surface, roll out 1/2 of pâte to an 8 x 12 x 1/8-inch rectangle. With a chef's knife, trim off uneven edges, then place on an ungreased baking sheet and prick lightly. Brush a 1-inch wide band around the edge with beaten egg. Spread cooled filling to within 1 inch of edge, being careful not to touch the band of egg.

Roll out rest of pâte, trim, prick, and place on top of filling. Press edges firmly to seal, brush with beaten egg, and with a sharp knife, make decorative slits in the top. Bake at 475-degrees for 5 minutes, then lower heat to 425-degrees and bake for another 20 to 30 minutes, or until puffed up and golden brown. If you want a glazed finish, dust with powdered sugar 10 minutes before the end of baking. Serve warm.

Aux Pommes (Apple) (VII-10a):
    12   ounces apples (about 2 medium-sized apples)
     1   cup compote de pommes (II-14)
    1/2 teaspoon vanilla extract
         pinch cinnamon

Peel, core, and dice apples. In a medium mixing bowl, stir together apples, compote, vanilla extract, and cinnamon. Prepare as above, substituting peach filling with apple filling. Serve warm.

Storage: Wrap in plastic and refrigerate 2 to 3 days. Can also be frozen, unbaked. Bake as directed above, without thawing, but allow about 10 minutes longer.

VII-11 TARTE AUX BANANES ET À LA NOIX DE COCO

An old Hindu legend affirms that the forbidden fruit of Eden wasn't really an apple, but a banana! Consequently, throughout the Indies, the banana tree bears a name best translated as "Adam's fig tree" A coconut topping complements the baked banana filling in this unusual pie.

(VII-11)
Tarte aux Bananes et à la Noix de Coco
(Banana-Coconut Pie)

Ingredients: (for one 10-inch pie)
Crust:

11	ounces pâte brisée (I-6) or pâte feuilletée rognures (I-8a)
	butter for pie plate

Filling:

4	medium bananas, ripe but firm
1/4	cup sugar
1	tablespoon rum
	juice of 1 lemon
1/4	cup sugar
1/2	cup flaked, unsweetened coconut
	juice of 1/2 lemon
1	egg
1	tablespoon rum
2	tablespoons coconut

In a medium mixing bowl, macerate sliced bananas, sugar, rum, and lemon juice for 1 hour, stirring from time to time. The lemon juice is essential because it accentuates the bananas' flavor, and keeps them from turning black during baking.

In another medium mixing bowl, whisk together sugar, coconut, lemon juice, egg, and rum. Place a collander over the bowl, and turn the macerated bananas into it so that the juice drains into the bowl. Mix well.

Preheat oven to 350-degrees. On a lightly-floured surface, roll out pastry to 1/8-inch thick, line a 10-inch buttered pie plate, and prick well so that it won't puff up in places during baking.

Line with foil and add a handful of dried beans or rice in the bottom. Bake for about 15 minutes, until the crust is half done. Remove foil and beans or rice. Spread bananas evenly in the bottom and pour the coconut mixture over it. Sprinkle with more coconut and return to oven for 30 minutes longer, or until the top is golden brown and set. Cool 15 minutes, then serve.

More→

(Tarte aux Bananes, Cont.)

Tarte aux Bananes aux Amandes (Banana/Almond) (VII-11a): Substitute 1/2 cup ground almonds for the coconut in the topping, and top unbaked pie with blanched slivered almonds and raisins macerated in rum.

> *Afterword: Joséphine Tascher de la Pagerie, a modest Creole who became Empress of France by her marriage to Napoleon Bonaparte, was known for her love of exotic fruits, and especially of the succulent bananas from her native Martinique. Her illustrious husband didn't discover them until his exile on the island of Sainte-Hélène, where they became one of his favorite desserts.*

VII-12 TARTE AU CITRON

Hercules, the mortal son of Zeus and Alcmene, won immortality by performing the twelve tasks demanded by Hera. One of them was the harvest of "golden apples" which, according to certain specialists in Greco-Roman mythology, were really lemons.

(VII-12)
Tarte au Citron
(Baked Lemon Pie)

Ingredients: (for one 10-inch pie)
Crust:
    14   ounces pâte sablée (I-7) or 11 ounces brisée (I-6)
            butter for pie plate

Filling:
    1/3   cup butter
      1   cup sugar
      4   eggs
            juice of 4 lemons
            finely-grated rind of 2 lemons
      1   lemon, thinly sliced

Preheat oven to 350-degrees. On a lightly-floured surface, roll out dough to 1/8-inch thick, line a buttered 10-inch pie plate, prick lightly, trim edge, and flute. Bake for 15 minutes or until half done.

In a small saucepan, melt butter, then whisk in rest of filling ingredients. Pour into pie shell, arrange lemon slices on top and bake for 30 minutes, or until filling is set and surface is lightly browned. Cool 1 hour before serving.

Storage: Can be frozen, unbaked. Bake unthawed pie as directed above, allowing about 10 minutes more.

VII-13   TARTE PRINCESSE AUX GROSEILLES

In medieval England, the sour red berries imported from Corinth were known, logically enough, as "raysons of Courante" (grapes from Corinth). Centuries of widespread use slowly changed and shortened the name to "currants".

In this delicious "princess pie", tart red currants are nicely set off by a topping of crème chiboust.

(VII-13)

Tarte Princesse aux Groseilles
(Red Currant "Princess" Pie)

Ingredients: (for one 10-inch tart)

14	ounces pâte sablée (I-7) or 11 ounces pâte brisée (I-6) or pâte feuilletée rognures (I-8a)
	butter for springform pan
2	cups fresh or frozen red currants
1	teaspoon kirsch
1/2	cup red currant jelly
4 1/2	cups crème chiboust (II-5)
	powdered sugar

Preheat oven to 350-degrees. Butter a 10-inch springform pan. On a lightly-floured surface, roll out pastry to 1/8-inch thick. With a fork or rolling pastry piercer, prick well, and line pan with dough. If you're using rognures, refrigerate 1 hour before baking. Line pan with foil and fill partially with dried beans or rice, pushing them up against the high sides to keep the pastry from sliding down during baking. Bake 15 minutes, then remove the foil and beans or rice and bake another 5 minutes, until the pastry is half baked. Cool.

While the crust is baking, prepare the crème chiboust (II-5). Set aside to cool.

Place currants in a medium mixing bowl. In a small saucepan, heat jelly to a boil, then turn down heat and simmer until jelly is thick. Pour over currants, add kirsch, and stir gently, just until blended. Spread in bottom of partially-baked pie shell.

Spread the crème chiboust over the fruit, then with a metal spatula, smooth the surface, making it as even and flat as possible. Dust with powdered sugar and return tart to oven until crust and crème are golden brown, about 30 minutes. Remove from oven, cool to room temperature, then carefully remove from springform pan, and slide onto a serving plate. Refrigerate until serving. Serve within 2 hours.

More➤

(Tarte Princesse, Cont.)

Tarte Princesse aux Ananas (Pineapple) (VII-13a):
- 1   medium can (about 1 pound) crushed pineapple, drained, or 1 fresh 1 1/2-pound pineapple, peeled, cored, finely chopped and drained
- 1   teaspoon rum or kirsch
- 1/2   cup abricotage (II-11a)

Prepare and bake as above, replacing filling with above ingredients. Simmer abricotage until thick, mix in pineapple and rum.

Tarte Princesse aux Pruneaux (Prunes) (VII-13b):
- 2 1/2   cups pitted prunes
- 1 1/2   cups armagnac or red wine
- 1/4   cup sugar

In a medium mixing bowl, combine prunes, armagnac or red wine, and sugar. Macerate overnight. Drain excess liquid into a small saucepan and simmer until thick. Mix with prunes. Prepare tart as above, replacing the currant filling with prune filling.

VII-14 CLAFOUTIS AUX CERISES

A leading Parisian fashion designer was so fond of this regional specialty from Limoges that he named his baby daughter "Marie Clafoutis". Originally prepared solely with black cherries, this nourishing fruit and custard pie can be made with almost any fruit you may have on hand, such as fresh apples or pears, raisins, or prunes.

(VII-14)
Clafoutis aux Cerises
(Cherry Fruit & Custard Pie)

Ingredients: (for one 10-inch pie)
Crust:

11	ounces pâte brisée (I-6) or pâte feuilletée rognures (I-8a)
	butter for pie plate

Filling:

1/2	pound fresh sour cherries
2/3	cup sugar
1/4	cup flour
1/8	teaspoon salt
1 1/2	cups milk
1	whole egg
3	egg yolks
1/4	teaspoon vanilla extract

Wash and pit cherries. Preheat oven to 350-degrees. On a lightly-floured surface, roll pastry out to 1/8-inch thick. Line a buttered 10-inch pie plate, prick lightly with a fork, and trim. If you're using rognures, refrigerate, untrimmed, for 1 hour before using so that it will relax and be less likely to shrink in the oven. Trim and use as above.

Line pan with foil and partially fill with beans or rice. Bake for 15 minutes, or until crust is half done. Remove foil and beans or rice.

In a large mixing bowl, stir together dry ingredients. Whisk in enough milk to make a smooth paste, then whisk in whole egg and yolks, followed by rest of milk, then vanilla extract. Pour into lined pie plate and sprinkle cherries over filling. Bake 30 to 40 minutes, or until top is lightly browned and custard is set. Serve warm or cold.

Storage: Refrigerate until serving. Serve within 48 hours.

Afterword: *Louis XV was said to have found a way of simultaneously enjoying his two weaknesses: pretty women and cherries. He insisted that his mistress, the Countess of Esparbes, peel his favorite fruit for him, which he rolled in sugar before eating.*

VII-15 TARTE AUX NOIX

The spectacular military conquests of Charlemagne which inspired the epic poem "La Chanson de Roland" are known the world over, but his passion for walnuts is less known. When he wasn't away at war, he enjoyed spending time on his domains in Aix-la-Chapelle, where he supervised the walnut harvesting and selected the choicest nuts for his personal consumption.

This recipe was given to me by an innkeeper from the Vercors, one of France's major walnut-producing regions. It originally called for a complicated caramel-making procedure, but I've adapted it so that brown sugar can be used without detracting from its original delicacy.

(VII-15)
Tarte aux Noix
(Walnut Pie)

Ingredients: (for one 10-inch tarte)
Crust:
    11   ounces pâte brisée (I-6) or pâte feuilletée rognures (I-8a)

Filling:
  1/2   cup (1 stick) butter
    1   cup lightly-packed brown sugar
  1/2   cup white sugar
    1   tablespoon flour
    2   tablespoons heavy cream
    2   eggs
    1   tablespoon sherry (optional)
    1   cup coarsely-chopped walnuts (or almonds)
        pinch salt

        butter for pie plate

Preheat oven to 350-degrees. On a lightly-floured surface, roll out the pastry to 1/8-inch thick, line a buttered 10-inch pie plate, and prick with a fork, Trim and flute. Bake for 15 minutes or until crust is half done.

In a medium saucepan, melt butter, then whisk in the rest of the ingredients. Pour into the pie shell and bake for 30 minutes, or until the filling is golden brown and set. This pie, which is equally good made with an equal amount of almonds **(Tart aux Amandes) (VII-15a)**, is best when served warm, either plain or with crème chantilly (II-1).

Tarte aux Noix au Chocolat(Chocolate/Walnut) (VII-15b): Over a double boiler or a pot of boiling water, melt 4 ounces semi-sweet chocolate with the butter. Whisk in the rest of ingredients and bake as directed above. This rich, fudgy pie is especially good served warm, with a scoop of vanilla ice cream.

Afterword: *In some regions of medieval France, peasants paid their taxes with their most important product: walnuts.*

VII-16   TARTE ANTILLAISE

"It's the king of fruits, which is doubtless why the King of kings placed a crown on its head: as an indication of its royalty." I don't see any reason for contradicting this affirmation made in the 16th century by a certain Father Dutertre. The fruit in question? The pineapple, *naturellement!* This pie is a combination of flavors from the French Antilles: coconut, pineapple, and rum.

(VII-16)

Tarte Antillaise
(Antilles Pie)

Ingredients: (for one 10-inch pie)
Crust:

14	ounces pâte sablée (I-7) or 11 ounces pâte brisée (I-6)
2	tablespoons frangipane (II-7)
	butter for pie plate

Filling:

1	cup finely-chopped fresh pineapple or crushed canned pineapple
2	tablespoons rum
1	tablespoon brown sugar
2 1/4	cups crème patissière (II-2)
1/2	cup flaked, unsweetened coconut
2	cups crème chantilly (II-1)
2	tablespoons toasted coconut

Drain pineapple, then place in a small mixing bowl with rum and brown sugar. Macerate for 1 hour.

Preheat oven to 350-degrees. On a lightly-floured surface, roll out pastry to 1/8-inch thick, line a buttered 10-inch pie plate, and prick. Spread frangipane in the bottom, trim, and flute edge. Bake 20 minutes, or until golden brown. Cool.

While pastry is baking, prepare crème patissière. Remove from heat, beat in coconut, and cool. Place collander or large strainer over the saucepan, and turn the pineapple mixture into it so that the juice drains into the crème patissière. Stir until smooth, then chill. Prepare crème chantilly, and, with a rubber spatula, fold about 1/2 cup into the cold crème patissière.

Spread pineapple evenly in bottom of pie shell, then spread on crème patissière. Spoon rest of chantilly into pastry bag and cover surface with rosettes of chantilly, or if you don't have a pastry bag, spread the chantilly carefully over the top, making small peaks. Sprinkle with toasted coconut. Chill 2 hours before serving.

Storage: Refrigerate until serving. Serve within 24 hours.

VII-17   TARTE AUX POMMES

Solon, the great Athenian statesman and poet, advised newlywed couples to eat an apple before retiring on their wedding night. Did he consider the apple to be a simple good luck token, or an aphrodisiac? History books generally neglect to mention one fact which leads me to opt for the latter possibility: Solon was the proud owner of a very successful...bawdy house!

(VII-17)
Tarte aux Pommes
(Apple Tart)

Ingredients: (for one 10-inch tarte)
Crust:

11	ounces pâte brisée (I-6) or rognures (I-8a)
	butter for pie plate

Filling:

1	cup compôte de pommes (applesauce) (II-14)
4	large apples
1/2	cup nappage

Preheat oven to 350-degrees. On a lightly-floured surface, roll out pastry to 1/8-inch thick. Line a buttered 10-inch pie plate, prick lightly with a fork, trim and flute edge. Spread compôte evenly in bottom of unbaked pie shell.

Peel and core apples, then cut in half, lengthwise. Place each half on the work surface, flat side down, and with a paring knife, cut widthwise in thin slices. Slice the rest of apples the same way, then arrange them on top of the compôte, starting with the outer edge, and going toward the center, working in a circular fashion.

Overlap the slices some, for good coverage. Bake 30 to 40 minutes, or until the crust is golden brown. The apples should be tender but not mushy, and should hold their shape. Cool 15 minutes, then brush with warm nappage and serve.

Storage: Can be frozen, unbaked. Bake, unthawed, as directed above, allowing about 10 minutes more.

VII-18   TARTE MERINGUÉE AU CITRON

Vitamin C may not have been discovered until recently, but its benefits have been known for much longer. Beginning in the 19th century, before leaving on long voyages, sea captains the world over laid in large supplies of citrus fruits to prevent scurvy. In fact, that's how British sailors came to be called "limies". Lemon meringue pie, one of America's all-time favorites, has also been enjoyed by generations of French families.

(VII-18)
Tarte Meringuée au Citron
(Lemon Meringue Pie)

Ingredients: (for one 10-inch tarte)
Crust:

14	ounces pâte sablée (I-7)
	butter for pie plate

Filling:

1/3	cup sugar
	pinch salt
4	tablespoons flour
1 1/3	cups milk
3	egg yolks
	juice of 3 lemons
	finely-grated rind of 1 1/2 lemons

Meringue:

3	egg whites
	pinch salt
3/4	cup sugar

Preheat oven to 350-degrees. On a lightly-floured surface, roll out pastry to 1/8-inch thick, line a buttered 10-inch pie plate, prick well and trim. Bake 20 to 30 minutes, until golden brown. Cool.

With the filling ingredients, make a crème patissière. That is, in a medium saucepan, mix together sugar, salt, and flour. Whisk in enough milk to make a smooth paste, then beat in the egg yolks. Stir in the rest of the milk, and cook, stirring constantly, over medium heat, until the mixture thickens and comes to bubble. Continue cooking for one or two more minutes, stirring, then remove from heat and stir in lemon juice and rind. Cover and set aside to cool.

In a large mixing bowl, beat egg whites and salt at high speed until soft peaks form. Add 1 tablespoon of the sugar and continue beating until stiff but not dry. Lower the speed and gradually beat in rest of sugar. If the sugar hasn't dissolved by the time it's beaten in, it will in the oven.

With a rubber spatula, carefully fold in 1/3 of meringue into crème patissière, then spread the filling in the cooled pie shell. Spoon the rest of the meringue into a pastry bag with a 1/8-inch star nozzle, and cover the surface of the pie

More➤

with small peaks of meringue. If you don't have a pastry bag, you can spread the meringue over the cooled filling (very gently, though, as the filling is soft).

Brown meringue under the broiler for 1 or 2 minutes, leaving the oven door open and watching closely as it browns. Chill at least 2 hours before serving.

Storage: Refrigerate until serving. Serve within 48 hours.

VII-19   TARTE ST. NICHOLAS
Did you know that St. Nicholas really existed? A 5th-century bishop from an eastern province of France, he was canonized—so the story goes—after having resuscitated three little children he'd discovered cut up and hung in a wicked innkeeper's salthouse. Small wonder he became the patron saint of children!

For many centuries thereafter, St. Nicholas Day was celebrated on December 6, with the exchange of small presents and especially gingerbread men in the form of the sainted bishop. In Normandy, where the custom still exists, the day is marked with different pastries, including this spicy apple pie. In this delicious deep dish pie, tart apples are hidden under a spicy, cake-like topping and a Calvados glaze.

(VII-19)
Tarte St. Nicholas
(St. Nicholas Apple Tart)

Ingredients: (for one 10-inch pie)
14 ounces pâte sablée (I-7) or 11 ounces pâte brisée (I-6) or 11 ounces pâte feuilletée rognures (I-8a)
butter for springform pan

Filling:
1 pound tart green apples (Granny Smiths or Pippins, for instance)
3 tablespoons sugar
1/4 cup raisins

Topping:
1/2 cup flour
1 1/2 teaspoons baking powder
pinch salt
1 teaspoon cinnamon

1/3 cup butter, softened
1/4 cup sugar
2 eggs
1/2 cup compôte de pommes (II-14) or cooked mashed apples
1/2 teaspoon vanilla extract

More→

(Tarte St. Nicholas, Cont.)

Glaze:
- 3/4   cup powdered sugar
- 1   tablespoon Calvados or water
- 2   tablespoons chopped toasted almonds or hazelnuts or prâlin (II-9)

Preheat oven to 350-degrees. Butter a 10-inch springform pan. On a lightly-floured surface, roll out pastry to 1/8-inch thick. With a fork or rolling pastry piercer, prick pastry well, then line springform pan and trim.

Filling: Peel, core, and dice apples. In a medium mixing bowl, stir together with sugar and raisins.

Topping: In a small bowl, combine dry ingredients. In a medium mixing bowl, beat butter and sugar until light and creamy, then beat in the whole eggs, compôte or mashed apples, and vanilla extract. Lower speed of mixer and beat in dry ingredients. Beat just until well blended.

Spread apples in unbaked pastry shell. Spoon batter into a pastry bag with a 5/8-inch nozzle, and cover the filling completely, starting at the outer edge, and piping around in a spiral.

Bake 40 to 50 minutes, or until pastry and topping are golden brown. Cool 30 minutes, then remove from pan.

Glaze: In a small bowl, beat together powdered sugar and Calvados or water until smooth. If the glaze is too thin, beat in a little more sugar; if it's too thick, beat in more liquid, a drop at a time. Drizzle over warm (not hot) tart. Sprinkle with chopped nuts or prâlin. Serve warm.

Tarte St. Nicholas aux Cerises (Cherry) (VII-19a): Prepare crust and topping as above. Replace apple filling with 1 pound sour cherries (washed and pitted) and 3 tablespoons sugar. Omit raisins. Finish preparation and baking as above. In glaze, replace Calvados with same amount of kirsch.

Tarte St. Nicholas aux Pêches (Peach) (VII-19b): Prepare crust and topping as above. Replace apple filling with 1 pound ripe yellow peaches (peeled and diced) and 3 tablespoons sugar. Omit raisins. Finish preparation and baking as above. In glaze, replace Calvados with peach brandy.

Tarte St. Nicholas aux Pruneaux (Prune) (VII-19c): Prepare crust and topping as above. Replace apple filling with 1 pound pitted prunes, soaked overnight in armagnac, red wine, or water. Drain well, place liquid in small saucepan with 4 tablespoons sugar and simmer until thick. Mix in with prunes. Omit raisins. Finish preparation and baking as above. In glaze, replace Calvados with armagnac.

VII-20 TARTE AUX MYRTILLES

The "myrtille", which has been prized for centuries by the Scandinavians for its medicinal properties and tangy taste, was probably introduced to the northeastern part of France a few hundred years ago, by traveling monks.

These juicy, flavorful berries are commonly called "huckleberries" in the United States. In some regions, you can find them canned, or even fresh. If not, you can use blueberries, a close relative. When using fresh berries, just replace the juice with 1/2 cup water.

(VII-20)
Tarte aux Myrtilles
(Blueberry or Huckleberry Tart)

Ingredients: (for one 10-inch tarte)
Crust:

14	ounces pâte sablée (I-7) or rognures (I-8a)
1	cup frangipane (II-7)
	butter for pie plate

Filling:

1	can (1pound) blueberries or huckleberries in light syrup (not prepared pie filling), about 1 1/2 cups fruit
3	tablespoons flour
1/2	cup sugar
1/4	teaspoon cinnamon
	pinch salt
3/4	cup reserved berry syrup
1	tablespoon lemon juice

Drain berries by turning into a large strainer or collander over a large bowl. Reserve 3/4 cup syrup (This is practically juice). In a medium saucepan, mix together flour, sugar, cinnamon and salt. Gradually stir in enough berry syrup to make a thick, smooth paste. Stir in rest of berry syrup, followed by lemon juice. Cook, stirring constantly, over medium heat until mixture thickens and boils. Add blueberries and cook a few minutes longer. Cover and set aside.

Preheat oven to 350-degrees. On a lightly-floured surface, roll out pastry to 1/8-inch thick, line a 10-inch buttered pie plate, and prick. Spread frangipane evenly in the bottom and bake about 30 minutes, until crust and frangipane are golden brown. Watch closely while baking. If the crust puffs up and becomes deformed, prick with a fork to release steam. When it's done, remove from oven and with a sharp paring knife, immediately trim edge of crust to 1/2-inch above frangipane. Cool.

Remove crust from pie plate, place on a serving plate, and pour partially cooled filling in the center, carefully spreading with a rubber spatula to cover frangipane. Cool completely before serving.

Storage: Refrigerate until serving. Serve within 48 hours.

VII-21 VAL D'ISÈRE
A "walnut measurer", a respected medieval professional, was responsible for sorting out walnuts and classing them according to their size, for the colporters who traveled year round from village to hamlet, selling the nuts' fresh "cuisses", or, literally "thighs". This rich dessert, a kind of creamy walnut pie topped with chocolate icing, was created on a ski resort in the Val d'Isère.

(VII-21)
Val d'Isère
(Glazed Walnut Cream Tart)

Ingredients: (for one 10-inch pie)
Crust:

11	ounces pâte brisée (I-6) or rognures (I-8a) or
	14 ounces pâte sablée (I-7)
	butter for pie plate

Filling:

1/2	cup butter, softened
3/4	cup powdered sugar
1	egg white
1	cup ground walnuts
3/4	cup ground almonds
	pinch salt
3	tablespoons kirsch

1/2	cup sirop à entremets au kirsch (dessert syrup) (II-12a)
8 to 10	biscuits à la cuillère (ladyfingers) (I-5)

6	ounces semi-sweet chocolate
2	tablespoons water
30-40	walnut halves

Preheat oven to 350-degrees. On a lightly-floured surface, roll out pastry to 1/8-inch thick, line a buttered 10-inch pie plate, and prick well. (If you're using rognures, refrigerate 1 hour before baking). Trim and flute edge, then bake 20 to 30 minutes, or until golden brown. Cool.

In a medium mixing bowl, cream butter and sugar until light, then beat in egg white, walnuts, almonds, salt and kirsch. Continue beating at high speed until light and creamy. Spread 1/3 of this mixture in the bottom of the pie crust.

Pour the sirop à entremets into a shallow dish and quickly dip the biscuits, turning once, and arrange on the crème in a solid layer, cutting when necessary to fit. Spread on rest of crème and refrigerate 30 minutes.

In a small saucepan, melt chocolate in water over very low heat, then stir until smooth. With a rubber spatula, spread evenly on the top, and decorate with walnut halves. Chill 2 hours before serving.

Storage: Cover and refrigerate until serving. Serve within 48 hours.

VII-22 TARTE AUX ABRICOTS

The coveted title of mistress to King Henri IV notwithstanding, Gabrielle d'Estrées refused to limit her services to her royal lover and give up the company of an occasional "galant", interludes which the king—a man of the world—generally chose to ignore. One evening, during an impromtu visit to his mistress, Henri suddenly began tossing candied apricots under the bed. When Gabrielle demanded an explanation, he answered nonchalantly, "My dear, everyone must make a living, n'est-ce pas?" And with a knowing smile, he pointed to a pair of feet protruding from under the bed.

Although this pie is made with canned or fresh apricots rather than candied ones, I can never serve it without thinking of "Good King Henri" and his "Belle Gabrielle".

(VII-22)
Tarte aux Abricots
(Apricot Tart)

Ingredients: (for one 10-inch pie)
- 11   ounces pâte brisée (I-6) or rognures (I-8a) or
       14 ounces pâte sablée (I-7)
       butter for pie plate

- 1 1/8   cups crème patissière (II-2)

- 2   pounds fresh ripe apricots
- 1/2   cup water
- 2   tablespoons sugar
- 1   teaspoon lemon juice
          or
       1 (28-ounce) can apricot halves in light syrup

- abricotage (apricot glaze) (II-11a)

Preheat oven to 350-degrees. On a lightly-floured surface, roll out pastry to 1/8-inch thick, line buttered pie plate, and prick well. If you're using rognures, refrigerate 1 hour before baking. Bake 15 to 20 minutes, or until half-baked. Remove from oven and cool.

Wash apricots, cut in fourths, and place in a large saucepan with water, sugar, and lemon juice. Cover and poach 10 minutes, or until tender. Drain. If you're using canned apricots, simply drain, then cut the halves in half.

Beat cold crème patissiére until creamy, then spread in pastry shell. Place the apricots, hollow side up, on the crème and bake until the tips of the apricots are browned and the pastry is completely baked, another 20 to 30 minutes. Cool, then brush with warm apricot glaze.

Storage: Refrigerate until serving. Serve within 12 hours.

VII-23 TARTE TATIN

Women pastry cooks were, and still are, a rarity in France. However, the Demoiselles Tatin became famous for their invention, which has since become a regional specialty of their native Sologne. This upside-down pie of caramelized apples and pâte brisée is traditionally served warm.

(VII-23)
Tarte Tatin
(Upside-Down Apple Tart)

Ingredients: (for one 10-inch pie)
Crust:

    11   ounces pâte brisée (I-6) or pâte feuilletée rognures (I-8a)

Filling:

    1/4   cup sugar
    2   tablespoons water
         butter and sugar for pan

    8   medium-sized apples
    1/3   cup sugar
    1/4   cup butter

    1/3   cup sugar
    2   tablespoons water

Caramelize sugar by heating in a saucepan with water until mixture begins to bubble. Lower heat and continue cooking. When the sugar begins to darken, rotate the pan slightly so that it will color evenly. Do not stir. Pour into 10-inch manqué pan and tilt in a rotating motion to coat the bottom with a thin, even layer of caramel. Butter and sugar sides of pan.

Peel and core apples. Cut 4 of them in half, and quarter the other four. Place apple halves, flat side down, in pan, then fill in spaces with quarters, cutting them smaller, when necessary, to make them fit. Sprinkle sugar over apples and dot with butter.

Preheat oven to 350-degrees. On a lightly-floured surface, roll out pâte brisée or rognures to 1/8-inch thick and, using a 12-inch cake board or dinner plate as a guide, cut out a disk of pastry. Place it on top of the apples, making several slits for steam. Place pan in a large baking dish half-filled with hot water and bake for 1 hour, or until pastry is golden brown and apples are tender. Pour off liquid which has formed during baking, and invert immediately on a wire cooling rack.

Immediately before serving, make more caramel and pour it over the apples, spreading quickly with a metal spatula before it hardens.

VII-24   FAR BRETON

If a time machine allowed us to enter an 18th century Parisian boudoir, we'd probably be surprised to hear the early morning litany, "A little prune from Tours, a little prune from Tours, a little prune..." A child's nursery rhyme? Morning prayers? The beginning of a recipe? No, just a sure method, according to the "élégantes" of the time, for beautiful lips!

This traditional custard-like dessert from the French province of Brittany can be made with either prunes or raisins.

(VII-24)
Far Breton
(Brittany Flan with Prunes or Raisins)

Ingredients: (for one 10-inch flan)

1	cup flour
2/3	cup sugar
1/8	teaspoon salt

2 1/2	cups milk
3	eggs
1/2	teaspoon vanilla extract

1   cup pitted prunes (preferably soaked overnight in water or red wine) or 2/3 cup raisins

butter for pan

Preheat oven to 325-degrees. In a large mixing bowl, stir together flour, sugar, and salt. Whisk in enough milk to make a thick, smooth paste, then whisk in the eggs, the rest of the milk, and vanilla extract. Pour into a generously buttered 10-inch manqué pan (or any other deep, round baking dish). Drop in prunes or raisins. Bake for 50 to 60 minutes, or until top is golden brown and a knife blade, inserted in the center, comes out clean. Cool 10 minutes, then slide out onto a serving plate. Serve warm or cold.

Note: In Brittany, flans (fars) are often served, liberally brushed with melted, lightly salted butter, which brings out the flavor of the fruit and custard.

Storage: Although best when eaten within a few hours, a flan (far) can be kept, tightly covered and refrigerated, for 24 hours.

Chapter VIII

Hot Desserts
(Desserts Chauds)

VIII-1   CRÊPES SUZETTE

Henri Charpentier, head cook to the Prince of Wales, took a deep breath, and, bracing himself, entered the royal dining room. "Did you ring for me, your highness?" he asked with a slight bow.

"These crêpes are exquisite!" the young prince exclaimed. "Is there a name for them?"

"Exquisite?" the chef repeated faintly. That's the last thing he'd expected to hear! A clumsy kitchen apprentice had burned the sauce usually served with the prince's favorite crêpes, and, in desperation, the head cook had garnished them with a hastily made orange sauce laced with rum. "I call them…ah…'Crêpes Princesse', your highness," he managed to stutter.

Always galant, the future Edward VII turned to his dinner companion and declared with a smile. "Mademoiselle Suzette is, in my estimation, a princess. From now on, these crêpes will be known as 'Crêpes Suzette'."

Few indeed are those who have never heard of this lovely crêpe dessert, which is just right for an intimate dinner on a cold winter evening.

(VIII-1)
Crêpes Suzette

Ingredients: (for about 8 servings)
Crêpes:

1	cup flour
	pinch salt
1	tablespoon sugar
1 3/4	cups milk
1/4	cup oil
3	eggs
1 1/2	teaspoons Grand Marnier
1 1/2	teaspoons rum
	finely grated rind of 1/2 orange
	butter for pan

Filling:

2 1/4	cups crème patissière (II-2)
	juice of 1/2 orange
	finely grated rind of 1 orange
2	teaspoons Grand Marnier

More➔

(Crêpes Suzette, Cont.)

Sauce:
- **1**   tablespoon butter
- **1/3**   cup sugar
-       juice of 1 orange
- **1/4**   cup Grand Marnier

- **1/3**   cup Grand Marnier

Crêpes: In a large mixing bowl, stir together dry ingredients. Stir in enough milk to make a smooth paste, then whisk in rest of milk, followed by rest of ingredients. Whisk vigorously until the batter is perfectly smooth. Cover with a cloth and let stand 30 minutes, to give the particles of flour time to swell. The crêpes will be less fragile, and much easier to cook. The batter, when ready to cook, should be the consistency of heavy cream. If it has thickened while standing, stir in a little milk. Heat a 9-inch crêpe pan over medium heat. It's ready when a drop of cold water bounces off the surface.

Drop in about 1/2 teaspoon butter and tilt the pan to coat evenly with melted butter. Pour in just enough batter to coat sides and bottom of pan—about 1/4 cup—and rotate it quickly to distribute it evenly. When the edges are brown and dry, turn and cook about 30 seconds longer. Turn out onto a plate, and repeat the process with the remaining batter, adding butter from time to time to prevent sticking. Cover crêpes and set aside.

Filling: Prepare crème patissière, remove from heat and stir in orange juice, rind, and Grand Marnier. Cover and set aside to cool.

Sauce: In a small saucepan, gently heat ingredients until butter and sugar are melted. Remove from heat and stir in Grand Marnier.

To serve: Drop a heaping tablespoon of filling in the middle of each crêpe and roll up, tucking in edges to seal. Place, seam side down, in a chafing dish (if you don't have one, a large, presentable skillet will do), and pour on the orange sauce. Heat until the sauce is thick and bubbly. In a small saucepan, gently heat 1/3 cup Grand Marnier, then light it and pour the flaming liqueur over the crêpes. They won't burn for long, so it's best to heat and flambée in front of your guests. If you must do it in the kitchen, add some rum to the Grand Marnier. The increased alcohol content will help the crêpes flame longer, and give you sufficient time to get to the dining room.

VIII-2 FRITURE AUX FRUITS

Since its pioneer days, America's language and culture have been enriched by those of its French settlers. An example: Our "fritters" were originally called "friture".

These flavorful fruit doughnuts make an excellent mid-afternoon snack, or a good dessert after a light evening meal.

(VIII-2)

Friture aux Fruits
(Fruit Fritters)

Ingredients: (for about 100 bite-sized fritters)
Fruit Mixture:

1 1/2	pounds mixed fruits (a combination of any of the following):

-prunes or dried apricots, soaked overnight in water and drained
-bananas, peeled and cut into bite-sized pieces
-pineapple, peaches or pears, peeled, cored, and cut into bite-sized pieces
-apples, peeled cored, and cut into bite-sized pieces or l/4-inch thick slices (thicker slices would only be half-cooked)

1/3	cup sugar
2	tablespoons kirsch, rum, or lemon juice

Batter:

3/4	cup flour
1/3	cup cornstarch
1/2	teaspoon baking powder
1/8	teaspoon salt

6 to 8	ounces liquid (milk, beer, or buttermilk)
1	egg
1	tablespoon melted butter

oil for frying
powdered sugar

Fruit Mixture: In a large mixing bowl, stir together sugar, alcohol (or lemon juice) and fruit. Cover and let macerate 1 hour. Stir from time to time.

Batter: In another large mixing bowl, stir together dry ingredients, then whisk in enough liquid to make a thick, smooth paste. Whisk in other ingredients, then rest of milk. The batter should be smooth but thick. (It will thin some as the fruit is dipped. If it gets too thin, whisk in a little flour). Drain fruit and drop several pieces at a time into the batter. Lift them out with a fork and drop them into the hot oil. Fry for about 1 minute, or until golden brown, turning once. Remove with a slotted spoon, drain on paper towels, dust with powdered sugar, and serve immediately.

VIII-3 CRÈMES FRITES

Paris. 1794. Twilight has begun to deepen into night, attenuating the harshness of the French capitol's most miserable quarter, where a man and a small boy trudge silently through the muddy streets. The Reign of Terror, begun less than a year ago, is ravaging the country, and times are hard. No one knows that better than a man with no real profession, a sick wife, and 15 children. At a busy intersection, the man stops and turns to his son.

"Go, my boy, go..." he begins. He falters in mid-sentence. The night before, abandoning his son had seemed like the only solution. Now, he's not so sure.

He takes a deep breath and goes on. "Misery is our lot in life. Leave us to our fate!"

Ten year old Marie-Antoine tries to speak, but one look at his father's anguished face stops him.

"The world is full of good professions. Find one and pursue it with passion!" The man falls silent for a moment, searching for the right words. Finally, he shrugs and murmurs, "Why go on? I see that you understand..." Without another word, he turns and walks away into the darkness. Marie-Antoine watches the receding figure until it disappears completely. He's old enough—and poor enough—to realize that he'll never see his family again.

Did Fate or simple hunger direct him to the nearest cabaret? Whatever the case, the amazing career of France's greatest gastronomist and chef began that night, when a compassionate cabaret owner took him in as his apprentice.

More➤

(Crèmes Frites, Cont.)

In his series of cookbooks still used by professional chefs, "Antonïn" Carême recommends crème frites as one of France's most traditional desserts. These squares of custard, hot and creamy on the inside, crispy on the outside, are delicious alone, or served with a hot apricot sauce.

(VIII-3)
Crèmes Frites
(Fried Custard)

Ingredients: (for about thirty-six 1 1/2-inch squares)

1/2	cup sugar
1/2	cup cornstarch
	pinch salt
2	cups milk
2	eggs
1/2	teaspoon vanilla

butter for pan

1	egg
	pinch salt
1	cup powdered bread crumbs

1   quart frying oil

abricotage (II-11a) (optional)

In a medium saucepan, stir together sugar, cornstarch, and salt. Whisk in enough milk to make a smooth paste, then whisk in whole eggs, followed by rest of milk.

Cook, stirring constantly, over medium heat, until mixture thickens and boils. Cook a minute more, stirring constantly. Remove from heat and stir in vanilla. Spread in a buttered 9 x 9-inch pan. Cool to room temperature, then refrigerate for several hours.

With a sharp knife, cut into about thirty-six 1 1/2-inch squares. In a soup plate or other wide, shallow bowl, beat whole egg and salt until frothy. In another soup plate, place bread crumbs. With a metal spatula, lift out squares (if you have trouble getting them out, dip the pan in hot water for a minute) dip them in beaten egg, roll in bread crumbs, and fry in hot oil for about 1 minute, or until golden brown. With a slotted spoon or skimmer, lift out crèmes and drain on paper towels. Serve immediately, plain or with hot apricot sauce.

Storage: Although the hot crèmes should be served immediately, the unfried preparation can be kept, tightly covered and refrigerated, for up to 48 hours.

VIII-4 OMELETTE SUCRÉE AU COULIS DE FRUITS

An exemplary working wife, England's Queen Victoria took time out from her busy schedule to cook for Prince Albert. One of his favorite dishes: omelettes, for which Victoria had over 70 recipes.

The recipe for this dessert omelette, flambéed and served with fresh fruit sauce, is similar to the one created by La Varenne, one of France's great pastry chefs.

(VIII-4)
Omelette Sucrée au Coulis de Fruits
(Dessert Omelette with Fresh Fruit Sauce)

Ingredients: (for one omelette, serving 6)

7	egg yolks
1/3	cup sugar
1	tablespoon rum, kirsch, or Grand Marnier
7	egg whites
1/8	teaspoon salt
2	tablespoons sugar
2	tablespoons butter for pan
	powdered sugar
2	tablespoons rum, kirsch, or Grand Marnier

Coulis de fruits, (Fresh Fruit Sauce) (II-13)

In a large mixing bowl, whisk together egg yolks, sugar, and alcohol of your choice.

In a deep mixing bowl, beat egg whites and salt at high speed until soft peaks form, then add sugar and continue beating until stiff but not dry. Beat a big spoonful of whites into yolk mixture, then carefully fold in rest of whites.

In an omelette pan, melt butter over medium heat, then pour in omelette. When the bottom is light brown (the top should still be soft), fold in half with a large wooden spatula and slide it onto a warm serving plate. Dust with powdered sugar. In a small saucepan, heat alcohol, then pour it over the omelette and flambée. If you're using Grand Marnier or kirsch, add a little rum to help it burn longer. Serve immediately with fresh fruit sauce.

VIII-5   SOUFFLÉ À LA VANILLE

Although the vanilla orchid was discovered during the Spanish Conquest, it didn't become widely used in France until the 19th century, when vast vanilla plantations were built in the French Antilles. The orchids flourished, but the growers encountered one major problem: The insects who played an essential role in the plant's pollinization had been left behind, in Central America. In 1841, a young slave found the solution: artificial pollinization, which became a standard procedure. In a normal work day, a "fécondeuse" can fertilize between 1000 and 1200 vanilla plants.

The recipe for this simple but delicious vanilla soufflé can also serve as a base for other flavors.

Soufflés: General Advice: Soufflés can look so easy to make. And they are! As long as you stick hard and fast to a few basic rules.

First of all, it's important to have the right kind of mold. Straight-sided, medium-sized, 1 1/2-quart porcelain, pyrex, stainless steel, or silver molds are all excellent choices. Why medium-sized? Because really large soufflés just don't rise correctly. If you want to prepare a soufflé for 8, simply double the recipe and bake it in two 1 1/2-quart molds or 8 individual ramekin molds.

Secondly, the egg whites must be beaten to the right consistency. You may have noticed that in many soufflé recipes, you're told to beat them until very stiff. I think this is a big mistake. Really stiff whites have had the life beaten out of them. In the oven—it's not surprising!—they have nothing more to give. Also, don't be too concerned about folding the whites perfectly into the batter. The less they're beaten and "handled", the better the soufflé will rise, and the longer it will stay up.

Now, the most important thing: Patience. Keep in mind the old saying "The soufflé doesn't wait for you. You wait for it." Take the time to preheat the oven correctly before putting in the soufflé, and don't give in to the temptation of opening the oven door during baking. This may not make the soufflé fall, but it will keep it from rising as high. Also, give it the time it needs to bake all the way through. A nicely puffed up soufflé isn't necessarily done, so test it with a knife blade before removing it from the oven.

More➔

(Soufflé à la Vanille, Cont.)

(VIII-5)

Soufflé à la Vanille
(Vanilla Soufflé)

1	cup milk
1	vanilla bean
1/2	cup sugar
1/3	cup flour
4	egg yolks
2	tablespoons butter
4	egg whites
1/8	teaspoon salt
2	tablespoons sugar

powdered sugar
butter and granulated sugar for mold

Preheat oven to 350-degrees. Butter and sugar a 6-inch soufflé dish. In a medium saucepan, heat milk and vanilla bean, split lengthwise, to a boil. Cover and simmer another 10 minutes, then remove from heat and allow to infuse until milk is lukewarm. Remove vanilla bean. In a small mixing bowl, stir together sugar and flour. Whisk into milk and return to heat, stirring constantly, until thick and smooth. Remove from heat and stir in butter. Cover and allow to cool 10 minutes, then stir in egg yolks. Cover.

In a deep mixing bowl, beat egg whites and salt at high speed until soft peaks form. Add the sugar and continue beating until whites are stiff but not dry. Don't overbeat. Beat a big spoonful of whites into warm crème, then add all this mixture to the whites and fold in carefully. Fill the mold, dust with powdered sugar, and bake about 25 to 30 minutes, or until a knifeblade inserted in the center comes out clean. Dust again with sugar and serve with one of the following: whipped cream and toasted sliced almonds, crème anglaise, or fresh fruit sauce.

Soufflé au Café (Coffee) (VIII-5a): Same as for soufflé à la vanille, replacing the vanilla bean with 2 teaspoons coffee extract. Cook sugar, flour, and milk over medium heat (as above), then stir coffee extract into mixture with the egg yolks. Bake as directed above, and serve with one of the following: whipped cream and grated chocolate, or crème anglaise à la vanille (II-3), or crème anglaise au café (II-3c).

Soufflé à la Noix de Coco (Coconut) (VIII-5b): Same as for soufflé à la vanille, omitting vanilla bean. Cook sugar, flour, and milk until thick (as above) and add 2/3 cup flaked, unsweetened coconut and 1 tablespoon rum to mixture, along with the egg yolks. Finish preparation and baking as above. Serve with whipped cream and diced pineapple macerated in rum, or more simply, with crème anglaise à la vanille.

More➔

(Soufflé à la Vanille, Cont.)

Soufflé aux Amandes (Almond) (VIII-5c): Same as for soufflé à la vanille, omitting the vanilla bean. Cook sugar, flour, and milk (as above), then stir in 1/2 cup blanched, chopped almonds and 1/4 teaspoon almond extract along with the egg yolks. Finish preparation and baking as above. Serve with whipped cream or crème anglaise, and toasted sliced almonds.

Soufflé aux Pistaches (Pistachio) (VIII-5d): Same as soufflé à la vanille, omitting the vanilla bean. Cook sugar, flour, and milk (as above), then stir in 2 tablespoons ground almonds, 1/3 cup chopped pistachios, and 1 tablespoon kirsch, along with egg yolks. Finish preparation and baking as above. Serve with whipped cream, crème anglaise, and chopped pistachios.

Soufflé Prâliné (Praline) (VIII-5e): Same as for soufflé à la vanille, omitting vanilla bean, and reducing sugar to 1/4 cup. Cook sugar, flour, and milk (as above), then stir in 1/2 cup powdered caramelized almonds and 1 tablespoon rum, along with the egg yolks. Finish preparing batter as above and fill prepared soufflé dish with half the batter. Sprinkle on top 1/3 cup powdered caramelized almonds, pour in rest of batter, and bake as directed above. Serve with whipped cream or crème anglaise and a sprinkling of caramelized almonds or toasted sliced almonds.

VIII-6 SOUFFLÉ AU CHOCOLAT

When chocolate first became known in Europe, its consumption was generally prohibited in monastaries and convents because it was believed to "heat the flesh and provoke unseemly thoughts".

Almonds, cocount, or extra chocolate can be added to this soufflé.

(VIII-6)
Soufflé au Chocolat
(Chocolate Soufflé)

Ingredients:

1	cup milk
1/3	cup sugar
1/3	cup flour

3	ounces semi-sweet chocolate
2	tablespoons butter
3	egg yolks

3	egg whites
1/8	teaspoon salt
2	tablespoons sugar

powdered sugar
butter and granulated sugar for mold

crème anglaise (II-3) or sauce au chocolat (II-15)

Preheat oven to 350-degrees. Butter and sugar an 6-inch soufflé dish. In a medium saucepan, stir together sugar and flour, then stir in enough milk to make a smooth paste. Stir in rest of milk and cook, stirring constantly, over medium heat until thick and smooth. Remove from heat, add chocolate, broken into small pieces, and butter. Cover and allow to cool 10 minutes. Stir to blend in melted chocolate, then stir in egg yolks.

In a deep mixing bowl, beat egg whites and salt at high speed until soft peaks form, then add sugar and continue beating until stiff but not dry. Don't overbeat. Beat a big spoonful of whites into warm chocolate mixture, then pour into rest of whites and fold together carefully. Pour into prepared dish, dust with powdered sugar, and bake 25 to 30 minutes, or until a knifeblade in the center comes out clean. Dust again with sugar and serve immediately.

Although this soufflé is delicious by itself, it can also be served with crème anglaise or sauce au chocolat. Beat 1/2 cup cold milk into the hot sauce of your choice, allow to cool, and present on the side in a small pitcher or sauceboat.

Double Chocolate Soufflé (VIII-6a): Fold 2 ounces grated or chopped chocolate into chocolate soufflé batter. Bake and serve as directed above.

More→

(Soufflé au Chocolat, Cont.)

Chocolate-Coconut Soufflé (VIII-6b): Fold 1/3 cup flaked, unsweetened coconut into chocolate soufflé batter. Bake and serve as above.

Chocolate-Almond Soufflé (VIII-6c): To chocolate soufflé batter, add 1/2 teaspoon almond extract, and 1/4 cup toasted, chopped almonds. Bake as directed above. Serve with whipped cream and toasted almonds, or as directed above.

***

VIII-7   SOUFFLÉ AU CITRON

During the Renaissance, elegant Italians—men included—often spent half their waking hours on their make-up, and since "venitian blonde" was the rage, some dyed their hair as often as twice a day! Jealously-guarded recipes called for an incredible variety of ingredients, such as peach extract, crusts of bread, and…vinegar distilled with horse dung. One of the most frequently cited ingredients, whether for a creamy complexion or for shiny hair: lemon juice.

***

Thank goodness for gourmets, citrus fruits have also been used, down through the centuries, for making excellent desserts, like this lemon or lime soufflé.

(VIII-7)
Soufflé au Citron
(Lemon or Lime Soufflé)

Ingredients: (for one 6-inch soufflé)

1/2	cup milk
2/3	cup sugar
1/3	cup flour

1/3	cup lemon or lime juice with pulp
	finely grated rind of 1 lemon or lime

1	tablespoon butter
3	egg yolks

4	egg whites
1/8	teaspoon salt
2	tablespoons sugar

powdered sugar
butter and sugar for soufflé dish

More→

(Soufflé au Citron, Cont.)

Preheat oven to 350-degrees. Butter and sugar a 6-inch soufflé dish. In a medium saucepan, mix together sugar and flour, then stir in enough milk to make a smooth paste. Stir in rest of milk, and cook, stirring constantly, over medium heat, until thick and smooth. Remove from heat, stir in juice, rind, and butter. Cover and allow to cool 10 minutes, then stir in egg yolks.

In a deep mixing bowl, beat egg whites and salt at high speed until soft peaks form. Add sugar and continue beating until stiff but not dry. Don't overbeat. Beat a big spoonful of whites into crème, then add this mixture to the rest of whites and fold together carefully. Fill the prepared soufflé mold, dust with powdered sugar, and bake 25 to 30 minutes, or until a knifeblade inserted in the center comes out clean. Dust again with sugar and serve immediately with whipped cream and strawberry or raspberry sauce.

VIII-8 SOUFFLÉ AUX POMMES

Although the apple was highly regarded by the ancient Gauls, it had to wait for the Roman conqueror to give it its definitive name: "pomum", a term which indicates the apple's importance, since it literally means "fruit".

This flavorful apple soufflé can also be made with pineapple.

(VIII-8)
Soufflé aux Pommes
(Apple Soufflé)

Ingredients:

1	cup milk
1/2	cup sugar
1/3	cup flour

2	tablespoons butter
3	egg yolks
2	tablespoons Calvados

4	egg whites
1/8	teaspoon salt
2	tablespoons sugar

2	small or 1 large apple
1	tablespoon butter
1	tablespoon sugar

4	biscuits à la cuillère (I-5)
2	tablespoons sirop à entremets (II-12) or Calvados

butter and granulated sugar for mold

Peel and core apples, then cut them into very thin slices. In a heavy skillet, melt butter, then sauté the apples over medium heat until transluscent. Sprinkle with sugar, and cook for another few minutes, until the sugar has melted and begun to caramelize. Cover and set aside.

More→

(Soufflé aux Pommes, Cont.)

Preheat oven to 350-degrees. Butter and sugar a 6-inch soufflé mold. In a medium saucepan, stir together sugar and flour, then stir in enough milk to make a smooth paste. Stir in rest of milk and cook over medium heat, stirring constantly, until mixture is thick and smooth. Remove from heat, stir in butter, cover and allow to cool 10 minutes, then stir in yolks and Calvados. Cover.

In a deep mixing bowl, beat egg whites and salt at high speed until soft peaks form. Add the sugar and continue beating until stiff. Don't overbeat.

In a shallow dish, place sirop à entremets or Calvados, and quickly moisten the biscuits à la cuillère, turning them quickly to avoid soaking.

Beat a big spoonful of egg whites into the warm crème, then pour this mixture into the rest of the whites, and fold in carefully. Fill the soufflé mold with a third of the batter, then place 1/2 the sautéed apples on top in an even layer. Crumble 2 biscuits over the apples. Repeat, finishing with the last 1/3 of batter. Dust with powdered sugar and bake for 25 to 30 minutes. To test for doneness, stick a knifeblade into the center. It should come out clean. Dust again with powdered sugar, and serve immediately.

Soufflé aux Ananas (Pineapple) (VIII-8a): Same ingredients and directions as for Apple Soufflé, but replace apples with 2/3 cup drained crushed pineapple (don't sauté). Replace Calvados with rum, in basic crème and for moistening biscuits.

VIII-9   SOUFFLÉ AUX MARRONS

In March, 1815, a chestnut tree in the Tuileries Garden suddenly burst into bloom, to celebrate—claimed ardent Bonapartists—Napoléon's brief political comeback to Paris. Royalists retorted that the tree owed its early blossoming to the Cossack army which, the year before, had camped in the Tuileries. Their kitchen had been set up next to the tree, which had simply benefited from frequent drenchings with dirty dishwater.

Naturally, the Bonapartists turned a deaf ear to this unromantic explanation, and for many years thereafter, as the tree continued to blossom long before the others, came from all over France to contemplate the tree which had blossomed especially for their emperor. Rum and diced chestnuts reinforce the flavor of this delicate soufflé.

(VIII-9)

Soufflé aux Marrons
(Chestnut Soufflé)

Ingredients:

3/4	cup milk
1	tablespoon sugar
1/4	cup flour
2	tablespoons butter
3	egg yolks
1	tablespoon rum
2/3	cup chestnut cream
4	egg whites
1/8	teaspoon salt
2	tablespoons sugar
1/2	cup diced candied chestnuts

powdered sugar
butter and granulated sugar for mold

Preheat oven to 350-degrees. Butter and sugar a 6-inch soufflé dish. In a medium saucepan, stir together sugar and flour, then stir in enough milk to make a smooth paste. Stir in rest of milk, and cook, stirring constantly, over medium heat, until thick and smooth. Remove from heat, stir in butter, cover and allow to cool 10 minutes. Stir in egg yolks, rum, and chestnut cream.

In a deep mixing bowl, beat egg whites and salt at high speed until soft peaks form. Add sugar and continue beating until stiff but not dry. Don't overbeat. Beat a big spoonful of whites into the warm crème, then pour into the rest of whites and fold carefully together.

Fill prepared mold with 1/3 of batter, then sprinkle on 1/2 the candied chestnuts. Add another 1/3 of the batter and sprinkle on the rest of chestnuts, then finish with the rest of batter. Dust with powdered sugar and bake 25 to 30 minutes, or until a knifeblade inserted in the center comes out clean. Dust with more sugar and serve immediately.

VIII-10   SOUFFLÉ AU GRAND MARNIER

One of the principal stockholders of the Ritz Hotel, a certain Mr. Marnier-Lapostolle, alternately irritated and amused his entourage with his pretentious manner. So much so, that before long, pompous Mr. Marnier-Lapostolle was more commonly known as "Monsieur Le Grand". Later, when he created an orange liqueur, he decided to dub it "Grand Marnier", in honor of his nickname. Grand Marnier adds its incomparable flavor to this delicate soufflé, served with orange sauce.

(VIII-10)
Soufflé au Grand Marnier
(Grand Marnier Soufflé)

Ingredients: (for one 6-inch soufflé)

1/2	cup milk
1/2	cup sugar
1/3	cup flour

1/3	cup orange juice with pulp
	finely grated rind of 1 orange
1	tablespoon butter
2	tablespoons Grand Marnier
2	egg yolks

4	egg whites
1/8	teaspoon salt
8	tablespoons sugar

powdered sugar
butter and sugar for soufflé dish

Preheat oven to 350-degrees. Butter and sugar a 6-inch soufflé dish. In a medium saucepan, mix together sugar and flour, then stir in enough milk to make a smooth paste. Stir in rest of milk, and cook, stirring constantly, over medium heat, until thick and smooth. Remove from heat, stir in orange juice, rind, and butter. Cover and allow to cool 10 minutes, then stir in Grand Marnier and egg yolks. Cover.

In a deep mixing bowl, beat whites and salt at high speed until soft peaks form. Add sugar and continue beating until stiff but not dry. Don't overbeat. Beat a big spoonful of whites into warm crème, then add all this mixture to the rest of whites and fold together carefully. Fill prepared soufflé dish, dust with powdered sugar, and bake 25 to 30 minutes, or until a knifeblade inserted in the center comes out clean. Dust again with sugar, and serve immediately with orange crème anglaise.

Orange Crème Anglaise: Prepare plain crème anglaise (II-3), omitting vanilla extract. Remove from heat and stir in 2/3 cup orange juice and 1 tablespoon Grand Marnier. Serve warm or cold, with soufflé.

Chapter IX

Cookies
(Petits Fours Secs)

IX-1   TUILES AUX NOISETTES

The shape of these popular hazelnut cookies is reminiscent of the curved terra cotta tiles (called "tuiles" in French) covering most rooftops in France. Professional bakers use special trench-shaped molds to give them their shape, but the homemaker must resort to what she has on hand—in most cases a rolling pin, which is fine, except that it can hold only 3 to 4 cookies at a time. Not always practical, when you have 8 hot cookies waiting to be shaped! Water glasses, slender wine bottles, and even glass baby bottles are good choices, but be sure that all "molds" are the same diameter so the cookies will have the same shape.

(IX-1)

Tuiles aux Noisettes
(Hazelnut "Tiles")

Ingredients: (for 24 small tuiles)
- 1/3   cup butter, softened
- 1/3   cup sugar

- 6   tablespoons flour
- 1/2   cup finely chopped (not ground) hazelnuts
- 2   tablespoons milk

Preheat oven to 350-degrees. In a medium mixing bowl, cream butter and sugar until light. Beat in flour, hazelnuts and milk.

Drop by scant teaspoons on lightly-floured baking sheets, no more than 8 per sheet. Dip a fork in water and flatten with a gentle patting motion. Re-wet fork occasionally, when it begins sticking to the dough. Bake 6 to 8 minutes, until cookies are dark brown around the edges.

While the cookies are baking, place a folded dish towel on the work surface and set the molds on top. (This will keep them from rolling around). Remove cookies from oven and let cool 30 seconds, then lift them off baking sheet with a metal spatula and place on molds, pressing sides gently with the cupped hand to help shape them. You'll have to work quickly, as the cookies harden rapidly. Cool, then lift cookies off molds. Time baking so that no more than one sheet comes out of the oven at any given time. If 2 sheets were ready at the same time, one would cool before you could get to it.

Note: These cookies are equally good made with sliced, untoasted almonds.

Storage: Store in a tightly-covered container for 1 week, or freeze in plastic bag for 1 month.

Variation: Make them twice as big and use as a "basket" for a scoop of ice cream, or fill with crème chantilly (II-1) and fresh fruit.

IX-2   PALETS DE DAMES

"Les Quatre Mendiants", or, literally, "The Four Beggars", was a popular dessert during the Middle Ages, named in honor of the four orders of mendicant friars. Simple enough to be enjoyed frequently by the common people, it had four components: figs, whose greyish color evoked that of the Franciscan friar's robes; almonds, whose whiteness symbolized that of the Dominican brothers'; hazelnuts, whose brown color imitated that of the Carmelite's; and dark violet raisins, reminiscent of the Augustines' robes.

These small raisin cookies bring to mind "palets de dames", or tokens used to play checkers.

(IX-2)
Palets de Dames
(Raisin Cookies)

Ingredients: (for 24 palets)

1/4	cup (1/2 stick) butter, softened
1/3	cup sugar
1	egg

1/2	cup flour
1/8	teaspoon salt
1/4	cup raisins, macerated in rum

butter for baking sheets

Preheat oven to 375-degrees. In a medium mixing bowl, cream butter and sugar until light. Beat in egg, then flour and salt. Stir in raisins, and drop by scant teaspoonfuls on lightly-buttered baking sheets. Bake 5 minutes. The palets should be dark brown around the edges and very light in the middle. Remove immediately with metal spatula and cool on racks.

Storage: Cover tightly for 1 week, or freeze 1 month.

IX-3 LANGUES DE CHAT

A cat-lover must have invented and named these delicate cookies, whose thinness and elongated form are reminiscent of a cat's tongue or "langue de chat". Serve them with champagne, fruit, or a creamy dessert such as oeufs à la neige.

(IX-3)
Langues de Chat
("Cat Tongues")

Ingredients: (for about 24 3-inch langues de chat)
- 1/4 cup (1/2 stick) butter, softened
- 1/4 cup sugar

- 1 egg yolk
- 1/3 cup flour

- 2 egg whites
- pinch salt
- 1 teaspoon sugar

Preheat oven to 350-degrees. In a medium mixing bowl, beat together butter and sugar until light. Beat in egg yolk, then flour. In another mixing bowl, beat egg whites and salt at high speed until soft peaks form, then add the teaspoon of sugar and continue beating until stiff but not dry. Add 1/2 of whites to yolk mixture and beat until well blended, then carefully fold in the rest of whites.

Cover baking sheets with waxed paper, using a dot of batter in the center and on the corners to make it stick. Spoon batter into a pastry bag with a 1/2-inch round nozzle and pipe out 3-inch long cookies, spacing them well to allow for spreading. Bake 8 to 10 minutes, until dark brown around the edges and very light in the center. With a metal spatula, remove immediately (if removed when cool, they'll break) and cool on metal racks.

Storage: Store in a tightly covered container for 2 to 3 weeks, or freeze in the same container for 1 month.

Variation I:
"Corbeilles" (Baskets) (IX-3a):
Ingredients:
- 1 recipe langue de chat batter
- butter and flour

Preheat oven to 350-degrees. Butter and flour 2 large baking sheets. Prepare langue de chat batter, spoon into a pastry bag with a 5/8-inch nozzle, and on the prepared sheets, pipe 12 mounds, about 3 inches in diameter. Bake about 10 minutes, or until dark brown around the edges and very light brown elsewhere.

More➤

(Langues de Chat, Cont.)

Remove from oven and with a metal spatula, flip cookies over, then place each cookie in a muffin cup. Press down in the center and pull the edges up, gathering slightly to make a high, fluted edge. As with the "surprise package", the important thing is to work quickly, before the cookies cool. If this happens, return them to the oven for a few minutes, to soften them and make them workable.

It's best to use these little baskets right away, filling them immediately before serving with fresh fruit salad, ice cream and hot fudge sauce, crème chantilly (II-1) and fruit, or crème chiboust (II-5) and fruit.

The next time you pay a visit to friends, surprise them with a cake wrapped in a crisp, edible casing:

Variation II:
Surprise Package (IX-3b)
Ingredients:

    1   **recipe langue de chat batter**
        butter and flour for baking sheet

    1   **5 to 6-inch loaf-shaped pound cake or fruit cake**

Preheat oven to 350-degrees. Generously butter and flour a 12 x 14-inch baking sheet. Prepare langue de chat batter, and with the spatula, spread evenly on baking sheet. Bake about 10 minutes, or until dark brown around the edges and very light brown in center. (The batter bakes, then burns, very quickly, so watch it closely).

Remove from oven and invert **immediately** onto work surface. Place cake in the center and fold the two wider edges around it, overlapping them in the center, and pressing gently with palms to mold in place. Then fold the remaining sides together and underneath, just as you would a paper-wrapped package.

You can go about it differently, if you prefer, the main thing being to get the cake attractively wrapped in a very short time, before the cookie "wrapping" cools enough to become hard and brittle. For a nice finishing touch, tie up your package with a bright ribbon and make a big bow on top. Your first "surprise package" may not be perfect, so you might want to plan to serve it to family...or understanding friends.

IX-4 DOIGTS DE FÉE

The Greek philosopher Plutarch claimed that a few almonds, if eaten immediately before a banquet, were effective in preventing drunkenness. It may not have helped, but then, unlike many other remedies of the time, it surely didn't hurt.

Chocolate icing gives extra dimension to these crunchy, almond-rich "fairy fingers".

(IX-4)
Doigts de Fée
(Fairy Fingers)

Ingredients: (for 24 cookies)

1/3	cup sugar
1/2	cup ground blanched almonds
2	egg whites
1/8	teaspoon salt
1	teaspoon sugar
1/3	cup finely chopped blanched almonds
1/3	cup powdered sugar
	butter and flour for baking sheets
3	ounces semi-sweet chocolate

Preheat oven to 325-degrees. Butter and flour baking sheets. In a small mixing bowl, stir together sugar and almonds. In a deep mixing bowl, beat egg whites and salt at high speed until soft peaks form, then add sugar and continue beating until stiff but not dry. Sprinkle sugar-almond mixture over whites and fold together carefully.

Spoon batter into pastry bag and pipe out twenty-four 3-inch long "sticks". Sprinkle with chopped almonds and dust with powdered sugar. Bake 7 to 8 minutes, or until very lightly browned.

With a metal spatula, immediately remove cookies from sheet to cool on a wire rack. In a double boiler, melt chocolate. Dip rounded sides of cookies, hold up over pan, and smooth with a small metal spatula. Cool, chocolate side up, on a wire rack.

Storage: Keep, tightly covered, in a cool, dry place (preferably not the refrigerator) for several days.

IX-5   PRETZELS GLACÉS

The first "brezel" made by an anonymous German pastrychef must have brought to mind a pair of crossed arms, since the name he gave to his invention is said to have been drawn from "brachium", the Latin term for "arms".

These delicious tea pretzels, Alsacian in origin, are made from butter-rich dough, then dipped in a rum glaze.

(IX-5)
Pretzels Glacés
(Iced Shortbread Pretzels)

Ingredients: (for about 30 2-inch cookies)
- 1/3 cup butter, softened
- 1/3 cup sugar

- 1 egg yolk
- pinch salt
- 1 1/3 cups flour
- 2 to 3 tablespoons milk

Glaze:
- 2 cups powdered sugar
- 2 teaspoons lemon juice
- 2 tablespoons rum
- 1 egg white

In a medium mixing bowl, beat together butter and sugar until creamy, then beat in egg yolk, salt and flour. Beat in milk, 1 tablespoon at a time, to make a firm but supple dough. Wrap in plastic and refrigerate 1 hour.

Preheat oven to 350-degrees. On a very lightly-floured surface, roll out dough to about 15 x 6 x 1/2-inch. With a chef's knife, cut thirty 6-inch long strips of dough. Roll each strip under palms to give them a rounded shape (the surface shouldn't be too floury, as the dough would just slide around rather than roll), then place on ungreased baking sheets and twist into pretzels, pressing well on ends to make them stick. Bake 8 to 10 minutes, until cookies are very light brown. Cool on a wire rack.

In a small mixing bowl, stir together glaze ingredients.

Submerge cooled cookies, one at a time, then lift out with a fork and hold sideways over the bowl to allow excess to drip off. Scrape bottom of cookie on side of bowl, to remove excess glaze, and set on a wire rack to set.

Storage: Cover tightly and store 1 week in a cool, dry place. Baked, uniced cookies can be frozen in plastic bags 1 month. Thaw 1 hour at room temperature, then ice as above. Dough can be wrapped in plastic and frozen 1 month. Allow to thaw overnight in refrigerator, then bake and ice as directed above.

IX-6 DIAMANTS

When Hortense Schneider, queen of Offenbach's comic operas, came on stage wearing her entire diamond collection, a roar went up from the gallery. Over the whistles, someone shouted, "She must have found a diamond mine!" An anonymous voice added mildly "...and quite a few miners..."

The edges of these tender cookies are encrusted with sparkling sugar crystals, which give them a diamond-studded effect.

(IX-6)
Diamants
(Diamond Studded Cookies)

Ingredients: (for 24 diamants)

14	ounces pâte sablée (I-7)
1/4	cup granulated sugar
2/3	cup crystalized sugar
1	egg, beaten with a pinch of salt

Preheat oven to 350-degrees. On a lightly-floured surface, knead dough with 1/4 cup sugar, then roll under palms to form a 12-inch long cylinder. Brush with beaten egg and roll in crystalized sugar. Place on baking sheets and freeze for 15 minutes, or until firm but not hard. With a chef's knife, cut into twenty-four 1/2-inch wide slices. Bake on ungreased sheets for 10 to 12 minutes, or until dark cream color. With a metal spatula, remove immediately and cool on a wire rack.

Diamants au Chocolat (Chocolate) (IX-6a): Knead dough with 2 teaspoons unsweetened cocoa and 2 tablespoons sugar. Finish preparing and baking as above.

Diamants à l'Escargot (Snails) (IX-6b): Divide dough in half. Set aside 1/2, and knead the other 1/2 with 1 teaspoon cinnamon or unsweetened cocoa and 1/2 tablespoon sugar. On a lightly-floured surface, roll out the 2 pieces of dough, each to about 6 x 14-inches. Brush the plain dough with beaten egg, then place the other piece of dough on top. Roll up tightly. With a chef's knife, trim off uneven ends. Brush the cylinder with egg and roll in sugar. Finish preparing and baking as above.

IX-7 SABLÉS AUX NOIX

As they come out of the church, newlyweds in some French provinces are given a walnut, with wishes that they be as closely united and inseparable as the two halves.

These crunchy walnut cookies are subtly spiced with ginger and cinnamon.

(IX-7)

Sablés aux Noix
(Walnut Cookies)

Ingredients: (for about 30 2-inch cookies)

1 1/4	cups coarsely ground walnuts
1	cup flour
1/4	teaspoon ground ginger
1	teaspoon cinnamon
1/4	teaspoon baking powder
1/2	cup butter, softened
1 1/3	cups lightly packed brown sugar
2	tablespoons milk

In a medium mixing bowl, stir together dry ingredients. In a large mixing bowl, beat together butter and sugar until creamy, then stir in dry ingredients. Stir in milk, a tablespoon at a time (you may need a bit more or less) to make a firm but supple dough. Cover and refrigerate 1 hour.

Preheat oven to 350-degrees. On a lightly-floured surface, roll out dough to about 1/4-inch thick. Cut out 30 cookies and place on lightly-greased baking sheets, spacing some to allow for slight expansion during baking. Bake 10 to 12 minutes or until golden brown. With a metal spatula, remove immediately and cool on wire racks.

Storage: Cover tightly and store in a cool, dry place for 1 week. The dough can be wrapped in plastic and frozen up to 1 month. Thaw overnight in the refrigerator and use as directed above.

IX-8 ALLUMETTES GLACÉES

Claude Gellée, an artist from the French province of Lorraine, is less known for his works of art than for his supposed invention of pâte feuilletée. This affirmation is based on one fact: during his youth, Gellée worked briefly as an apprentice pastry cook.

These slender pastries topped with royal icing are called "matchsticks" because of their shape.

(IX-8)
Allumettes Glacées
(Iced Matchsticks)

Ingredients: (for 40 allumettes)

    8   ounces pâte feuilletée classique (I-8)

    1   cup powdered sugar
    1   egg white
    4   drops lemon juice

In a small mixing bowl, beat together powdered sugar, egg white and lemon juice until mixture is very smooth and light. If it's really soupy, beat in a little more sugar. Cover and set aside.

Preheat oven to 400-degrees. On a lightly-floured work surface, roll out pastry to a 12 x 15-inch rectangle. Using a ruler and a sharp chef's knife, cut the pastry into two 15 x 6-inch rectangles. Dust one piece lightly with flour, place on a baking sheet and refrigerate while working with the remaining piece of pastry.

Place on an ungreased baking sheet and with a small metal spatula, cover with a thin (about 1/16-inch) even layer of icing. With a damp chef's knife, cut the pastry into twenty 3 x 1 1/2-inch strips. Ice and cut the other piece of pastry the same way. Place the strips on 2 baking sheets. In the corners of the sheet to be baked, place 4 small 3/4-inch high tartlet pans, then place a wire rack on top, so that the allumettes will be of uniform height.

Place in oven and crack door with a wooden spoon. Bake, one sheet at a time, about 10 minutes, until golden brown. During baking, the allumettes will shrink slightly and separate. If the icing runs and makes them stick together, cut them apart during baking.

Storage: One week in a tightly closed container.

IX-9 PALMIERS

Were these caramelized flaky pastry "palm leaves" created in honor of the French Antilles' most common tree? In some parts of continental France, they're also known as "little pig's feet" or "elephant prints", depending, of course, upon their size.

(IX-9)
Palmiers
(Glazed Palm Leaves)

Ingredients: (for about 40 medium-sized palmiers)
    8   ounces pâte feuilletée classique with 4 tours (I-8)

    2/3   cup powdered sugar

Dust work surface generously with powdered sugar and give the dough the last two turns. Whenever necessary, redust work surface and dough with the sugar, using it as you would flour. Place dough on baking sheet and freeze 10 minutes, then roll out into a 15 x 20-inch rectangle. Fold over one side of the dough 2 1/2-inches, lengthwise, then fold it over another 2 1/2-inches. Do the same thing with the other side, then fold in 1/2 again, to form a long, 6-layer thick strip. Place on a baking sheet and freeze another 10 minutes, or until dough is very firm but not hard.

Preheat oven to 375-degrees. With a chef's knife, cut the strip of dough into forty 1/2-inch wide slices. Place on ungreased baking sheets, spacing some to allow for spreading during baking. Return unbaked dough to the freezer until ready to use. Bake one sheet at a time. Bake about 10 minutes, then turn with a wide metal spatula and finish baking. The palmiers should be golden brown. Remove immediately with a metal spatula and cool on a wire rack. Don't pile up warm palmiers or allow them to stand on the baking sheet. The caramel formed during baking would cause them to stick.

Note: Be sure to use classical flaky pastry rather than quick flaky pastry, whose very slight unevenness in layering makes it unsuitable. If you wish to make smaller or larger palmiers, simply make the folds larger or smaller, accordingly.

Storage: Can be kept in a tightly-sealed container for 1 week. Unbaked palmiers can be frozen for 2 months. Freeze on a tray or baking sheet, then store in a plastic bag. Bake unthawed palmiers as above, allowing about 5 minutes more baking time.

IX-10 PAPILLONS

In 13th century France, those with frivolous, unstable personalities were dubbed "papillon", literally "butterfly". There's evidence that the old custom has survived: Henri Charrière, author of a bestseller recounting his escape from the most dreaded prison in French Guiana, was more commonly known as..."Papillon".

These butterfly-shaped pastries, which also ressemble golden brown bow ties, differ only in shape from palmiers.

(IX-10)
Papillons
(Butterflies)

Ingredients: (for about 40 papillons)
- 8 ounces pâte feuilletée classique (I-8) with 4 tours
- 2/3 cup powdered sugar
- 1 egg, beaten with a pinch of salt

Dust work surface generously with powdered sugar and give the dough the last two turns. Whenever necessary, redust work surface and dough with sugar, using it as you would flour. Place dough on a baking sheet and freeze 10 minutes, then roll out into a 15 x 20-inch rectangle. Using a ruler and a chef's knife, cut dough into three 5 x 20-inch pieces. Press the side of the rolling pin lengthwise into the center of one piece of dough. Brush the indentation with beaten egg.

Place a second rectangle of dough on top of the first and press the center to make another indentation and seal the rectangles together. Brush the second indentation with more egg, place the last rectangle of dough on top, and press the center to seal the three layers of dough together.

Place on a baking sheet and freeze 10 minutes, or until dough is very firm but not hard. Preheat oven to 375-degrees. With the chef's knife, cut the dough into forty 1/2-inch wide strips. Pinch the center of each strip and give it a 1/2 twist. Place the twisted strips on baking sheets, with the center flat on the sheet. With a finger, hold down the center of each strip and gently separate the 3 layers.

Space the papillons about 2 inches, to allow for spreading. Return sheets of unbaked papillons to freezer until ready to use. Bake 1 sheet at a time, about 10 minutes, then turn with a metal spatula and finish baking. The papillons should be golden brown. Remove immediately with a metal spatula and cool on a wire rack.

Storage: Can be kept in a tightly-sealed container for 1 week. Unbaked papillons can be frozen for 2 months. Freeze on a tray or baking sheet, then store in a plastic bag. Bake unthawed papillons as above, allowing about 5 minutes more baking time.

IX-11 ARLETTES

Arlette, a popular girl's name in France around the turn of the century, has recently fallen into disuse. And yet, the French nation owes one of its greatest military leaders to a lady by that name: Arlette de Falaise, the domineering, ambitious mother of William the Conqueror.

Arlettes are yet another variation of traditional palmiers.

(IX-11)
Arlettes

Ingredients: (for 40 arlettes)
- 8 ounces pâte feuilletée classique (I-8) with 4 tours
- 2/3 cup powdered sugar

Dust work surface generously with powdered sugar and give the dough the last two turns. Whenever necessary, redust work surface and dough with the sugar, using it as you would flour. Place dough on baking sheet and freeze 10 minutes, then roll out into a 15 x 20-inch rectangle. Roll up dough tightly, to a 20-inch long cylinder. Place on a baking sheet and freeze 10 minutes, or until very firm but not hard.

With a chef's knife, cut into forty 1/2-inch thick slices. Lightly dust work surface with powdered sugar. Place a slice of dough on the work surface and tuck free end underneath. Dust with sugar, and, with the rolling pin, flatten the slice into a 1/8-inch thick disk.

Preheat oven to 375-degrees. Place arlettes on baking sheets, spacing about an inch to allow for expansion. Return sheets of unbaked arlettes to freezer until ready to use. Bake, one sheet at a time, about 10 minutes, then with a wide metal spatula, turn and finish baking. The arlettes should be golden brown. Remove immediately with metal spatula and cool on a wire rack.

Storage: Can be kept in a tightly-sealed container for 1 week. Unbaked arlettes can be frozen for 2 months. Freeze on a tray or baking sheet, then store in a plastic bag. Bake unthawed arlettes as above, allowing about 5 minutes more baking time.

IX-12 SACRISTAINS

The sacristan gave his title to these sugar and almond-studded twists, which bring to mind one of that church official's most important tools: a corkscrew used for opening the sacrificial wine.

(IX-12)

Sacristains
(Sacristans)

Ingredients: (for about 40 cookies)
- 1/2   pound pâte feuilletée classique (I-8) or
       pâte demi-feuilletée (I-9)
- 2/3   cup coarsely broken rock candy, or crystalized sugar
- 1/2   cup chopped, blanched untoasted almonds
- 1   whole egg, beaten with a pinch of salt (egg wash)

Since it's difficult to make twists with soft dough, you must work quickly, while the dough is as cold and stiff as possible. Preheat oven to 350-degrees. On a lightly-floured surface, roll out dough into a 6x16 1/2x1/16-inch rectangle. With a chef's knife, cut dough in half, lengthwise. Refrigerate one of the halves while you work with the other.

Brush dough with beaten egg. Sprinkle with 1/4 of the sugar and the almonds. With the hands or a rolling pin, press sugar and almonds lightly into dough. Turn dough over and repeat process. (If the dough has become very soft, refrigerate 10 to 15 minutes). Cut into twenty 3/4 x 2 3/4-inch strips. Twist each strip slightly to form "corkscrews", place on an ungreased baking sheet, and bake 20 to 25 minutes, until puffed and golden brown.

While first sheet of cookies is baking, prepare and then bake second half of dough, as described above.

Storage: Will keep, tightly covered, for several days.

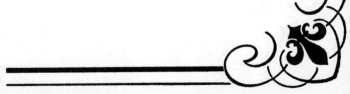

IX-13 FINANCIERS

In some parts of rural France, farmers reject new ideas and still call upon a water diviner when they decide to dig a well. Of course, no modern instruments are used. Only a hazelnut divining rod will do, because of its reputed power to "smell out" water.

These tender cake-like cookies, rich with ground hazelnuts, can also be dressed up with whole almonds, jam, or chocolate.

(IX-13)
Financiers

Ingredients: (for 24 financiers)

4 1/2	ounces hazelnuts (about 1 cup)
2/3	cup flour
1/2	cup sugar
1/3	cup butter, softened
1/4	teaspoon vanilla extract
1/2	cup milk
2	egg whites
1/8	teaspoon salt
1	tablespoon sugar
	butter for muffin tins

Preheat oven to 350-degrees. Using a pastry brush, butter 24 muffin tins. In blender, grind hazelnuts. In a medium mixing bowl, stir them together with flour and sugar, then beat in butter, vanilla extract, and milk. Beat just until batter is well-blended and smooth.

In a deep mixing bowl, beat egg whites and salt at high speed until soft peaks form. Add sugar and continue beating until stiff but not dry. Beat a big spoonful of whites into the batter, then add all of this mixture to the rest of whites and fold together carefully. Divide batter between the prepared muffin tins and bake for 8 to 10 minutes, or until light brown, and edges pull away from tin. Turn out immediately onto a wire rack. Serve warm.

Financiers aux Amandes (Almond) (IX-13a): Prepare as above. Immediately before baking, place a whole blanched almond in the center of each financier. Bake and serve as above.

Financiers à la Confiture (Jam) (IX-13b): Prepare as above. Before baking, place 1/2 teaspoon apricot jam (or another flavor of your choice) in the center of each financier. Bake and serve as above.

More→

(Financiers, Cont.)

Financiers Glacés au Chocolat (Chocolate) (IX-13c): Prepare and bake as above. Cool, then ice with semi-sweet chocolate. In a double boiler, melt chocolate, then, leaving the chocolate over hot water to keep it soft, dip in the browner side of each financier. Hold up over pot, smooth with a fork, then drag the tines across to create a ridged effect. If the ridges aren't well-defined enough, allow the chocolate to cool some, then scrape again.

Storage: Keep, tightly covered, for several days.

IX-14   FLORENTINS

These crunchy almond tartlets studded with candied fruit and crowned by a tangy chocolate icing evoke the elegance and refinement of Italy's most renowned Renaissance city: Florence.

(IX-14)
Florentins
(Florentines)

Ingedients: (for 8 Florentins)

1/2	cup heavy cream
1/4	cup sugar
1/4	cup butter
3	tablespoons honey
1/2	cup chopped candied fruit
1 1/2	cups blanched sliced almonds
1/2	cup flour
1	tablespoon Grand Marnier
	butter for pans
6	ounces semi-sweet chocolate

Preheat oven to 325-degrees. In a medium saucepan, heat first 6 ingredients to a boil. Remove from heat and beat in flour and Grand Marnier. Divide batter between eight 4-inch buttered tartlet pans. Place on a baking sheet and bake 20 to 30 minutes, until florentins are lightly-browned and edges pull away slightly from sides of pans. Cool a few minutes, then turn out onto a wire rack.

In a double boiler, heat chocolate gently until melted. Remove from heat, but leave the chocolate over the hot water so it will stay soft. Ice the side of the florentin which touched the pan (it's smoother and browner than the top). Hold cooled florentins by the edges and dip them in the melted chocolate. Lift up over the pot and smooth surface with a fork, then drag tines across the

More➜

(Florentins, Cont.)

surface for a ridged effect. If the ridges aren't well-defined enough, let the chocolate cool some, then repeat the operation. Present the florentins on an oblong plate, alternating chocolate sides with plain sides.

Storage: Refrigerate florentins in an airtight container for several days. Uniced florentins can also be frozen, flat on a tray or a baking sheet, then in a plastic bag. Heat unthawed florentins for 5 minutes in a preheated 300-degrees oven, then cool and ice as directed above.

IX-15   ROCHERS CONGOLAIS

Everyone knows that many American parents threaten unruly children with a visit from the "boogy man". In France, it's "croquemitaine", while Spanish children are warned about "coco". The unnerving hairy "face" looking out from a grocer's fruit stand must have frightened more than one Spanish child, because the new tropical fruit was quickly dubbed "coconut".

These small pyramids of chewy coconut are very quick and simple to make, and are a big success with children.

(IX-15)
Rochers Congolais
(Congolese Coconut Cookies)

Ingredients: (for about 24 rochers)

4	egg whites
1 1/3	cups sugar
1	tablespoon lemon juice
4	cups flaked unsweetened coconut

Preheat oven to 350-degrees. Over a double boiler, beat egg whites and sugar until hot, for about 5 minutes. Beat in lemon juice, then coconut. If the dough isn't stiff enough, beat in a little more coconut.

On lightly-greased baking sheets, drop dough by tablespoonfuls. Wet fingers and shape into small pyramids. Bake 20 minutes. The rochers should be moist and chewy on the inside, and a very light brown on the outside.

Storage: Cover tightly and store in the refrigerator for 1 week.

IX-16 MADELEINES

"Your Majesty, I would like to have a word with you, if I may…It really is very urgent!" Pale as death, the head cook at the Château de Commercy was clearly on the verge of hysteria.

Suddenly called away from the dinner table, King Stanislas of Poland shot his cook a penetrating look and drew him to one side. *"Well?"* he demanded shortly, not about to waste time on niceties, especially with a mere domestic.

"The pastry cook and I had a…minor disagreement." There, it was out!

The king's eyebrows shot up. *"Minor?"*

"Well, it was actually somewhat violent," the cook admitted, nervously twisting his white chef's hat. *"The man is impossible, I tell you, impossible!"*

All too aware of the rivalry between his head cook and pastry chef, King Stanislas gritted his teeth, knowing he had every reason to dread the worst. *"And?"* he asked impatiently, glancing back towards the banquet hall, where jugglers were entertaining his royal guests.

"He threw his apron in my face, your majesty! In my face!" Indignation made his eyes fairly pop out of his head, but the king's fierce expression made him forget about his injured pride and hurry on. *"But worst of all, he gathered up all the pastries and stormed out the door, shouting like a crazy man that he was going to throw them all in the river Meuse! Le misérable!"* The wadded chef's hat landed on the flagstones and was stomped to shreds.

Accustomed to these periodic fits of rage, King Stanislas fought back an overpowering urge to strangle the cook, and waited for him to regain a semblance of composure. *"This is no small problem,"* he finally agreed, *"especially with the dessert only a few courses away…"*

"If I dared suggest…" the cook began, then stopped as though rejecting a sudden inspiration.

The order thundered down. *"Go on!"*

"A young girl who works in the kitchen…a simple scullery maid, if you must know…"

The monarch cut him off with the wave of a hand. *"Can she cook?"*

"Indeed, your majesty, I do not really know. But she does claim to know the recipe for a pastry that would please even royalty…"

"Thanks to you and your love for fighting like a ragpicker with all the other personnel," Kind Stanislas interrupted acidly, *"we have no choice but to hope that she's telling the truth. Give her all the equipment and help she asks for, and whatever you do, don't pick a fight with her, she's our last hope. And hurry!"* Without another word, he turned and strode back towards the banquet hall, where the jugglers were taking their final bow.

More→

(Madeleines, Cont.)

Shortly thereafter, large baskets preceded by a heavenly lemon aroma made their appearance on the royal tables. The king and his guests, delighted with the tender, shell-shaped cakes, clamored for more, and, finally satiated, insisted upon congratulating the pastry chef. Beaming with pride, but modest, the young girl admitted that, to her knowledge, the pastry had no name.

The king came forward and took her hand. "What is your name, my dear?"

"Madeleine, your majesty."

He smiled and turned halfway to his guests. "Then from now on, Madeleine, it will bear your name. And to show my appreciation, I will provide you with an ample dowry when you come of age to marry."

So whoever said that fairy tales never happen?

(IX-16)

Madeleines

Ingredients: (for about 24 madeleines)

1/2	cup (1 stick) butter, softened
2/3	cup sugar
3	eggs
	finely-grated rind of 1 lemon
2/3	cup flour
1/4	teaspoon salt
1/4	teaspoon baking powder, sifted if lumpy
	butter and flour for molds

Preheat oven to 350-degrees. In a large mixing bowl, cream butter and sugar until light. Beat in whole eggs, one at a time, then lemon rind. If the mixture separates, place the bowl over a pot of hot water and continue beating until creamy.

In a small bowl, mix together dry ingredients, then beat into butter mixture just until well blended. Fill buttered and floured madeleine molds to about 1/2, and bake 10 to 12 minutes, until golden brown.

Note: The traditional peel can be replaced by vanilla extract (1/2 teaspoon) or 1 tablespoon rum.

Storage: Wrap in plastic and store in a cool, dry place for several days, or freeze for up to 1 month. Heat gently for a few minutes before serving.

IX-17 SABLÉS À LA CONFITURE

George Sand, the 19th century author who shocked—and secretly delighted—all of Europe by wearing men's clothing, smoking cigars, and changing lovers as often as she pleased, led a surprisingly sober life in her native province. Among her daily tasks: overseeing the preparation of jams and jellies in the family manor's vast kitchen.

Although Ms. Sand was never known for her gourmandise, her numerous houseguests may well have enjoyed these attractive jam-filled sandwich cookies, a favorite in French homes of the day.

(IX-17)
Sablés à la Confiture
(Jam-Filled Sandwich Cookies)

Ingredients: (for 24 cookies)
- **14** ounces pâte sablée (I-7)
- **2/3** cup smooth apricot or raspberry jam (or 1/3 cup each)

      powdered sugar

Preheat oven to 350-degrees. On a lightly-floured surface, roll out pastry to 1/8-inch thick. With a 2-inch round pastry cutter (with scalloped edge, if possible), cut out 48 disks. With a thimble, cut a hole in the center of 24 disks. Place on ungreased baking sheets and bake 8 to 10 minutes, or until light brown. Remove to wire racks and cool.

If the jam isn't perfectly smooth, whirl it in the blender until it is. In a small saucepan, heat jam to a boil, then reduce heat and let it simmer until jam has thickened slightly. Remove from heat and cool until lukewarm. With a pastry brush, cover the solid disks with jam. Take care not to spread on too much, as it would run over the sides. With a sugar dredger or a small strainer, dust the other cookies. Holding them carefully by the edges, place the dusted cookies on top of the jam-coated cookies.

Storage: Ungarnished cookies can be frozen in a plastic bag for 1 month. Thaw at room temperature 1 hour, then place on a baking sheet and heat 5 minutes in a 200-degree oven. Fill and dust as directed above.

IX-18 GALETTES FRIVOLES

The French word "galet" designates a kind of small flat stone, commonly found on beaches of the Côte d'Azur. By extension, the name was applied to many kinds of cakes and cookies, whose round, flat shape bring to mind that of the "galet".

These "frivolous" shortbread cookies can be made with an array of toppings.

(IX-18)
Galettes Frivoles
(Filled Shortbread Cookies)

Ingredients: (for 24 cookies)
14	ounces pâte sablée (I-7)
3/4	cup chopped blanched almonds
	garnish of your choice (see below)

Preheat oven to 350-degrees. On a lightly-floured surface, roll dough under palms to form a long cylinder. Cut in half, then cut each half into 12 pieces. Place chopped almonds in a shallow dish. Roll pieces of dough into balls, then roll in almonds. Place on baking sheet, spacing some to allow for spreading, and with the thumb, press the center of each ball to flatten slightly and form a small "well". Bake about 15 minutes, or until cookies are golden brown. Cool partially, remove with a metal spatula, and place on wire racks to finish cooling. Garnish with one of the following:

Garnishes:
Cerise-Ananas (Cherry/Pineapple) (IX-18a):
2 1/2	slices pineapple (fresh or canned)
6	candied cherries, sliced in fourths
1/3	cup abricotage (apricot glaze) (II-11a)

Cut the pineapple slices into small wedges (about 10 per whole slice), and cut cherries in four. In a small saucepan, heat abricotage to a boil (this thickens it and helps the fruit stick better), then remove from heat. Drop about 1/4 teaspoon abricotage into the well of each cookie, place a pineapple wedge (with the narrower end in the center) and place a piece of cherry on top of the end in center. Brush fruit lightly with apricot glaze.

Cerise (Cherry) (IX-18b):
1/3	cup abricotage (apricot glaze) (II-11a)
12	candied cherries

Cut cherries in half. In a small saucepan, heat abricotage to a boil, then remove from heat and drop about 1/4 teaspoon into each well. Place a cherry half of top. Brush with apricot glaze.

More→

(Galettes Frivoles, Cont.)

Chocolat (Chocolate) (IX-18c):
- 3 ounces semi-sweet chocolate
- 2 tablespoons heavy cream or strong coffee

In a small saucepan, heat chocolate and cream or coffee over very low heat until chocolate is melted. With a fork, stir until smooth. Allow to cool 10 minutes. Drop about 1/2 teaspoon chocolate into each well.

Raisin (IX-18d):
- 1/2 cup raisins
- 1/2 cup fondant (II-10)

In a small saucepan, heat fondant very gently, beating vigorously all the while with a wooden spoon. When it's barely warm, remove from heat and drop about 1/2 teaspoon into each well. Top with several raisins.

Confiture (Jam) (IX-18e):
- 1/2 cup apricot or raspberry jam

In a small saucepan, heat jam to a boil, then remove from heat and fill the wells.

Storage: Cover tightly and store in a cool, dry place for 3 to 4 days.

French Index